Financial Crises:
Lessons from the Past,
Preparation for the Future

THE WORLD BANK GROUP

THE INTERNATIONAL MONETARY FUND

THE BROOKINGS INSTITUTION

This book is based on the sixth annual financial markets and development conference held April 26–27, 2005, in Washington, D.C. The conference was cosponsored by the World Bank Group and Brookings Institution.

The previous volumes in this series are available from the Brookings Institution Press:

Financial Markets and Development: The Crisis in Emerging Markets (1999)

Managing Financial and Corporate Distress: Lessons from Asia (2000)

Open Doors: Foreign Participation in Financial Systems in Developing Countries (2001)

Financial Sector Governance: The Roles of the Public and Private Sectors (2002)

The Future of Domestic Capital Markets in Developing Countries (2003)

The Future of State-Owned Financial Institutions (2004)

GERARD CAPRIO
JAMES A. HANSON
ROBERT E. LITAN
Editors

Financial Crises:
Lessons from the Past,
Preparation for the Future

BROOKINGS INSTITUTION PRESS
Washington, D.C.

Copyright © 2005
THE BROOKINGS INSTITUTION
1775 Massachusetts Avenue, N.W., Washington, D.C. 20036
www.brookings.edu

Library of Congress Cataloging-in-Publication data
Financial crises : lessons from the past, preparation for the future / Gerard Caprio, James A. Hanson, Robert E. Litan, editors.
p. cm.
Summary: "Analyzes the efficacy of attempts to recover from past crises and their lessons for the future, assesses the current state of international financial markets and examines policy options for reducing systemic vulnerability, and addresses pension system reform"—Provided by publisher.
Includes bibliographical references and index.
ISBN-13: 978-0-8157-1289-3 (pbk. : alk. paper)
ISBN-10: 0-8157-1289-8 (pbk. : alk. paper)
1. Financial crises. International finance. 3. Monetary policy. 4. Economic policy. I. Caprio, Gerard. II. Hanson, James A. III. Litan, Robert E., 1950–III. Title.
HB3722.F546 2005
332'.042—dc22   2005027077

9 8 7 6 5 4 3 2 1

The paper used in this publication meets minimum requirements of the American National Standard for Information Sciences—Permanence of Paper for Printed Library Materials: ANSI Z39.48-1992.

Typeset in Adobe Garamond

Composition by Circle Graphics
Columbia, Maryland

Printed by Victor Graphics
Baltimore, Maryland

Contents

GERARD CAPRIO
JAMES HANSON
ROBERT E. LITAN

1

Introduction

The calm before the storm? That question dominated the stage at the seventh annual conference on emerging markets finance, cosponsored by the World Bank and the Brookings Institution and held at Brookings in late April 2005.

At the time of the conference, it had been a little less than eight years since the onset of the Asian financial crisis, an event that had depression-like effects throughout much of Asia and, for a time, seemed to threaten global economic stability. That this outcome never happened can be attributed to a combination of aggressive monetary easing by the Federal Reserve Board in the United States, emergency lending to the countries in the region by the International Monetary Fund (IMF) and other international institutions, the concerted rollover of some of Korea's private external debt, and a dose of good luck.

The Asian economies have since recovered from their financial crises to varying degrees, as have the other major emerging-market countries that suffered their own crises shortly afterward: Argentina, Brazil, Russia, and Turkey. What has been learned since these crises in key parts of the developing world? How exposed are countries in different parts of the world to another, perhaps entirely different kind of financial and economic crisis?

These are among the questions that the conference papers address. This introduction provides a brief overview of their main findings. The subsequent chapters contain the papers as well as a summary of the panel discussion with private sector representatives of commercial banks and rating agencies and select portions of the discussion by the roughly 100 financial experts from around the world who attended the conference.

James Hanson led off the conference by examining the challenges and economic vulnerabilities in East Asia and Latin America. Countries in both regions suffered financial crises in the 1990s and the early part of this decade. In chapter 2, Hanson discusses the common features of the crises in both regions and the very different paths that countries in each region have taken since their crises.

Almost all of the crises in the 1990s and post-2000 in both regions were not just external crises; they often began in the domestic banking sectors, and banking sector problems complicated policymaking in all cases. In the typical case, runs on banks quickly turned into runs on currencies, forcing central banks to abandon attempts to peg the exchange rate and deal with bank failures. In some, but not all, cases, excessive government borrowing contributed to the crises, unlike the 1980s-era Latin American crises, where excessive government borrowing was the dominant cause.

There also were common elements among the policy responses to the more recent financial crises. Governments typically bailed out bank depositors. They incurred massive debts to the banking systems in the process, since governments also had to pick up the tab for losses on unpaid bank loans that typically were transferred to separate asset management companies. On the macroeconomic front, pressure from the market and the IMF, which provided emergency finance to many of the countries in both regions, sooner or later forced the governments to tighten monetary and fiscal policy.

Hanson does not add to the well-known and vigorous debate over these policy responses; instead he focuses factually on what happened in the economies as a result. One of the postcrisis macroeconomic outcomes, common to both regions, was a dramatic drop in inflation, an unusual experience for Latin America, where much higher inflation rates had been common. Lower inflation rates helped the working of the financial system after the crises in all the countries.

In terms of growth, the postcrisis experiences have differed between (and within) regions. The East Asian countries generally have rebounded from their crisis-induced downturns. Annual growth recently has been in the 4–6 percent range, good for developing countries, but below their growth rates in the first half of the 1990s. Korea recovered the most rapidly, using the unorthodox strategy of promoting consumption, but its growth then slowed as the approach reached its limits. Indonesia suffered the most from its crisis, in part because of the political turmoil surrounding the end of the Suharto regime and realignment of the political economy as the country developed a democratic government. The Latin American countries that suffered crises in the 1990s recovered quickly. Nonetheless, despite their upswing in 2004, their average growth remained low.

Another sharp contrast between the two regions relates to their external debt. Since the 1997–98 crises, the average ratio of external debt to GDP in East Asia has fallen. The opposite has occurred in Latin America, where the ratio of external debt to GDP in 2004 stood above the level of the mid-1990s. Borrowing from the World Bank and the IMF by Latin American governments is one factor contributing to this difference in external debt patterns. Other factors include an apparent increase in the risk tolerance of investors, coupled with improving economic prospects in many Latin American countries since 2000, which has enabled governments to sell their debt more easily. Indeed, by early 2005, the spread on interest rates on emerging-market bonds relative to those on U.S. treasury bonds stood at an eight-year low. The lower spread, coupled with the lower level of U.S. rates, has eased the debt service of all emerging-market borrowers. It remains to be seen whether, and to what extent, high-borrowing countries will be able to keep on servicing their debts if interest rates rise. In contrast to Latin America, the East Asian crisis economies generally have taken advantage of the benign external financial environment since their crises to run tight fiscal policy, reduce their debt, and substantially increase their foreign exchange reserves. They should have an easier time avoiding future difficulties than their counterparts in Latin America.

Hanson points to a number of interesting structural developments in both regions during the past few years. While countries in both regions continue to rely heavily on banks for intermediation, pension funds have grown increasingly important in Latin America (Peru and Chile, in particular). Domestic currency government and private corporate bond markets have also developed in both regions, although trading in secondary markets remains low. Banks have recovered, but Latin American bank deposits remain low. In Latin America and Indonesia, banks' holdings of government debt have increased relative to deposits, crowding out private credit. This represents a major challenge to growth and development since private credit is a major factor in growth.

Banks also face some risks. The government debt carries market risk and is not free from default risk. Private loans are riskier than they were, with the most creditworthy private sector borrowers financing themselves abroad or in the domestic bond markets. Banks may lack the risk management capacity to deal with their expansion into consumer, small-scale, and mort-gage lending, a problem that hit Korea. Many borrowers in Latin America continue to borrow in dollars, exposing themselves to currency risk, which contributed to previous banking crises. Improvements are slowly occurring in banks' risk management techniques and the information and legal frame-works on which sound lending depends.

State-owned banks, which were major factors in the previous crises, also continue to be important financial institutions in both regions and are even growing in some cases. In the current environment of tight fiscal and mone-tary policy, governments face political pressure to use public sector banks as economic policy instruments. The costs of this strategy are already becoming clear in some Asian countries. Meanwhile, the well-known international banks that once were thought to be a way to improve financial sector perfor-mance have become less interested in expanding into most developing coun-tries. Regional banks are expanding, but they offer fewer benefits than the well-known international banks.

Finally, governments in both regions have strengthened prudential reg-ulation of their banks, prodded and supported by the IMF–World Bank Financial Sector Assessment Program. Most countries also have indicated their intention gradually to adopt the about-to-be-implemented Basel II capital standards. It remains to be seen whether these measures will prove sufficient to prevent or minimize the damage from future financial crises, especially given the political constraints facing their application.

Central and Eastern Europe, too, were touched by financial crises of their own, but these were largely due to a wave of bank failures that arose as their economies were transformed from centrally planned to market-based economies, as discussed in chapter 3 of this volume by Fernando Montes-Negret and Thomas Muller, both of the World Bank.

The "banks" that existed prior to this transformation were banks in name only; in fact, these institutions were administrative agencies that sim-ply held credits from state-owned enterprises on their "books." When the institutions were converted into "banks," as part of the transformation to market-based economies, these bookkeeping credits proved largely worth-less. The banks thus found themselves with insufficient assets to back the deposits that individuals and firms held in them.

At the same time, household assets were relatively liquid because the shortage of goods in centrally planned economies left them with little alter-native other than to hold their meager income as bank deposits or buy foreign exchange. The new governments therefore faced a macroeconomic problem as well as a structural one: with a monetary "overhang," the new freedoms could have unleashed a wave of spending unmatched by the production of goods, causing a major bout of inflation. Central banks attempted to reduce that overhang by tightening credit, forcing so-called hard-budget constraints on enterprises that were not used to them. The predictable result was a wave of bankruptcies, which only reinforced the structural problems in the "banks" that had once extended them credit.

The economies in the region took very different approaches to "cleaning up" their banking sectors, particularly in terms of transparency. In all cases, however, some form of government infusion of funds was required to make good on the deposits and compensate for the inevitable writedowns of the banks' previous credits. Most governments also attempted to introduce some semblance of sound bank supervision, consistent with international practice. But understandably, the countries did not have the expertise to carry out this program effectively, especially as long as the banks remained state owned and thus followed the directions of government leaders rather than market norms.

A number of countries in the region tried to offset the domination of their state-owned banks by allowing new entrants into commercial banking. But, as Montes-Negret and Muller discuss, many of these entrants were too small to be efficient, lacked experience, and were undercapitalized and thus the source of additional banking problems.

Notwithstanding all of these difficulties, the costs of banking problems in Central and Eastern Europe, computed as a fraction of total output, turned out to be substantially below the costs suffered by the crisis-ridden countries in East Asia and Latin America and by Turkey and even Japan. The authors suggest that in the European countries, the financial sectors were relatively much smaller to begin with, so they suffered and caused less damage than in countries where banks played a more central role in the economy.

Although the economies in the region during the transition period have performed very differently, the authors suggest that certain common conclusions can be drawn from their experiences. For example, after suffering initial downturns following the end of central planning, Central and Eastern European economies generally have enjoyed real growth, as have their financial sectors. At the same time, all countries in this part of the world could benefit from increased financial depth (measured by the ratio of financial assets to GDP) as well as stronger capital markets to supplement the dominant role being played by banks.

As for the country-level differences, the authors note that eight Eastern European countries that later joined the European Union (EU) in 2004 outperformed, along several dimensions, other formerly centrally planned economies that have transitioned toward some capitalism. They suggest that the prospect of EU accession encouraged reforms and foreign capital inflow that made this superior performance possible. Russia has benefited from favorable commodity prices and fiscal discipline since its 1998 crisis, but its banking and financial systems remain underdeveloped relative to those of other countries in the authors' survey. Central Asian economies, in the authors' words, seemed trapped in a "low-level equilibrium," with underdeveloped financial institutions and regulatory oversight. In Southeast Europe, financial sector development is very uneven, with Slovenia furthest ahead, having joined the European Union; finance in the countries that formerly made up Yugoslavia continues to be held back in the aftermath of civil conflict in the 1990s; and the financial sector is perhaps most underdeveloped in Albania and Macedonia.

The well-known association between financial crises in the developing world and external debt raises the obvious questions of whether external debt is going to lead to a new crisis and, more fundamentally, whether sovereign borrowing is an aid or a hindrance to economic growth. Indermit Gill and Brian Pinto of the World Bank address these questions in chapter 4 of this volume.

What is the likelihood of a sovereign debt–induced financial crisis in the developing world in the near future? The authors suggest that, in light of the frequency of past episodes, future crises always remain possible. Public debt (external and internal) remains high in the major developing countries with market access. Nonetheless, the authors argue that risks have receded for several reasons.

Taking the East Asian crisis economies first, along with reasonably strong growth, many of them have improved government balance sheets and now have strong fiscal positions (except the Philippines). The buildup of international reserves should provide protection against "sudden stops" in capital inflows.

The other four major crisis economies of recent years—Argentina, Brazil, Russia, and Turkey—have taken very different roads to recovery. All four got into trouble because of unsustainable exchange rate pegs, excessive sovereign borrowing, and, in the last three cases, weak financial systems. When the governments could not service foreign currency–denominated debt, they abandoned the currency pegs; Argentina went further and stopped payment on its debt and later restructured it (to the consternation of its creditors). Russia also restructured its debt, but through more of a negotiation than the unilateral actions taken by Argentina. Brazil and Turkey adopted much tighter fiscal policies. Since these actions, all of the economies have rebounded to varying degrees. Primary fiscal surpluses (budget accounts minus interest payments) now exist, in the cases of Brazil and Turkey at unprecedented rates. The countries are building up hard currency reserves, and the adoption of more flexible exchange rates also will help (by discouraging excessive foreign currency borrowing). However, debt ratios remain uncomfortably high, especially in Brazil and Turkey, and the sustainability of debt depends on continued high primary surpluses, low international interest rates, and market confidence that translates into continued low sovereign spreads.

Perhaps the best test of the success of measures taken so far is how the market, specifically bond investors, has perceived them. By this test, the verdict, at least at the time this paper was presented, looked good: for virtually all of the countries that experienced a crisis within the last decade, interest rates relative to U.S. treasury bond rates have fallen significantly since the time they were in trouble.

Does sovereign debt help or hinder growth? Government borrowing (like private sector borrowing) can add to growth, provided borrowing occurs in moderation and the proceeds are used for investment rather than consumption. Crises, related to high debt, obviously slow growth. But even without a crisis high debt can slow growth as a result of direct crowding out of private investment, concerns about debt overhang, and reduced fiscal space for public investment and social spending.

The authors do not identify a specific debt-to-GDP threshold that should trigger concern, but they observe that the debt ratio seems high in a number of prominent market access countries. Countries are responding, to varying degrees, with fiscal discipline, changes in institutions to lock in fiscal discipline, and reforms to speed growth.

An important challenge for developing-country governments in the future is to manage foreign exchange risk and thus the risk of currency crises. One response, in some cases related to financial sector bailouts, has been to develop a domestic currency debt market and borrow more in domestic currency. Innovations in debt instruments can help: one idea is to issue bonds with interest payments tied to GDP growth (to help avoid unsustainable interest rate burdens in years when the domestic economy may be performing poorly for exogenous reasons, such as a slump in commodity prices). However, it appears that such instruments and markets will not play a major role in easing the burden of developing-country debt for some time.

Peering into the future is a lot more difficult than explaining the past, but Morris Goldstein of the Institute for International Economics takes up the challenge in chapter 5 of this volume, speculating on what the next emerging-market-economy financial crisis (banking, currency, or both) might look like. Admittedly, at the time of this exercise, the likelihood of such a crisis seemed lower than it had for some time: GDP growth in emerging markets in 2004 was the best in twenty years, primary prices were high, and borrowing rates were low.

But Goldstein warns against complacency: very good times often precede bad times. And the healthy averages conceal wide variation in country performance: in 2004 more than fifty developing countries had current account deficits exceeding 5 percent of GDP. And then there is the looming presence of the "haircut" that Argentina forced its creditors to take on foreign currency debt earlier this decade. When the next crisis occurs, investors may rightly fear the same thing happening to them and thus bolt for the exits at the earliest sign of trouble.

Of all the myriad things that could go wrong in the near future, Goldstein singles out two for special attention: a bursting of the apparent "investment bubble" in China and a sudden run from the U.S. dollar on account of the large U.S. current account deficit. Moreover, the two events are not mutually exclusive; they could happen simultaneously and thus have potentially synergistic negative effects on the world economy, emerging markets included.

China and the United States account for roughly 12 and 21 percent of the world's output, respectively, based on purchasing power parity exchange rates. In 2003–04, the two economies together accounted for nearly half of the world's expansion in output. Clearly, therefore, a slowdown in one or both economies could have potentially serious ripple effects on much of the rest of the world.

The main risk that could arise from China comes from the likely slowdown in its very high rate of investment, which as a share of GDP recently hit an all-time record of 46 percent of GDP. Although Chinese officials initially denied that investment spending posed a problem, more recently, the government has attempted to tighten monetary policy (through administrative controls and higher interest rates) in an effort to curb spending generally, which had pushed GDP up almost 10 percent in 2004. Of course, another risk is the impact of a change in exchange rate policy. (After the conference, this issue became more important when China announced a slight revaluation of its currency in July 2005.) Goldstein lays out the pros and cons of each of three possible future scenarios for the Chinese economy: a soft landing, a hard landing, and a long (but gradual) landing. He sides with the long-landing view, implying that China's GDP growth in 2006–07 could be 3–4 percentage points lower than in 2004.

Goldstein also outlines alternative "landing" scenarios for the U.S. current account deficit. As his Institute for International Economics colleague Michael Mussa (former chief economist of the International Monetary Fund) has argued, one way or another, the U.S. current account deficit will have to be reversed, and when that occurs, three interrelated things must happen: (1) the dollar must depreciate against a basket of foreign currencies, (2) domestic demand in the United States must grow more slowly than production to make room for the additional exports that a weaker dollar will stimulate, and (3) domestic demand elsewhere in the world will have to grow faster than output to reduce net exports from the rest of the world. Yet when and how fast these adjustments will take place is highly uncertain.

How will emerging markets fare if and when the Chinese and the U.S. economies slow down or, worse, suffer sharp corrections? Clearly, the effects will be negative, but they will be manifested in several ways. One is through a decline in exports to a slumping China and the United States; through this channel, Hong Kong and Korea, the largest exporters to China, would suffer disproportionately, as would much of Latin America, which exports commodities to the United States and recently to China. European emerging economies would be the least adversely affected.

A second channel through which emerging economies could suffer is through higher interest rates in the United States, which the Federal Reserve has been engineering and which is likely to slow capital flows to emerging economies as a by-product. A higher U.S. dollar interest rate could also be a by-product of a slowdown in China's accumulation of U.S. government debt. In a worst case, the contraction of capital flows and higher domestic interest rates could precipitate another financial crisis, especially in countries with weak banking systems. The negative impact could also spread to other countries through "contagion" effects, similar to those displayed during the Asian financial crisis of the late 1990s. The countries that will suffer the most from high interest rates are those that still have high debt ratios, many of which are countries that still have not recovered fully from earlier crises.

Emerging-market economies may be somewhat defenseless against shifts in economic fortune because it is difficult for them, in a global environment, to run independent and effective countercyclical macroeconomic policies. Countries with relatively low levels of sovereign debt to begin with are likely to be best able to carry out effective countercyclical economic policy (because foreign investors will not necessarily flee from the country when its government attempts to offset a downturn with stimulus).

What do institutions with real money at risk believe about the outlook for emerging economies? A panel of three experts from major commercial banks and rating agencies offered their views at the time of the conference, which are summarized in chapter 6.

David Wyss from Standard and Poor's was much more optimistic about the general outlook for emerging markets than Goldstein. While he acknowledged that credit ratings are not perfect, he found it nonetheless a significant sign of optimism that the ratings of emerging markets had improved markedly in recent years. Wyss also was much less alarmed than others at the conference about the U.S. federal budget deficit, which he noted was not out of line with the deficits of other industrial countries. He was more concerned, though, about the large and growing U.S. current account deficit and the danger that foreign central banks would suddenly be unwilling to continue buying large volumes of U.S. government debt, thereby removing the financing of the large U.S. current account deficit and the associated large demand for U.S. assets.

Don Hanna of Citigroup noted that foreign central banks that are buying U.S. dollars are doing so out of their free will and presumably are making rational decisions in doing so. Indeed, in countries such as China where formal domestic interest rates are lower than in the United States, the central banks are making money in the short run through such purchases (although they are also assuming the risks of capital losses in the future if the dollar should decline in value).

On another subject, although better regulation supports higher credit ratings on Asian securities, Hanna questioned how much transparency in financial reporting had really improved in the region since the 1997–98 crisis. Furthermore, enforcing legal rights in some countries, such as China, can still be quite expensive.

Khalid Sheikh of ABN Amro was more nervous than the other two panelists, highlighting the possibility that some unforeseen event could trigger an economic downturn in emerging markets. In particular, since other Asian economies have become so dependent on the Chinese market, any slowdown of China's economic growth could have significant negative effects in the rest of the region. Furthermore, some of the countries that have been buying dollars have also had difficulty sterilizing the dollar inflows, which creates a danger of inflation.

The financial sector, and the banking system in particular, has been at the heart of the financial crises discussed in this volume. To what extent have countries since introduced reforms to address the weaknesses that contributed to their difficulties in the first place? This is the topic of chapter 7, by Gerard Caprio and Patrick Honohan of the World Bank.

The authors observe that, in most cases, banks in crisis countries took speculative or unhedged foreign exchange positions that later contributed to their difficulties and to problems in the financial sectors generally, when governments were forced by events (and dwindling reserves) to float their currencies. In a few cases, like the Dominican Republic and Venezuela, outright fraud played an important role in the banking crises.

The authors discuss several features of how the financial crises in these countries were resolved. Although there were many differences among countries, the authors note that there also were common features. For example, with a few exceptions, banking difficulties in the crisis countries were confined to a minority of institutions and were not widespread throughout entire banking systems. In addition, problems arose at both public and privately owned banks. Governments rarely addressed banking problems quickly and all at once; instead they tended to recapitalize failed institutions in successive waves. Sharp currency depreciations typically affected the timing, nature, and scale of these recapitalizations.

The authors examine the postcrisis performance of thirty-eight countries that have suffered crises (a few more than once) since 1994. Again, despite the country variations, some interesting common features stand out. On average, GDP growth in the three years following the crisis was lower than in the three years preceding it; the same was true with inflation (suggesting that, with less pressure from domestic demand, prices were not pushed up as rapidly as in the precrisis period). Almost all countries increased their "financial depth" postcrisis—that is, deposits flowed into the banking systems, during and as they were repaired. The experience with bank credit postcrisis was much more varied; in some cases it grew, while in others it shrank (suggesting that government debt rose rather than loans to private borrowers, partly because of the postcrisis bank restructurings). At the same time, interest rate margins—the "spreads" between banks' earnings from interest and the costs of funds—have fallen pretty uniformly since the crisis episodes. In addition, the crises have moved varying amounts of ownership of banks into private and, especially, foreign hands.

One silver lining to the black cloud of financial crises is that experience has produced a reasonable degree of consensus about how to resolve troubled financial institutions. Ideally, the process should be clear and transparent, and banks' nonperforming assets should be removed as quickly as possible and sold to private investors. Parallel work should be done on strengthening the banks' main clients, the corporate sector. Losses should not be fully socialized. Government aid should "fill the hole" in the balance sheets of failed banks created by the loan and other losses that contributed to the failures, but only as part of recapitalization plans that draw in new, private capital and management to run the bank thereafter. Although foreign capital and expertise can often make a real difference, it is not always a panacea. If capital and management—domestic or foreign—cannot be attracted, then the institutions should be liquidated. The authors discuss specific additional principles for special situations, such as what to do with failed state-owned banks, how to realize value most efficiently and profitably for the banks' nonperforming assets, and how and to what extent to protect depositors.

In reality, countries varied in how closely they conformed to these "best practices." The authors suggest that many deficiencies in the implementation of "resolution policy" can be attributed to limited administrative capacity and limited independence from political elites who run the countries.

In addition to these lessons for authorities whose financial system has just emerged from a crisis, the authors conclude with a series of broader recommendations for developing countries in building productive and stable financial sectors in the future, including the advisability of attracting foreign banks and other financial institutions, reducing the reliance on banks, encouraging more intermediation through capital markets, and relying more heavily on markets than on regulators to discipline banks and prevent them from taking undue risks. They note that the lack of access to financial services in many developing countries is a source of vulnerability for emerging markets, not least because it could prompt calls, already being heard, for the return of development banks and subsidized credit schemes, which the authors warn could, as in the past in many countries, undermine financial sector development.

Finally, looking ahead, one of the larger financial challenges confronting all emerging-market economies (and developed countries too) is the pension system. Populations are aging, but the traditional way of providing support for the elderly—the extended family—is being eroded by migration and urbanization. At the same time, the standard pay-as-you-go pension systems for government and formal sector workers have become costly in many developing countries. Many countries have followed Chile and put in place some sort of fully funded system of individual pension accounts, but questions have arisen about these systems. In chapter 8, the last paper in this volume, Robert Holzmann of the World Bank examines these issues, drawing on a longer study by a World Bank team.

Holzmann argues that successful reform of pensions depends first of all on a careful consideration of whether the macroeconomic and fiscal environment can support the reform. It also depends on a credible commitment arising from the political economy of the country and a buy-in by the country's leadership. Finally, it depends on creating appropriate regulatory and supervisory arrangements and building capacity and governance to deal with the complex, intertemporal problems of providing retirement income. In reforming pensions, careful attention to the secondary developmental benefits of pensions is also necessary. Pensions are, after all, a claim on future economic output and should therefore be designed to leverage positive impacts from saving and financial market development and to reduce potential negative impacts on labor markets and macroeconomic stability.

Holzmann suggests that pension reform is now becoming based on five subsystems or pillars. In addition to the three well-known pillars—a public system linked to earnings and usually with pay-as-you-go financing; a mandatory, fully funded, and privately managed system (essentially an individual savings account or variant of the Chilean model); and voluntary savings for retirement—there is a basic, "zero" pillar to deal with poverty among the elderly and a nonfinancial pillar that involves intrafamily support, access to health care, the housing status of the elderly, and so forth. To be sure, this is an ideal system, and not every country has the resources to have all pillars—pension systems must be affordable and not create macroeconomic instability—but the full system is something to which all countries can aspire.

Holzmann concentrates the latter part of his chapter on three areas of the mandatory, fully funded, privately managed pillar that have drawn attention: country readiness and regulatory and supervisory issues, containment of fees and costs, and annuities for retirees, an often overlooked issue when systems are set up. Generally, most countries are ready to implement some sort of fully funded, privately managed pillar. The exceptions are countries with chronic macroeconomic imbalances. A credible macroeconomic framework and a sound banking system are preconditions for a sound pension system. For countries with immature markets, tight regulation and supervision of investments and close attention to provision of information for the contributors are desirable initially. As the system and capital market develop, the limitations on investments can be relaxed.

Fees have become an issue for contributors to private pension systems. High fees not only reduce the returns to retirees but also reduce the system's attractiveness to potential contributors outside the formal economy. The most successful approaches to containing fees seem to involve reducing costs by using a unified clearinghouse system for managing the accounts, limiting the incentives for marketing expenditures, and limiting the fees via competitive bidding or passive investment options.

The provision of annuities is becoming an issue as pension systems age and more contributors retire. Typically, the insurance sector is the most likely provider. However, information on insurance companies or specialized annuity providers is often opaque and needs improvement. A crucial issue, which has not yet been resolved, is to determine who will bear the risk of rising life expectancy and uncertain future investment income. So far, a combination of three approaches has been used: regulation of the insurance-annuity sector, the creation of variable annuities, and minimum pension guarantees by the government.

Much has happened in emerging markets, mostly for the good, since the financial crises of the late 1990s and the early part of this decade. At the same time, however, some of the conditions that allowed those crises to come close to getting out of hand, such as poor transparency and inadequate regulation, remain. Furthermore, some countries have not taken sufficient advantage of the current, benign conditions to strengthen their debt positions and their financial markets to better withstand future crises. Finally, there are significant global imbalances in saving and investment that may not be sustainable. It seems odd that the emerging markets are financing the leading economic power in the world. True, the United States may offer high returns, but so should many emerging markets themselves. At some point, the appetite for U.S. dollar investments may wane, and if it does so too rapidly, the economic fallout for the entire world will not be pleasant.

JAMES A. HANSON 2

Postcrisis Challenges and Risks in East Asia and Latin America

Where Do They Go from Here?

Beginning in the mid-1990s, Latin America and East Asia were rocked by a series of financial sector and currency crises. The Mexican crisis began in late 1994 and then spread quickly to Argentina, where damage was limited by sound policy and efforts to strengthen the financial system.[1] Jamaica also suffered a severe crisis in the mid-1990s, following a poorly managed financial liberalization. In 1997 crises unexpectedly hit Asia. The "miracle" countries—Indonesia, Korea, Malaysia, and Thailand—were hit hardest, the Philippines was less affected. China, which continued to grow rapidly, is not considered a crisis country and is not treated extensively in this chapter; its substantial effects on world growth and finance are discussed in Goldstein's contribution to this volume (chapter 5). In 1998 Brazil was hit by a crisis, following the Russian crisis. Soon after, banking crises of varying severity began in Colombia, Ecuador, and Peru, among other Latin American countries, as international lending dried up and premiums on high-risk debt rose in industrial-country markets. Chile managed

The author thanks Jerry Caprio and Patrick Honohan for comments and Ying Lin and Roman Didenko for their excellent assistance.

1. The dating of the crises in this paragraph refers to when each crisis became open. In some cases, this was very close to the end of the year. In most cases, GDP growth only declined after the year of the crisis.

to avoid a crisis, but its growth slowed noticeably.[2] In late 2001 Argentina's excessive domestic and international debt and high international rates finally turned into a full-fledged, old-fashioned debt crisis; Uruguay was hit immediately by contagion to its banking system. Beginning in late 2001, Brazil came under currency and debt rollover pressure but survived without a default. In 2003 a major financial crisis hit the Dominican Republic.

Various explanations have been offered for the crises, and different mixtures of the explanations apply to each country. Krugman's first-generation model of crises focuses on the current account and seems inappropriate for the most recent round of crises.[3] Another type of explanation relates to excess debt, "sudden stops" in capital inflows, and liquidity and insolvency problems, in particular, in the case of Argentina but also for countries that had relatively high ratios of debt to GDP. The question remains why countries that were able to borrow so much in international markets were suddenly cut off. Contagion and multiple equilibria are possible explanations. However, these theories neglect the financial sector element of the crisis. Some critics have argued that financial markets are prone to overshooting and bubbles, which must eventually lead to crashes.[4] A more recent perspective emphasizes the role of liability holders' subjective estimates of net worth: when a government's contingent liabilities suddenly appear more likely to become actual liabilities, its subjective net worth falls sharply, and domestic and foreign asset holders respond by attempting to liquidate their holdings in the country quickly.[5] Finally, many of the crises reflected massive underlying problems in the banking systems related to the lending of public and private banks to "well-connected parties" for activities that proved unproductive. These problems eventually led to runs on the banks and the currency, because of political as well as economic factors.[6]

This chapter discusses the policies with which East Asian and Latin American governments dealt with their crises and how the crises may affect their financial systems into the twenty-first century, the different rates at which growth resumed in the countries after the crises and other macroeconomic developments, developments in international debt and reserves

2. In 1998, to reduce the risks of contagion from Asia and encourage capital inflows, Chile eliminated the special reserve requirements that had been used to deter short-term inflows (Edwards 1999).

3. Krugman (1979).

4. Kindleberger (2000); Minsky (1992).

5. Dooley (2000).

6. World Bank (2000, 2005a).

after the crises, and the current situation in the financial systems of East Asia and Latin America, including the risks and challenges they face. It also discusses particular risks, such as the resurgence of public sector banking in developing countries, the recent reduction in interest of well-known international banks in expanding into developing countries, the issues related to cross-border expansion of regional banks, and the possibilities for reducing risk through regulation and supervision, market discipline, and improvements in the legal framework, issues discussed in more detail elsewhere in this volume, notably in chapter 7 by Gerard Caprio and Patrick Honohan. The last section offers a brief summary.

Policy Response to the Crises and Financial Sector Overhang

All the crises in East Asia and Latin America included currency crises; the new element was how many of these crises involved, if not originated in, banking and financial sector crises. This pattern contrasts with most of the crises of the early 1980s, which largely reflected the inability of governments to roll over the external debt of the public sector.[7] In many of the recent cases, the banking and financial crises preceded the currency crises.[8]

In the crises of the 1990s, banks were hit by withdrawals of deposits and cuts in external credit lines. Initially, central banks typically responded with lender-of last-resort support for weak institutions; in some cases, monetary policy was loosened to deal with sectoral problems.[9] Although a standard policy response, lender-of-last-resort support was fraught with the well-known difficulties of distinguishing between illiquid and insolvent banks. Another issue was the possibility that well-connected insiders attempted to loot their banks or take funds out in response to increasing political risks, and lender-of-last-resort support allowed them to do so. In some cases,

7. The Chilean crisis of 1982 is an exception.

8. Kaminsky and Reinhart (1999).

9. A significant literature exists on whether credit crunch existed in East Asia during the crisis; see the works cited in Coe and Kim (2002), for example. As discussed below, some evidence suggests that central banks were increasing their domestic credit fairly rapidly, interest rate policy was not particularly tight, and funds were flowing out of the countries rapidly. See World Bank (2000); Kenward (2002), and various papers in Coe and Kim (2002). Moreover, a lot of credit continued to exist; it just went bad. However, cutbacks in foreign credit and closure of banks and other intermediaries probably did reduce the availability of credit to some borrowers.

notably Indonesia and the Dominican Republic, lender-of-last-resort support far exceeded the precrisis capital of banks.

The 1990s runs on the banks and the support for the financial sector typically turned into runs on the currency and the loss of international reserves. The runs on banks reflected depositor and creditor pressure to reduce their holdings and obtain foreign assets, not just switch banks.[10] East Asia was one obvious set of cases—massive amounts of new central bank domestic credit were roughly matched by losses of reserves, producing a complete change in the composition of central bank assets but not much change in the money base.[11] The lender-of-last-resort support tended to increase the supply of domestic assets, the demand for which was falling, and so translated into additional pressure on the exchange rate. In addition, central bank support may have generated concerns about the state of the financial system and the government's targets and policies (for example, Thailand's fixed exchange rate), further increasing the demand for foreign assets. This process may explain why financial crises often precede currency crises.[12] In open economies facing bank runs and capital flight, the central bank must decide whether to maintain the exchange rate by selling reserves, allow depreciation, or tighten money generally to offset the liquidity support given to a few intermediaries, which puts pressure on borrowers indebted in local currency and their lenders. Typically, central banks in the 1990s did a bit of all three, allowing some depreciation, but limiting it by using reserves and by tightening money from time to time.

A second, more lasting, impact of the crises on the financial system was the massive increase in government debt in domestic banking systems. As shown in figure 2-1, government debt rose in almost all the banking systems that suffered crises, in most cases substantially.[13] Governments typically bailed out depositors in weak banks with deposit guarantees—few depositors lost much in local currency terms. The bailout process typically involved transferring bad loans from weak banks to an asset management or recovery company. The asset management company, in turn, put new debt into the banks,

10. This outcome contrasts with the standard analysis of a lender-of-last-resort facility in a closed economy, where depositors shift their funds to other banks or currency. Public sector banks sometimes gained deposits in the crises; despite the well-known poor performance of their portfolios, depositors considered these banks to have the full backing of the government.

11. World Bank (2000).

12. Kaminsky and Reinhart (1999).

13. In Korea and Thailand, government debt in the banks did not rise substantially, but the government took over the external debt of the banks and other intermediaries, shrinking their balance sheets.

Figure 2-1. *Bank Deposits and Public Sector and Central Bank Debt as a Share of GDP in Major Latin American and East Asian Countries, 1995 and 2000*[a]

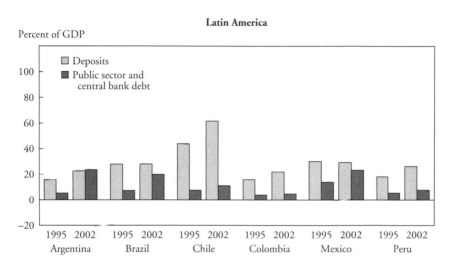

Source: IMF (various years).

a. With the exception of Argentina, for which the postcrisis date is 2002.

implicitly or explicitly guaranteed by the government.[14] The resultant bank was either merged with another bank or banks (often in the public sector) or kept open—under old or new management or, in some cases, under the asset management company—and eventually sold. Whatever initial optimism existed regarding recovery of the bad loans proved false—typically the recovery was 20 percent or less of face value. The governments eventually had to put their debt into the banks to replace the debt of the asset management company. The implications of this process for banking systems postcrisis are discussed below.

The Macroeconomic Recovery: Low Inflation and the Return of Growth

Inflation remained surprisingly low despite the crises and, in some cases, fell even lower afterward. In East Asia, inflation traditionally had been low and remained in single digits in almost all cases during the crisis. The exception was Indonesia, where inflation jumped to more than 50 percent after the large devaluation. However, Indonesian inflation fell back to about 6 percent in 2003 and 2004. Latin America historically had high inflation, with inflationary spurts, and the associated inflation tax on depositors was often used to finance governments and clean up bank balance sheets. However, in a break with history, Latin American inflation dropped sharply in the 1990s. Most Latin American emerging-market borrowers, which often had experienced three- or even four-digit inflation at the beginning of the 1990s, dropped to single-digit inflation in 2000, despite their crises.[15] The crises in Argentina and Uruguay that began in 2001 were associated with large real devaluations and inflation that rose to the 20–30 percent range, but by 2004 their inflation returned to single digits. The crisis in the Dominican Republic that began in 2003 was associated with an even sharper rise in inflation, but after July 2004 inflation was largely halted by a sharp appreciation of the peso.

14. Banking data from the International Monetary Fund's *International Financial Statistics* typically do not show the rise in government debt from the crisis until the government actually puts its debt into the system. In Mexico, for many years, some of the debt from the asset management company remained in the system with a government guarantee that was renewed annually by congress.

15. Mexico experienced a rise in inflation after the crisis at the end of 1994, but by 2001 its inflation was down to the 4–6 percent range. Jamaica reduced its inflation after the large outburst in 1992 and, with a sharp fall in 1997, began a run of single-digit inflation. Colombia also maintained single-digit, declining inflation after 1999. The exceptions are Ecuador and Venezuela, where inflation remained high.

The general prevalence of single-digit inflation has had some benefits. Low inflation reduces the need for high nominal interest rates, the pressures for government intervention to favor particular borrowing groups, the massive subsidies associated with interest rates that were kept well below inflation, the attention to financial engineering rather than efficient production, and the allocation of credit to activities that benefit from inflation. Low inflation has largely eliminated the issue of whether financial intermediaries charge reasonable real interest rates; the issue has become more one of ensuring loan repayment.

The recovery of growth after the East Asian crises has left the crisis countries with average annual growth in the 4–6 percent range since 2000. This is relatively high by developing-country standards, but less than these countries enjoyed in the first half of the 1990s. Except for Korea, all the crisis countries are well below their previous growth path (figure 2-2).[16] Investment ratios have fallen from their high levels of the early 1990s, but proportionately not as much as growth has declined.

Among the East Asian countries, Korea recovered most rapidly and had roughly returned to its previous growth path by about 2002, but growth has since slowed to an average of less than 4 percent a year. Korea's financial crisis was, relative to GDP, the second smallest of the East Asian countries, and it benefited from a large international support package and an agreement among major international creditors to roll over a substantial part of their outstanding loans. Korean imports fell dramatically initially, and the country began to accumulate international reserves; by 2001 it had prepaid its debt to the International Monetary Fund (IMF) and much of its crisis-related external debt. Korea is also generally considered the East Asian country that reformed the most. Some chaebols (conglomerates) were allowed to go bankrupt, others were forced into major restructurings, and a few banks were sold to foreign investors.

A major factor in Korea's rapid recovery was a rise in household consumption. With a slowdown in traditional export markets and competitive pressures from China, the government elected to stimulate the economy by encouraging a rise in consumption, including a major expansion of credit cards. Although banks eventually suffered losses on consumer credit and one

16. Barro (2001) finds that output loss after the financial crisis in East Asia was larger than in a broad sample of crisis countries, the recovery was strong, and the previous growth path may not be resumed. Cerra and Saxena (2003) also find a quick recovery from the crisis, but some permanent loss of output.

Figure 2-2. *Precrisis and Postcrisis Growth in Select East Asian Countries,*
1991–2004

Index of GDP 1997=100

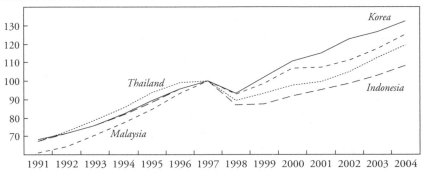

Sources: IMF (various years); World Bank estimates.

of the largest non-bank credit card companies went bankrupt and had to be
bailed out, principally by Korean Development Bank, the consumption-led
growth strategy was initially successful in supporting a rapid return to Korea's
earlier growth path. When world growth increased, Korean exports and capital account receipts also increased, and the buildup in international reserves
increased massively. However, consumption is now lagging, household
indebtedness is high, and, with high oil prices, GDP growth seems likely to
be less than 5 percent in 2005, after 4.6 percent in 2004.

Thailand's recovery was slow until, as in Korea, its consumption picked
up in 2002, followed by sharp rises in exports in 2003 and 2004. The government that took office in 2001 adopted a somewhat populist strategy,
putting a moratorium on rural debts, offering new lending after write-offs of
old loans by public sector banks, and providing funds for revolving credits in
villages, low-cost medical care, and incentives for home buying. The government also resisted industrial restructuring or execution of collateral on past-
due debts. However, the fiscal accounts actually tightened after 2001, and
monetary policy was largely unchanged. Thailand has reduced its international debt by one-third since 2000 and paid off its IMF debt in 2003, two
years early. The government is now promising a push on infrastructure, but
high oil prices and the tsunami that devastated the country in December
2004 are limiting growth in 2005 to less than 5 percent.

In contrast to Korea, Indonesia has recorded average growth much slower
than in the first half of the 1990s and hence has fallen well below its previ-

ous growth path. Indonesia suffered the worst crisis of the Asian countries.[17] In 1998 democracy replaced the long-lived regime of President Suharto and his cronies, which meant a complete restructuring of Indonesia's political economy and major adjustments in the economy. Recently, the country was unable to take advantage of the rise in petroleum prices and reduce its fiscal deficit or increase public investment or social spending, because of a large subsidy of domestic oil prices, a long history of underinvestment in petroleum production, and a generally unfavorable climate for foreign direct investment, all of which had turned the country into a net importer of petroleum. The election of a new president was associated with a rise in growth, and construction in Jakarta is picking up, but the tsunami may slow growth again, and foreign investors still cite many issues, including security. Malaysia and the Philippines have also remained below their precrisis growth path.

In the Latin American crisis countries, growth has resumed, but most countries remain below their relatively slow precrisis growth paths, despite 2004 bringing the highest growth in Latin America since the 1980s (figure 2-3). In many of the Latin American countries the crises were smaller, relative to GDP, than in East Asia, and hence the recoveries did not have to be as large. In addition, the crises in some of the Latin American countries started after 1997, which meant that the recovery periods coincided with a pickup in the world economy and growing markets for primary products. However, Latin American growth rates were much slower than in East Asia, and, until 2004, the Latin American economies seemed to have benefited less from the rise in world growth than the East Asian economies. Although the Latin American economies recently benefited from the increased world demand for primaries, many Latin American economies still face significant adjustment problems in their manufacturing sectors as a result of globalization. Investment rates in most Latin American countries are 20 percent of GDP or less, which is somewhat lower than investment rates in East Asia today and much lower than East Asian rates in the first half of the 1990s.

Regarding individual Latin American countries, Peru did better than most, increasing its growth rate and rising above the previous growth path. Peru suffered a relatively small financial crisis that it managed well. Despite a major political upheaval in 2000, Peru maintained a strong fiscal stance and a market orientation, while continuing to limit government intervention in the economy. Mexico also seems to have risen above its growth

17. Some indicators suggest that postcrisis growth and exports may be underestimated, particularly in forestry and related industries, because of the growth in illegal logging after the end of the cronies' control of logging concessions, which was related to their monopoly on plywood exports.

Figure 2-3. *Precrisis and Postcrisis Growth in Select Latin American Countries, 1994–2001*

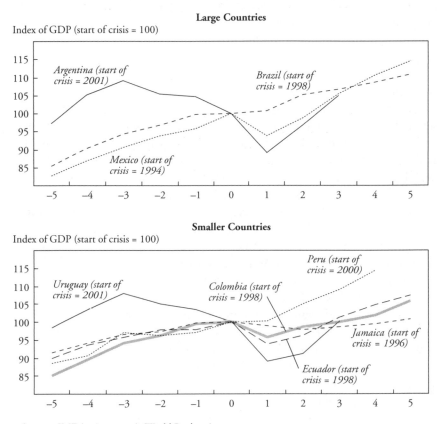

Large Countries

Index of GDP (start of crisis = 100)

Smaller Countries

Index of GDP (start of crisis = 100)

Sources: IMF (various years); World Bank estimates.

path prior to the 1994 crisis (not shown in figure 2-3, where the last date for Mexico is 1999). Jamaica also is above its former growth path, but its growth remains less than 3 percent a year.

Argentina and Uruguay rebounded quickly from the large losses in output after their crises; it remains to be seen whether they can sustain growth in coming years. Argentina suffered a recession before the 2001 crisis, especially after Brazil's devaluation in 1999 (figure 2-3). Many observers attribute that recession to Argentina's declining competitiveness because of the peso's link to the dollar. Both Argentina and Uruguay suffered sharp declines in output following the Argentine debt-financial crisis that began in late 2001. Since then, Argentina has benefited, at least temporarily, from its default, and its exports have become much more competitive since it broke the link between the peso and the dollar. Uruguay has benefited from Argentina's recovery. And both countries, along with Brazil, have benefited from the rise in demand for major agricultural exports such as meat and soybeans. Brazil managed to avoid a debt default in 2002–03, and export-led growth has picked up. The other crisis countries, Colombia and Ecuador, have recovered but continue to suffer from country-specific problems that limit their growth.

International Debt and Reserves

Globalization of financial markets has given international debt and reserve issues an important role in both financial intermediation and crises. International borrowings played a major role in financing the private sector up to the mid-1990s in many of the larger developing countries.[18] Excessive external debt and "sudden stops" in inflows played an important role in the crises of the 1990s.

Since 1997, among the "emerging markets,"[19] the average ratio of external debt to gross national income (GNI) in East Asian countries has declined to roughly the 1995 level; in Latin America, the average ratio has risen since 1997 and exceeds the levels of the mid-1990s (figure 2-4). The fall in East Asia reflects sharp declines in the amount of external debt in Korea and Thailand—and a smaller decline in Indonesia—as well as real growth and real exchange rate movements. The rise in the average debt ratio in Latin America since 1997 reflects the sharp rise in the debt ratios of the crisis countries of Argentina, Dominican Republic, and Uruguay, because of real exchange rate depreciations and declining output (compared to 1997). In the other emerging-market crisis countries of Latin America, the amount of debt in dollars was roughly constant, and the ratios of external debt to GNI tended to rise less sharply than in the other crisis countries and, in some cases, were roughly constant, reflecting changes in the real exchange rates

18. Hanson (2003).
19. The term "emerging markets" refers to countries that have issued international bonds; as used here, these are Indonesia, Korea, Malaysia, Philippines, and Thailand in East Asia and Argentina, Brazil, Chile, Colombia, Costa Rica, Dominican Republic, Ecuador, Jamaica, Mexico, Panama, Peru, Uruguay, and Venezuela in Latin America.

Figure 2-4. *Ratio of Average External Debt to Gross National Income in East Asia, Latin America, and Emerging Markets, 1980–2003*[a]

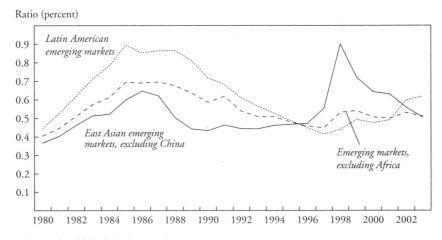

Ratio (percent)

Source: World Bank (various years).
a. The figure covers thirteen emerging markets in Latin America and five in East Asia.

and GNI growth as well as the absolute change in external debt since 1997. Nonetheless, it is worth noting that the average external debt ratio in Latin America has risen since 1995, even excluding Argentina, Dominican Republic, and Uruguay, while it has fallen in East Asia since 1997, even excluding Korea and Thailand, basically because of the reduction in the ratio of debt to GNI in Indonesia. Thus less has been done to reduce the postcrisis overhang of external debt in Latin America than in East Asia.

One element in the overhang of debt from crises is the growth of IMF and World Bank debt in some countries (table 2-1). In Argentina in 2004, IMF and World Bank debt became even more important in relative terms, with the reduction in private debt values. The IMF and the World Bank have preferred creditor status. Hence their large position in a few countries may even deter the entry of new private borrowing, which would face substantial default risk because of the large overhang of indebtedness of these countries to the IMF and the World Bank. In addition, some observers have criticized the IMF for not being tough enough on Argentina, one of its largest borrowers.

In 2003, and even more in 2004, net external borrowing by East Asian and Latin American countries rose, with measured net private external lend-

Table 2-1. *Select Countries with Large Exposure to the IMF and World Bank, 2003*

Percent

Ratio of	Argentina	Brazil	Indonesia	Uruguay
IMF debt to total external debt	9.3	12.0	7.6	20.5
IMF debt to public sector debt (medium and long term + IMF)	10.8	13.1	9.2	23.4
IMF debt to GNI	12.7	6.0	5.2	22.4
World Bank debt to total external debt	4.5	3.6	7.3	6.1
World Bank debt to public sector debt (medium and long term)	7.6	9.0	13.3	9.7
World Bank debt to GNI	6.1	1.8	4.9	6.7

Source: World Bank (2004).

ing turning increasingly positive.[20] Moreover, borrowing plus net errors and omissions was substantially higher than in the mid-1990s, indicating that nonregistered flows were following the same pattern as registered flows, not offsetting them in capital flight, as occurred in the mid-1990s.

The rise in private flows reflected private lenders' search for higher yields than were available in industrial countries.[21] In 2003 and 2004, private lenders shrugged off Argentina's default and the more recent problems in the Dominican Republic and drove down spreads on debt of emerging-market countries, notably Brazil, where market opinion reversed itself on the new government. In 2004 Uruguay even managed to issue $150 million of external bonds, despite a debt restructuring in 2003.

The recent rise in borrowings also involved a wider menu of instruments than in the past. Various kinds of debt were collateralized. Domestic currency bonds were issued internationally by Colombia and a few Brazilian banks. In their search for higher yields, private lenders even began to participate in local debt markets in developing countries. For example, in Brazil,

20. World Bank (2005b).
21. Another factor may have been the need for oil exporters to invest their higher earnings: even if these funds were recycled back to industrial-country markets, the downward pressure they exerted on interest rates there may have encouraged other investors to move into developing-country instruments.

an estimated 10 percent of domestic debt was held by nonresidents in 2004. These new trends raise questions about the reasons for the previous concentration of developing-country debt denominated in foreign currency— so-called "original sin."[22]

In addition to the lenders' higher tolerance for risk, the flow of new debt and the declining spreads also reflect improvements in country ratings and performance. Moreover, lower interest rates on external debt have lowered costs and improved fiscal performance.

By February 2005, the spread on emerging-market bonds over U.S. treasuries hit a record low, and the spreads on Brazil's debt were back to the levels of 1997. Latin American countries took advantage of the decline in spreads to increase net borrowing, replace old, high-interest-rate debt, and lengthen maturities, to some extent. East Asian countries tended to go slowly on new borrowing and simply amortized debt. Even in 2003, before the full impact of the lower interest rates and the replacement of old debt was felt, average interest rates being paid on the stock of long-term external debt fell 50 to 100 basis points for the major emerging-market countries in Latin America and East Asia.

For private borrowers in developing countries, the impact of these trends was delayed somewhat. For example, in banks in many of the major emerging markets in Latin America and East Asia, the net overseas asset position improved after 2000 as the banks increased their offshore holdings and creditor banks reduced their lending. In 2003 private sector total external borrowing in most developing countries was still down, relative to 2000, as was the countries' short-term external debt. By 2004, however, private borrowers in developing countries also began to increase their offshore borrowings.

---

22. Eichengreen and Hausmann (2004) argue that a major factor in financial crises has been the denomination of emerging-market countries' debt in industrial countries' currency, which they term "original sin" and attribute to some sort of market failure. The denomination of borrowing in an industrial country's currency imposes a massive cost if the borrowing country has to devalue in a currency crisis. However, as discussed in Hanson (2002), there are incentives for a country to denominate its debt in foreign currency—the low up-front interest cost and the corresponding longer effective maturity of the debt compared to a local currency bond that would carry high interest rates that include a large devaluation premium—even given the foreign currency–related risk to the issuer that, of course, only becomes an actual cost over time. The recent appearance of bonds in Colombian pesos and external investor interest in Brazilian reais bonds, both currencies that recently appreciated substantially relative to the dollar, raises the issue of whether what appeared to be "original sin" simply reflected incentive-based decisions, not some sort of market failure.

To what extent could sudden changes in international markets—in particular, increases in U.S. interest rates and depreciations of the U.S. dollar—generate new external debt–related problems in East Asia and Latin America similar to those that began in the mid-1990s? The still-high external debt levels raise the issue of vulnerability, particularly in Latin America, where debt ratios remain higher than in East Asia.

Rising international interest rates, as predicted by the U.S. yield curve, would raise the costs of new external borrowing directly as well as indirectly, if investors redirect their funds to the United States.[23] In addition, spreads would probably widen on emerging-market debt, particularly for countries with high external debt. A short-lived example of the turbulence that such developments could create occurred in early 2005. Rises in U.S. interest rates, a rise in oil prices, and concerns about U.S. growth were followed by rises in developing-country rates, leading some countries to postpone their bond issues.

Vulnerability to rising international interest rates seems limited by a number of factors, however. First, current international interest rates are low by historic standards. For example, the rate on long-term U.S. government bonds has remained below 4.5 percent for much of 2005 and even dipped below 4 percent in the early summer, compared to an average rate of about 6.5 percent in 1995–96. Thus not only are spreads on developing-country debt low, but interest rates on them are low historically. Even a 2-percentage-point rise in U.S. rates, plus an associated increase in spreads, would only bring rates back to about 1995–96 levels. Moreover, many countries have "locked in" recent low interest rates and longer maturities to some degree, thereby reducing future external borrowing needs. Nonetheless, countries that are still highly indebted, that did not lock in low rates, and that did not take advantage of the period of low interest rates to raise fiscal surpluses enough to reduce their excessive debt could encounter difficulties.[24] In addition, countries' borrowing costs would tend to rise because of the sympathetic rise in local currency rates on the debt issued in domestic markets, which is often short term.

23. Whether investors would redirect funds to the United States is not clear; it depends not only on rises in U.S. interest rates but also on investors' expectations of future U.S. dollar devaluations.

24. The optimal level of debt depends on expectations of future rates. Thus reducing debt, even in a period of low interest rates, may make sense. If the current stock of debt is excessive, then using the fiscal gains from low interest rates to reduce the stock of debt to optimum levels is a politically easy approach.

A depreciation of the U.S. dollar against major currencies would tend to reduce the burden of most countries' debt, not directly worsen their situation.[25] Such a decline has occurred since 2002. However, sudden depreciations of the dollar could make it more difficult for developing countries to earn foreign exchange, because of a slowdown in the world economy and a loss of competitiveness in those countries that allow their currency to appreciate relative to the dollar.

Another element reducing the vulnerability to current debt levels and to "sudden stops" in new inflows is the large accumulation of international reserves in many countries, particularly in East Asia, combined with limited growth or even declines in measured short-term debt. The average ratio of short-term debt plus external interest payments to reserves has declined about 20 percent since the mid-1990s (figure 2-5). Moreover, most countries also show an improvement; the outliers in 2002 and 2003 were mainly crisis countries.

The biggest improvements were in East Asia, reflecting mainly sharp rises in reserves, although declines in short-term debt and interest costs also played a role. In Korea, reserves increased nearly 500 percentage points between 1996 and 2004 (figure 2-6). Reserves also increased by 65–150 percent in Indonesia, Malaysia, and the Philippines. The sharp rises in reserves in East Asia reflect a combination of (a) maintenance of the exchange rate with respect to the dollar to maintain export competitiveness, despite large capital inflows, and (b) a deliberate policy to build up a shock absorber, for example, in Korea. One issue, however, is the extent to which this growth in reserves reflects capital inflows in expectation of an appreciation and how quickly currency inflows could turn to outflows after an exchange rate adjustment.

In Latin America, the buildup of reserves has been much less than in East Asia and occurred mainly in 2003 and 2004. To some degree, the differences between Latin America and East Asia reflect the more recent dates of the Latin American crises. But they also reflect slower growth of reserves in

---

25. A dollar depreciation, given constant export prices, makes it easier to earn enough foreign exchange to repay the debt. A dollar depreciation would not affect the ratios of reserves to debt, except to the extent that debt was not in U.S. dollars. Much of emerging-market external debt is in dollars. Not only have some countries been trying to refinance their debt to reduce interest costs, but some have been converting their stock of debt into dollars, to avoid a potential capital loss (in dollars) on non-dollar-denominated external debt. Of course, a dollar depreciation would reduce the value of developing-country reserves relative to domestic currency, assuming the country did not also depreciate and thus possibly reduce its ability to cover a bank run.

Figure 2-5. *Ratio of Short-Term Debt plus Interest to Reserves in Emerging-Market Economies, 1986–2003*

Ratio (percent)

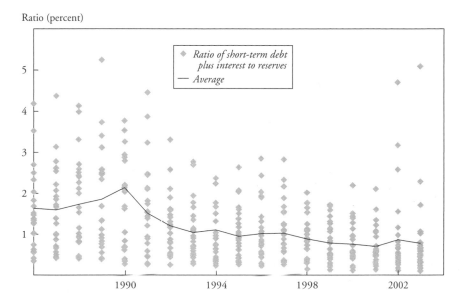

Sources: IMF (various years); World Bank (various years)

Latin America, even recently. In Latin America, much of the improvement in the ratio of debt and interest to reserves reflects slow growth of short-term debt and the recent dampening of interest costs, not strong growth of reserves.

A final issue in the area of international debt is the implication of the recent Argentine default. To some extent, Argentina's case is unique. Nonetheless, the default, and the events leading up to it, could affect international financial transactions during the next few years (box 2-1).

Risks and Challenges in Domestic Financial Systems in East Asia and Latin America circa 2004

Banks continue to dominate the financial systems of East Asia and Latin America. However, private pension systems have become large relative to banks in some Latin American countries—for example, in Peru, pension system assets are now roughly one-third as large as bank assets, and in Chile, the system with the longest, most successful history, they are roughly as

Figure 2-6. *Reserve Accumulation Index in the Crisis Countries of East Asia and Latin America, 1996–2004ᵃ*

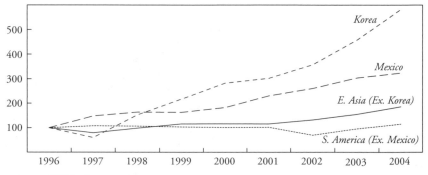

Reserve accumulation index (1996 = 100)

Source: IMF (various years.)
a. East Asia includes Indonesia, Malaysia, Philippines, and Thailand. South America includes Argentina, Brazil, Colombia, Ecuador, Peru, and Uruguay.

large as those of banks.[26] Other non-bank intermediaries, such as the finance companies in Korea, Malaysia, and Thailand and the mortgage banks in Colombia, suffered problems in the financial crises and are being wound down to various degrees.[27] Government bond markets in local currency have developed in almost all of the "emerging markets" of East Asia and Latin America.[28] Their development in some cases—for example, Indonesia and Jamaica—is the result of the large volume of government debt arising from the crisis. Markets in central bank debt also exist in some countries. Secondary trading in government and central bank debt remains small, however, because most investors simply buy and hold and because the legal framework for repos, forward transactions, and security-based lending is poorly developed. Private bond markets have also developed in some countries, helped by various combinations of increased GDP growth, the development of the government bond market, and the demand from

26. In theory, private pension funds transfer risk to their contributors, unlike banks where depositors are usually insured. However, in many countries, governments guarantee a minimum pension, which represents a contingent liability. Another risk is in the insurance companies. The retirement of workers enrolled in these private pension funds, who generally will buy annuities from the insurance companies, will increasingly make the soundness of the insurance companies an issue.

27. The crisis-related problems of Thailand's finance companies are not new—in the early 1980s, they suffered from problems prior to the banking crisis, and many were closed (Baliño and Sundarajan 1991).

28. The exceptions are the Dominican Republic and Ecuador.

Box 2-1. *The Possible Consequences of Argentina's Recent History*

Argentina is unique to a large extent. In the early 1990s Argentina ended a series of currency crises and hyperinflation by converting short-term deposits into longer-term debt, adopting a currency board, and resolving an external debt default with a Brady Plan restructuring. Growth was strong for some time but turned negative because of what many observers see as a loss of competitiveness, especially after Brazil devalued in 1999. Despite close relations with the IMF during the 1990s, Argentine government debt soared, partly because of deficits, but largely because of debt injected into its pension system to cover privatization and judicial reversal of earlier government cuts as well as to resolve arrears on suppliers' credits. In 2001 Argentina defaulted on its debt, asymmetrically converted banks' dollar deposits and loans into pesos, and then converted much of the deposits into longer-term instruments. In June 2005 it completed an agreement with 76 percent of its bonds holders that cut these obligations to 34 percent of their face value and accrued interest. This has left the IMF and World Bank holding a substantial fraction of Argentina's debt. Nonetheless, total debt remains $120 billion (about 75 percent of GDP).

Argentina's recent history may have at least five possible implications:

1. Currency boards will be less attractive.

2. International banks will have less interest in large-scale expansion in the banking markets of developing countries.

3. The large discount on Argentina's restructured debt may set a benchmark for future restructurings.

4. Individuals' small-scale purchases of developing-country debt will be unlikely, although sophisticated investors seem unfazed—Argentina was upgraded to a B–rating by Standard and Poor's and is rumored to have received offers of new loans.

5. The IMF and the World Bank will be more careful about future large exposures.

pension funds. Large corporations, which financed themselves offshore in the first half of the 1990s, are now using domestic bond markets to some degree; pension funds and insurance companies, as well as banks, are buyers of these instruments. As with the government bond market, the secondary market in private bonds is small. Securitized instruments have not developed because of legal and tax issues. In response to the loss of highly rated borrowers, banks in the two regions are increasingly moving into consumer credit and mortgages, a process that has occurred in industrial countries. Equity market capitalization has risen in both Latin America and East Asia, but trading (turnover) remains low, particularly in Latin America.

Listings have actually declined in most Latin American countries since the mid-1990s, while rising in East Asia.[29] Hence equity markets, particularly in Latin America, have not been a major source of funding.

As discussed in this section, the main developmental challenge facing banks is in Latin America: limited financial intermediation between depositors and private borrowers,[30] because of low deposit mobilization, the absorption of deposits by government, and debt held by the central bank. Credit to the private sector has been identified as a major positive factor in growth by a number of studies,[31] which suggests that the lack of intermediation is and will be a factor limiting Latin America's growth. Corporations can offset the lack of bank intermediation to the extent that they can finance themselves by selling bonds to non-banks (for example, pension funds and insurance companies) and the public. However, small borrowers, particularly those in rural areas, will face limited access to credit because of limited intermediation as a result of low deposit mobilization and crowding out by government and central bank debt.

Various risks and vulnerabilities also exist in Latin America, because of the high levels of government debt and dollarization—and, to a lesser extent, in East Asia—as well as the standard problems of credit quality in the banks in both regions. Informational and legal frameworks, on which credit quality and access depend, are improving but remain weak. Public banks are growing again, and their nonperforming loans have been costly in the past. Well-known international banks, which at one time were thought to be a solution to many of the problems in the banking sector, are less interested in expanding to developing countries; instead regional banks are expanding across borders, creating their own problems. To deal with the risks and credit quality in the banks, governments have attempted to strengthen regulation and supervision, as well as market discipline, but technical and, more important, political issues are likely to hamper these efforts.

Developments in Banking after the Crises

In East Asia, banks have largely recovered from the 1997 crisis, and intermediation remains high, except in Indonesia. The ratio of bank deposits to

29. World Bank (2005a). To some extent, the decline in listings in Latin America reflects the multinational takeovers of major local firms, such as telephone companies.

30. Banks' credit to the private sector reflects not just intermediation of deposits but also intermediation of foreign funds and the use of bank capital.

31. See King and Levine (1993); Levine (1998, 2003); Levine, Loayza, and Beck (2000), and works cited there.

GDP remains large, although it has declined in Indonesia, the Philippines, and Thailand since 2000 (figure 2-7). Banks' holdings of public sector and central bank debt have fallen relative to bank deposits in all countries, compared to 2000. Bank credit to the private sector (relative to GDP) is larger than in either 1995 or 2000 in Korea (although some of this credit now represents consumer credit) and is about the same as in Malaysia. However, in Malaysia, total credit to the private sector has declined because its non-bank sector has declined since the crisis. In Thailand, private sector credit is lower than in either 1995 or 2000, reflecting the decline of both bank deposits and the non-bank sector. Finally, private sector credit is lower in the Philippines and substantially lower in Indonesia than in either 1995 or 2000, reflecting the declines in deposits and, particularly in Indonesia, the large volume of recapitalization bonds in the banking system.[32]

In six major Latin America countries, bank deposits were still only a small fraction of GDP in 2004 and have not grown much since 2000.[33] Deposits averaged only 38 percent of GDP in 2004, compared to 73 percent in East Asia. Only Chile's banking sector is similar in size to that of the East Asian countries. Deposits stagnated, or fell, as a percentage of GDP in four of the Latin American countries between 2000 and 2004 and rose only slightly in the other two. Moreover, banks' net foreign borrowing declined in all six countries except Chile. Hence banks in Latin America are generally raising fewer funds to intermediate to the private sector than they were in 2000.

Latin American banks in the six countries also hold more public sector debt (almost wholly government debt, net of government deposits) and central bank debt compared to private deposits than they did in 2000. Public sector debt and central bank debt rose relative to deposits on average and in every one of the countries, except Mexico. Bank credit to the private sector, as a percentage of GDP, has fallen in all six countries since 2000, from its already low levels compared to levels in East Asia.

---

32. In cases of crises, assessing the contribution of private sector credit to economic growth involves both a measurement issue and, more substantively, a productivity issue. The measurement issue occurs because, after a crisis, large volumes of private credit typically are transferred from banks to an asset management company. Hence private sector credit declines in banks but rises by an equal amount in the asset management company—that is, no change occurs in the overall volume of private credit. Measuring the volume of private-sector credit correctly means taking into account the loans held by the asset management company. Substantively, there is a productivity issue. The prices that the asset management company eventually realizes for the credits (or the collateral on them) are often less than 30 percent of their face value, not to speak of accrued interest at market rates. Hence the economic value of these private sector credits is substantially less than their face value. This reflects the fact that the use made of these credits does not contribute substantially to growth after the crisis.

33. The following analysis applies to Venezuela and the smaller Latin American emerging markets.

Figure 2-7. *Bank Deposits and Public Sector and Central Bank Debt as a Share of GDP in Major Latin American and East Asian Countries, 2000 and 2004*

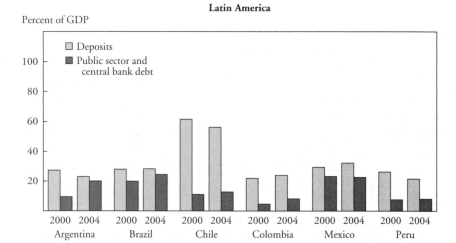

Source: IMF (various years).

The small size of deposits of Latin American banks largely reflects history. Years of high and variable inflation, high taxes, and bank defaults generated a lack of public confidence in bank deposits. Latin American corporations and wealthier individuals placed their deposits offshore—in regional centers or the United States—to avoid these problems. Dollarization and the recent history of low inflation and institutional change that supports it led to a rise in the ratio of deposits to GDP in the 1990s, but deposits still remain a much smaller fraction of GDP than in East Asia (figure 2-7).[34]

The growth of government and central bank debt in Latin America reflects four factors. First, crises in Latin America—particularly in Argentina and in Jamaica and Uruguay among the smaller countries—led to a rise in government debt. Moreover, many of the crises were more recent in Latin America than in East Asia, meaning that there has been less time for growth to reduce the relative size of government bonds that were injected during the crises.[35] Second, the increase in government debt in Latin America reflects the interest on the overhang of debt from the 1990s and a fiscal policy that was not sufficiently tight to offset it, compared to East Asia, where governments have run small surpluses. Third, Latin American governments have taken advantage of growing domestic debt markets and the lower interest rates in them to issue more debt locally, reducing their currency risk.[36] For example, Peru, which did not have a government debt market in 2000, now plans to amortize some offshore debt with funds raised locally. Finally, the monetary policy of central banks has led to substantial and rising amounts of debt, for example, in Mexico, Brazil, and Peru, where in the latter two cases it represents more than one-third of private sector deposits.[37]

The small size of Latin America's small deposit base and its absorption by public sector and central bank debt mean decreasing room for private sector credit. To some extent, corporations can find other sources of funding: domestic bond issues and external borrowing, particularly by the multinationals that took over local firms in the 1990s. However, small borrowers

---

34. World Bank (2005a).

35. The differences also reflect the approach of Korea and Thailand, which took over banks' external debt, rather than injecting government debt into the banking system.

36. Unfortunately, some governments and central banks still have substantial currency risk, not just in their international debt, but because of foreign currency hedges offered to borrowers onshore, either directly or through sales of foreign currency–denominated bonds in domestic markets. These practices, particularly the former, may be creating risky, nontransparent contingent liabilities for governments.

37. Central bank debt is also a large fraction of deposits in Chile, to some extent dating back to the approach taken during the 1982 financial crisis.

suffer from this crowding out. Thus slow growth of private credit represents a challenge to growth in Latin America and, to a lesser extent, in East Asia.

The Challenges and Risks of Government and Central Bank Debt in Banks: Mainly a Latin American Issue

Latin American banks often are criticized for not lending to the private sector, but this criticism neglects the implications of the large inelastic supply of government and central bank debt.[38] Banks' holdings of government and central debt do not reflect banks' unwillingness to lend to the private sector nor the attractiveness of government and central bank debt to banks because of their low capital requirements, liquidity, and likelihood of repayment. Rather, the main reason for these holdings is a macroeconomic constraint—the large outstanding stock of government debt must be held by someone. This stock and the new bond issues to amortize it and cover interest on it are essentially unresponsive to the interest rate.[39] Similarly, central banks, pursuing monetary policy, are inelastic net suppliers of debt in sufficient quantities to reach their target interest rate. In some countries, this central bank debt has accounted for a substantial and growing portion of banks' assets, as the central banks have tried to (a) sterilize capital inflow, while holding the exchange rate roughly constant, and (b) roll over their previous issues of debt. Thus government and central debt crowd out private borrowing, because the interest rate on private debt must be high enough to "create space" for the entire inelastic supply of government and central bank debt.[40]

The recent rise in government and central bank debt has had some benefits. It is less risky than private sector debt—in theory, the government could always print money to pay the bonds, although the resulting inflation would be an effective default. Government debt can also be used as riskless collateral for central bank liquidity support or be sold in markets to raise liquidity, although government debt markets remain thin.

---

38. Also, in some countries, banks face liquidity requirements to hold government or central bank debt.

39. Any responsiveness comes from the government choosing to borrow offshore rather than onshore or to finance the deficit by issues of money, both of which are out of favor. Many governments, particularly in Latin America, are increasing their reliance on domestic borrowing because low interest rates have allowed them to reduce their currency risk at low cost. Governments' ability to use inflationary finance has been curbed by independent central banks with inflation targets.

40. Private pension funds may also hold central bank debt, easing the crowding-out pressure on banks, but not macroeconomic crowding out, except to the extent that their growth has increased the net demand for financial assets and overall saving.

At the same time, the rise in government and central bank debt also represents a challenge (low intermediation) and two risks (default risk and market risk). The challenge represented by government and central bank debt is that it reduces the already low level of bank intermediation between private depositors and borrowers in Latin America: crowding out. Recent studies show that low levels of deposits (M2) and low levels of credit to the private sector are related to slower GDP growth in the future. To some degree, corporates can use direct offshore funding, which was important in the first half of the 1990s, bond market finance, which has grown, and equity market finance, which has grown in Asia, to offset the lack of bank finance. However, these substitutes are available mainly to large corporations. The limited options of small borrowers mean that crowding out affects them heavily.

Government and central bank bonds are less risky than private sector debt, but they still have default risk and market risk. Default risk arises because governments may not be able to service their debt fully, as occurred in Argentina, a case that perhaps has overly focused bank regulators on government default risk. Market risk arises because bond prices may fall relative to banks' liability prices. Moreover, government bonds are repriced in markets relatively frequently, and the capital loss on bonds is more obvious to depositors than the loss on loans, where the asset values are obscured.[41]

The well-publicized defaults on government debt in Argentina have led bank regulators to discuss ways to reduce the risk of government default, but these approaches neglect the macroeconomic constraint mentioned above. Suggestions for reducing government default risk often involve increases in capital requirements or limits on financial institutions' holdings of government debt. However, raising the capital requirements on government debt merely raises the cost of inelastic government borrowing (to allow banks to cover the cost of additional capital). Since the same amount of government debt must still be held, raising capital requirements on government debt simply leads to a rise in the loan rate on private borrowings at which the crowding out occurs.[42] Limits on banks' government debt holdings may simply

41. Even though secondary market trading of government bonds is limited, new issues and the yield curve allow regular revaluations of government bonds. Loans have to be classified according to bank regulations, and this information is increasingly public. However, banks are often able to hide deteriorations in credits by restructuring loans and "evergreening," despite regulation and supervision.

42. Raising the capital requirement may also reduce the attractiveness of government debt to banks, relative to pension funds, corporations, and individuals. Other than pension funds, the participation in government debt markets in developing countries is limited. Nonetheless, this policy would probably lead to a shift of government debt to non-banks and a corresponding transfer of the risks on it. In any case, such a rise in non-banks' holdings of government debt would not affect the overall availability of funding for the private sector, just increase funding from banks and reduce funding from non-banks.

push borrowing offshore. But excessive government borrowing, whether external or internal, will lead eventually to a crisis. As the crisis approaches, domestic financial institutions will get into difficulties, even if their government debt holdings are limited—no economy does well when its government goes bankrupt. Attempts to protect the financial system from excessive government borrowing from banks—limits or disincentives to hold government debt—are the wrong instrument to deal with a problem of excessive government debt and fiscal deficits. These policies are effective in reducing the fiscal costs of crises only to the extent that requiring more bank capital may transfer more of the costs of any default on government debt to bank owners.

Market risk on government bonds is potentially a major issue for Latin American banks in coming years, when international interest rates rise and push up domestic interest rates. A rise in interest rates will reduce the value of government debt holdings. Governments, and some central banks, have been taking advantage of the development of domestic debt markets and low interest rates to extend the maturities of their domestic debt, to lock in low rates, and to reduce their rollover risk. However, this process transfers risks to financial intermediaries that hold the debt, particularly to banks, which have liabilities that have relatively short maturities, have fixed prices, and must pay higher rates as interest rates rise.[43] The risk to banks is limited somewhat by the existence of stable "core deposits." Nonetheless, at a minimum, the capital loss on longer-term debt will cut into bank earnings and could create substantial losses of bank capital. Forcing bank owners to put in more capital may be difficult, particularly given the source of the problem. Moreover, bank depositors, concerned about bank solvency, may withdraw deposits and put them overseas.

Attempts to reduce market risk on government bonds have taken two paths—the accounting for gains and losses on debt and the placing of disincentives on mismatches. With regard to accounting, regulators typically allow banks to separate their holdings of government debt into portfolios for trading and for holding to maturity. The trading portfolio is marked to market, and, to various degrees, profits and losses on it are recorded. The hold-to-maturity portfolio is typically valued at original cost, which means that losses due to rising interest rates are not recorded. Nonetheless, (a) the costs

---

43. Pension funds and mutual funds holding government debt simply transfer to their investors the effective loss from not being able to convert their long-term government debt into higher-interest-rate assets.

of the deposits needed to hold this debt rise with interest rates, reducing earnings on the debt, and (b) capital is lost, even though the loss does not show in accounting terms. With regard to the disincentives to take such risks, regulators may require capital in the case of maturity mismatches between deposits and government debt holdings. However, the capital requirement is likely to be small relative to the potential loss. An alternative to reduce market risk, from the side of the government, would be to issue floating-rate domestic debt, but few governments have made such issues.[44] Ultimately, the issue comes back to the government's need to issue enough debt to cover its rollovers and deficits. Either the government or the financial institutions and the public must take the risk of rollovers and higher interest rates. Currently, the rise in domestic government debt is transferring the risk to banks and, through pension funds, to the public.

Credit Risk and Dollarization: Old Problems of Vulnerabilities

Credit risk of bank portfolios is a traditional vulnerability issue. In East Asian banks, it remains very important given their large volume of private sector credits. Moreover, in some East Asian countries, the link between banks and large, well-connected borrowers remains because postcrisis reforms have been limited. Such links contributed to the crises of the 1990s. In Latin America, the large presence of government and central bank debt has reduced the overall portfolio risk. However, credit risk remains an issue for Latin American banks. Credit risk also exists in pension funds and insurance companies and, through them, for the public and the government (to the extent that it guarantees a minimum pension).

It seems likely that the loan portfolios of commercial banks (excluding credit to governments) are becoming riskier. One reason is that the better borrowers migrated offshore in the first half of the 1990s or have begun to raise funds in local markets (bonds in Latin America, bonds and equity in East Asia). Correspondingly, there has been a reduction in the better borrowers' use of bank credit, a process that has been occurring in industrial countries. In response, banks have increased their lending to other clients.

---

44. Few countries in East Asia or Latin America have issued floating-rate debt, although this is probably a best practice from the standpoint of reducing market risk for banks (see Honohan 2005). In Indonesia, some of the recapitalization bonds originally carried floating rates; to make the intervened private banks more attractive to potential buyers, their fixed-rate recapitalization bonds were converted to floating-rate debt.

Often these new loans have taken the form of consumer credit, mortgages, and, in some cases, loans to microenterprises and small and medium firms, again a process that is occurring in industrial countries.

Consumer credit, mortgages, and micro- and small business credit can be risky for traditional banks. The traditional business of developing-country banks was loans to large firms. Lending to these firms depended on the balance sheet and evaluation of prospects (if they were not part of the bank's financial-industrial conglomerate). In contrast, consumer credit, mortgages, and micro- and small business credit depend on an evaluation of the likelihood that the borrower will repay and, more generally, group probabilities of repayment. In the past, some micro-credit institutions, such as MiBanco in Peru and Credi-Fe in Ecuador, have successfully kept nonperforming loans low by relying heavily on a costly evaluation of individual borrowers. Another approach for loans for consumer durables and mortgages has been to rely on repayments through deductions from wages and salaries earned in the formal sector, where employment is typically steady. However, large banks that wish to expand consumer credit and mortgages may find that such "micro" procedures are too expensive or reach too small a client base.

In some cases, consumer lending has been expanded simply by issuing large numbers of credit cards, hoping that the average default rate will be covered by the high rates of interest being charged. However, this procedure has sometimes proved costly, for example, in Korea, as noted. Expansion of mortgages is an even more complicated issue, given the possibility of a weak credit culture as a result of the previous dominance of public sector banks in the mortgage market and the weak legal framework.

A second element of the credit risk problem is related to the still-large stock of foreign currency loans and deposits—henceforth dollarization. Dollarization developed as a way to recognize the buildup of foreign currency in the economy and to capture some of the demand for foreign currency assets and liabilities in the domestic banking system.[45] Despite a recent reduction in inflation and more stable monetary policy, dollar deposits have remained large in many countries. To cover the foreign currency deposits, banks have issued foreign currency loans, an elementary risk management scheme.[46] Banks did not have to force borrowers to take these loans; foreign currency loans have

45. See Hanson (2002) and Savastano (1992, 1996) for discussions of the reasons for dollarization. Honohan and Shi (2003) provide data on the buildup of dollar deposits over the 1990s.

46. Since the crises, the banks in many countries have shifted from being net international borrowers of foreign exchange to net holders of assets offshore. These assets provide insurance against a devaluation.

a lower cost than domestic currency loans until a devaluation occurs, they have a longer effective maturity than domestic currency loans with their higher interest rates, and there is always the possibility of a government-ordered bailout for borrowers in foreign currency.[47]

Thus the risk from financial sector dollarization is usually credit risk owing to borrowers' lack of assured access to foreign exchange that can be tapped in the event of devaluation, not a mismatch of foreign currency loans and assets in bank portfolios. With devaluation, debt servicing problems arise among nonexporters, whose earnings and asset values typically do not rise proportionately to the devaluation. Even if such borrowers have access to foreign currency assets—for example, offshore—they may not be willing to use them to repay foreign currency loans, because of hopes of a favorable restructuring. The risk for banks is being exacerbated, since the smaller borrowers, who make up more of banks' portfolios, usually do not have easy access to foreign exchange but often borrow in dollars. Indeed, since government debt in local markets is increasingly sold in local currency, these smaller borrowers increasingly represent a counterpart to dollar deposits in the financial system. These trends may have been mitigated to the extent that highly rated borrowers have returned to borrowing from domestic banks when external private-to-private credits declined after 1997. At the moment, with many developing countries facing appreciation rather than depreciation, this credit risk is low. However, the situation could change, perhaps quickly.

Of course, local currency loans would also have credit risk, and their credit risk would tend to rise when interest rates rise sharply with rising expectations of devaluation. Hence the solution to reducing credit risk associated with dollarization is not simply to reduce dollar lending and deposits by fiat. Such a policy would reduce deposits and limit the availability of credit, on average, especially in periods when expectations of devaluation increase and credit risks on local currency loans rise.

---

47. As discussed in Hanson (2002), interest rates on foreign currency credits avoid the high, up-front cost of an expected devaluation that is factored into local-currency interest rates even though the devaluation may not occur for some time—the "peso problem." The lower interest rates on dollar loans improve cash flows (lower deficits for governments using cash accounting) and increase the loan's effective maturity. Moreover, if and when devaluation occurs, its cost is spread out over the amortization period for dollar loans. For these reasons, it is not surprising that governments borrow externally, and many countries—for example, Mexico in 1994 and Brazil and Turkey recently—have indexed some domestic debt to foreign currency. For private firms, in addition to the attractions described above, the hope exists that a devaluation may lead to a government bailout, either by a favorable takeover of foreign currency loans or by an asymmetric conversion of domestic foreign currency debts and deposits to local currency, as occurred in Mexico (1982) and Argentina (2002).

To deal with credit risk, both the traditional kind and risk due to dollarization, banks in developing countries are slowly improving their risk management systems. Not surprising, this will take time. Bank regulators and supervisors are encouraging better risk management, and the more complex levels of Basel II make evaluation of risk management by the banks part of supervision. However, improving risk management and reducing credit risk also will depend on some changes in the informational and legal framework for lending.

Reducing credit risk, and expanding access to credit, will depend heavily on improvement of the information framework. Banks' development of risk management techniques is based on information about the potential borrowers, particularly for consumer and small business loans. An information framework of borrowers' credit histories is also important because it creates an incentive for borrowers to pay on time—development of the intangible asset of a good credit record. Based on a substantial information base of borrowers' histories, U.S. banks have expanded consumer credit without large losses. The ongoing growth of credit bureaus in Latin America and East Asia will generate a similar information base and allow a similar approach to expanding consumer credit. However, the development of credit bureaus depends on sharing information on even the small loans made by banks and on maintaining that information on debtors for some time.[48] Often credit bureau development is limited by legal protections of privacy and the unwillingness of large banks to share information on their best clients to other banks. Moreover, since many potential credit card customers will not have borrowed from the financial system, information on borrowers will need to include data on their payments for telephone service, public utilities, and credits from stores.

Improvement in the legal system is also important to reduce credit risk. Improvements are needed in titling, defining collateral, and executing collateral promptly. In some countries, such as Mexico, special courts have been created to deal with debt default cases, thereby speeding up the execution of collateral. These improvements are not solely to make it easier for banks to take over assets. Banks are in the business of taking deposits

---

48. Politicians may mistakenly seek to reduce the length of credit histories to help defaulters by eliminating their bad credit records after a short time. However, shortening credit histories not only reduces the value of the credit bureau to lenders, it also reduces the intangible asset value of a good credit record to potential borrowers. As a result, their borrowing costs will increase and their access to credit will decline.

and making loans, not managing assets. Collateral that is taken over is usually not worth as much to a new buyer as it was to the borrower, and thus
its sale may not bring enough to repay the loan. Rather, the value of these
legal improvements to banks is to create a credible threat that collateral
will be executed and thus to create an incentive for on-time debt service
by borrowers.

Vulnerabilities and Risks in the Renewed Growth of Public Sector Banks

Public sector commercial and development banks still play a major role in
many East Asian and Latin American countries, and, in some cases, their role
is growing, reflecting the politics of postcrisis recovery. Public sector banks
have a long tradition in Latin America and East Asia. Governments wanted
to use public sector banks to lead the development "takeoff," particularly
industrial development; reduce the power of private bank owners, who were
often foreigners; and provide funds to underserved groups and government
supporters, as well as the public sector itself. Public sector banks also have
often had a major role after financial crises, even though their bad lending
was often a major factor in the crises.[49]

In Latin America in the 1990s, after a history of multiple, costly bailouts
of public sector banks, a wave of bank privatizations occurred along with the
general move toward market-based economies. However, major public sector banks often were not privatized. For example, in Argentina, most provincial banks were privatized after 1995.[50] Nonetheless, public sector banks
constituted more than 30 percent of the system in 2000, reflecting the large
size of Banco de la Nación, Banco de la Provincia de Buenos Aires, and Banco
Hipotecario.[51] In Brazil, Banco do Brasil and Caixa Economica Federal
received large injections of fiscal resources. They remain among the top five
banks and account for about 30 percent of the commercial bank system, even
as the state banks were sold off, closed, or turned into agencies between 1996
and 2002. In addition, BNDES (Banco Nacional de Desenvolvimento
Econômico e Social), a development bank that relies on borrowing and
low-cost pension fund money for resources, had assets that would place it

49. Hanson (2004).
50. Clarke and Cull (1999, 2002).
51. Figures are based on Barth, Caprio, and Levine (2001a, 2001b) and refer to the share of government ownership in commercial banks in 150 countries, as reported by the country's central bank.

among the top five banks. In Chile, despite its commitment to the private sector, Banco del Estado accounts for more than 10 percent of the banking sector. The development bank, CORFO (Corporación del Fomento de la Producción), remains active, particularly as a second-tier lender for small-scale finance. In Mexico, Nacional Financiera, a development bank, remains a major force in the financial market, even though the commercial banks that were taken over in 1982 were privatized in the first half of the 1990s, renationalized after the crisis, and then reprivatized. Peru also made a major effort to get rid of public sector banks—all but COFIDE (Corporación Financiera de Desarrollo) and Banco de la Nación, the government's international and domestic agents, were closed in the early 1990s, and the activities of those two banks were circumscribed. In some countries, privatization never really occurred. In Ecuador, public sector banks (Corporación de Fomento Nacional and Banco Nacional de Fomento) remained large, although lending operations have been limited since the crisis. In Uruguay, Banco de la República and Banco Hipotecario together represented more than 50 percent of the system in 2000.

East Asia did not experience a Latin American–type privatization wave in the 1990s,[52] but the relative importance of public sector banks declined as a result of their own problems and the growth of private sector banks and non-bank intermediaries. For example, in Indonesia, the share of public sector banks in loans fell from 55 percent in 1991 to 45 percent in 1995. In Thailand, Bank Krung Thai continued to be the second largest commercial bank, and the government continued to operate other financial institutions, such as the Savings Bank and various development banks. However, their importance as a source of loans to the private sector declined in the first half of the 1990s, as did the importance of all banks, with the growth of the finance companies.

The crises hit the public sector banks hard. Indonesia is probably the costliest recent example of weak lending by public sector banks. Indonesia's crisis is estimated to have cost more than 50 percent of GDP, with the public sector banks estimated to account for half or more of the total and the cost of cleaning up one public sector bank, Mandiri, equal to nearly one-fifth of GDP. In 2001 the Brazilian Finance Ministry recapitalized the federal banks in various ways to offset their bad loans at an estimated cost of more than $30 billion (before recoveries on bad loans). In the Uruguayan

52. Sales of equity occurred in some cases, but the governments retained a controlling interest, if not a majority of the capital.

crisis, Banco Hipotecario, with assets of almost $3 billion, collapsed because of the mismatch between deposits indexed to dollars and peso-denominated mortgages that, in many cases, had not even been finalized legally.

Despite their weak lending, governments have often used public sector banks as part of the crisis resolution process, sometimes in concert with asset recovery companies. Public sector banks also were used to take over the remnants of private banks and other intermediaries, for example, in Argentina, Indonesia, and Thailand. In Indonesia, public sector banks bought some of the failed banks' assets that were sold by the asset management corporation. Some consolidation also occurred in public banks in the 1990s. For example, in Indonesia, Bank Mandiri was formed from four public sector banks just before the crisis, and a fifth was added after the crisis. In Uruguay, Banco de la República took over the deposits of the bankrupt Banco Hipotecario after the crisis.

This process, as well as postcrisis policies to stimulate growth, has led to an increased role of public sector banks, or public sector–controlled banks, in many countries. It has taken a long time to sell off intervened banks because of the technical complexities of privatization, concerns about getting a reasonable price in a depressed economy, and the politics of sales when either the former owners or foreign banks are the most likely buyers. For example, in Indonesia, it took nearly six years from the founding of the asset management company, IBRA (Indonesian Bank Restructuring Agency), to sell off all the banks, with most of the sales coming in the last two years. In Jamaica, it took nearly five years to sell off the intervened banks. In Uruguay, rather than sell off the banks, a new public sector bank, Banco Comercial Nuevo, was formed from the consolidation of the remnants of Banco Comercio, Banco Crédito, and Banco Montevideo, which collapsed in the crisis, although that is now being privatized.

In addition, public sector entities are returning to credit markets. For example, in Peru, government agencies have become involved in lending— AgroBanco was set up in 2001 to begin limited agricultural lending; Mi Vivienda has become a dynamic force in second-tier lending to finance small-scale mortgages, using the funds that remained after Banco Vivienda's closure; and Banco de la Nación has been reauthorized to expand its deposit-taking and lending in areas that are underserved by private banks. Indonesia created numerous small-scale lending programs, despite having one of the most successful small-scale lenders in the world: the public sector Bank Rakyat Indonesia. And public sector bank credit has been expanding. Indonesia's Bank Mandiri, Indonesia's regional development banks, and Thailand's

Bank Krung Thai and other public sector banks were exhorted to increase their lending in recent years. Despite these exhortations, in all these cases loans have grown only slightly faster than overall bank lending, which has been rising fairly rapidly. In Brazil, also, lending by Banco do Brasil and BNDES has been growing slightly faster than bank lending in general.

These recent developments reflect the traditional motives for public sector banking, probably enhanced by restrictions on economic policy facing the new governments. The sale of public sector banks has always been complicated by issues of political power, particularly sales to foreigners. Governments have always regarded public sector banks as a policy instrument to jump-start development. Governments are impatient to increase credit, even if much of the lack of credit relates to government debt's crowding out of private sector borrowing. Governments have also always regarded public sector banks as a way to channel credit to groups that have lacked access and to political supporters. Political pressures for such directed credit tend to rise as private credit becomes scarce. Moreover, these traditional arguments and pressures for public sector banking are probably felt more strongly in today's world when governments have limited room for maneuver—fiscal deficits are limited by IMF programs and the need to keep borrowing costs low to maintain country ratings, while monetary expansion is limited by the inflation targets of independent central banks. In these circumstances, the resurgence of public sector banking and interventions in credit markets are not surprising.

At the same time, the costs of such public sector pressure for expanded lending are also becoming evident. For example, the costs of the Indonesian small-scale credit programs as well as the write-offs of old small-scale credits have been large. The defaults on Korean credit cards have been costly to banks and to the government-owned Korean Development Bank. Bank Mandiri of Indonesia experienced substantial losses on the loans it purchased from the Indonesia Bank Reconstruction Agency; the central bank ordered it to increase its provisioning substantially, even though the loans were reported to be performing. Since the election, a substantial amount of bad loans was discovered, often linked to well-connected parties. Bank Krung Thai was similarly required to increase provisioning by Thailand's central bank recently. The other Thai government banks have also experienced nonperforming loans of 10 percent or more, in part reflecting their leadership in the government's village fund and low-cost credit schemes. Thus the resurgence of public sector banks represents a risk to governments because of the weaknesses of their lending.

Risks in the Slowdown of Major International Banks' Expansion and the Entry of New Players

A standard recommendation of the 1990s to ease the problems of the financial system was to privatize public sector banks and allow the entry of well-
known international banks. It was thought that these banks would increase
competition and lending to underserved groups with their lending expertise and skills. Moreover, they were likely to absorb costs of any losses without expense to the government rather than suffer a reputational loss. In
Latin America in the 1990s, the presence of well-known international
banks and major Spanish banks grew substantially, through purchases of
private and public sector banks, direct entry, and growth of existing offices.
In East Asia, in contrast, most countries limited the presence of such banks,
and their shares of the banking market rose little over the first half of the
1990s. For example, in Indonesia, the share of foreign and joint venture
banks in total credit remained about 9 percent over the period 1991–96.[53]

Once the international banks entered the countries, their performance
was good, but not as good as their strongest proponents had claimed. These
banks did indeed bring new approaches, often played important roles in
developing the new government bond markets, and stimulated competition
for the best borrowers. They also did not impose any costs on the countries
during the crises of the 1990s.[54] However, credit to underserved sectors did
not expand substantially after these banks entered the market. Critics of large
international banks have argued that they basically focus only on large, well-
known borrowers, and it is generally agreed that they have lowered costs and
improved service to these customers. However, foreign banks with a large
presence have also tended to provide at least as much small-scale lending as
large local banks, according to the only econometric study on the issue.[55]

53. Indonesia eased bank entry significantly in 1988, and the number of domestic and international
banks rose significantly. However, because of difficulties in enforcing contracts in the Indonesian legal
system, international banks usually signed their loans offshore; the local bank offices focused mainly on
client services and loan origination.

54. One exception was Banco Comercial in Uruguay, which went bankrupt in the crisis that began
in 2001. It was run by local and Argentine investors, who had 25 percent of the capital, but well-known
international banks had 75 percent of the capital. The case has generated various lawsuits. Two international banks did leave Argentina after the government generated massive losses in the banking system by an asymmetrical conversion of dollar deposits and loans into pesos.

55. Clarke and others (2005). The same study shows that international banks with a small presence
did not lend to small businesses as much as small domestic banks, but such international banks were
probably set up as offices to service international clients.

Both types of banks have faced two major problems in expanding credit to underserved borrowers. First, public sector banks offer loans to these groups with low interest rates and do not pressure borrowers to repay. For example, agricultural lending in Brazil, Mexico, and Uruguay and mortgages in Brazil and Uruguay have been the province of public sector banks, which charge low interest rates and allow easy rescheduling and defaults. Lending in those sectors, even to those borrowers that did not obtain loans from the public sector banks, probably face high default risks owing to the credit culture and the weaknesses of the local legal system in enforcing loan contracts and executing collateral.[56] Second, international banks have been frustrated by the lack of information on borrowers, as have local private banks. However, progress is occurring in the informational and legal areas in many countries. This progress, together with the loss of business of the best borrowers to international and domestic bond markets, has led international banks, as well as local banks, to expand consumer, small-scale, and mortgage lending, for example, in Brazil, Mexico, and Peru.[57] Citibank has played a major role in issuing credit cards in Indonesia and other East Asian nations.

In any case, the ability to use well-known international banks to resolve potential financial system problems largely became moot, because these banks have been less interested in such expansion. There are probably two reasons for this change. First, profits in developing markets have not been as high as expected, particularly since the crisis in Argentina. Second, recent strategies of some of the large international banks have focused on domestic markets in the United States (Citibank, the consolidations of Bank of America) or expansion within the European Union (Santander, Banco Bilbao Vizcaya Argentaria [BBVA]). In Latin America, the net result has been either outright withdrawal, such as the withdrawal of Bank of Boston from Latin America after it was absorbed by Bank of America and the withdrawal of Santander from banking in Peru when it switched its investment into pension fund management, or decisions to base growth solely on capital

---

56. In Ecuador, the bankruptcy of the public sector intermediaries left room for a dramatic growth of private intermediaries focused on small credits in the last two years, for example, by Credi-Fe, a subsidiary of Banco Pichincha. These intermediaries' loan expansion has been based on a strategy of identifying clients who will repay and has been highly profitable.

57. "Mexican Banks Ride a Strong Wave of Lending: After Years of Stagnant Growth the Industry Is Seeing a Dramatic Upturn," *Financial Times,* March 3, 2005; "Brazil's Banks Adjust View of Their Market," *New York Times,* April 9, 2005.

generated by the existing bank assets in the country, which seems to be Citibank's strategy. In East Asia, Indonesia's sale of eight intervened banks between 2002 and 2004 brought bids from only one well-known international bank, which eventually bought one of the banks; other well-known international banks were not interested in expanding their existing operations in Indonesia with a merger. Korea's sale of banks initially went to investment banks, not well-known international banks, although recently Citigroup has bought the Carlyle Group's holdings in KorAM and Standard Charter bought Newbridge Capital's holdings in Korea First. Well-known international banks may still be interested in expansion in some markets, such as Brazil, China, India, Korea, and Mexico. However, interest in expanding elsewhere has been limited, particularly where the political and legal environment is uncertain.

While expansion of well-known international banks has slowed, some new players have offered bids in privatizations, and banks from developing countries have expanded regionally. For example, Lone Star, Newbridge Capital, and Carlyle purchased equity in the Korea Exchange, Korea First, and KorAM banks, respectively. Salvadoran banks have expanded in Central America; Banco Pichincha of Ecuador has expanded into neighboring countries. Royal Bank of Trinidad and Tobago purchased one of Jamaica's intervened banks and is expanding in the region. Salvadoran banks are expanding in Central America. In East Asia, Singapore's state investment arm, Temasek Holdings, and Malaysian banks have expanded through purchases of intervened banks.

While providing capital and new techniques, these banks may not have great concern for their international reputation and are difficult to supervise by local authorities. After international expansion, if problems occur in their home markets, they may simply withdraw, leaving the government to resolve the issues with depositors and manage the loans. Problems such as these occurred with Serbanco of Chile in Peru and with Banco Galicia of Argentina in Uruguay. Regarding supervision, it may be hard to evaluate even the capital of these banks, since the bank often is legally owned by an entity located in an offshore financial center with limited cross-border supervision. It is true that in Korea the banks were turned around by their new owners and later sold to reputable international banks, but it is easy to imagine different scenarios that might have occurred. Hence these banks, unlike the well-known international banks, may pose as much risk to the government as local banks or even more.

Reducing Risks: Prudential Regulation and Supervision, Market Discipline, Information, and Legal Improvements

After crises, governments have typically attempted to reduce financial sector risks by strengthening prudential regulation and supervision. The intent is to limit the expansion of weak banks and the tendency of bank managers to adopt high-risk, high-return lending strategies that leave the depositors and the government at risk. In both East Asia and Latin America, the 8 percent ratio of capital adequacy to risk-weighted assets rule (CAR) was widely adopted where it was not already in place, and in some Latin American countries where the requirement existed it was raised. The classification of nonperforming loans and provisioning also was strengthened, and exposure limits were reduced. East Asian crisis countries also strengthened their regulation and supervision after the crisis.[58] In addition, the high ratios of government debt to deposits represent collateral for liquidity support in the event of a bank run on performing assets unless there is a government default. Of course, at the same time, the high level of government debt (typically with a zero risk weight) also means that not much capital is needed to comply with the 8 percent CAR. Hence the capital at risk by bank owners that is available to buffer losses to depositors is sometimes very low compared to the regulatory figure of 8 percent.

Prudential supervision has been strengthened as well. The process of improving prudential regulation and supervision has been supported by the IMF–World Bank Financial Sector Assessment Program, which provides governments with a confidential evaluation of the country's prudential financial regulation and supervision, including the Basel core principles for supervision, the International Organization of Securities Commissions principles for capital markets, and the principles for systematically important payments systems.[59]

The international comparisons with other countries and the pressures from international bond markets and, in some cases, the IMF have contributed to improvements in prudential regulation and supervision. Most countries have indicated their intention to adopt Basel II standards gradually. Among other things, Basel II would link bank capital to operational as well as credit risk and encourage banks to develop better risk management

---

58. See Lindgren and others (1999).

59. However, Indonesia, Malaysia, and Thailand have not participated in the Financial Sector Assessment Program.

systems. In addition, some countries have begun to consolidate supervision of banks, other financial intermediaries, and capital markets in a single agency, in an attempt to improve supervision. However, these complicated changeovers may create a distraction from the current need to improve supervision and may even weaken supervision during their implementation.

The issue, however, is whether the changes in prudential regulation and supervision will provide more protection from crises than in the past, given the problems of ensuring compliance. Perhaps the worst example in the past is the case of Indonesia. The 1988 financial liberalization was followed by a strengthening of prudential regulation, including higher capital ratios and tighter exposure limits.[60] However, the capital requirement was phased in for public sector banks, where nonperforming loans were high, and the reduction in exposure limits was largely evaded by portfolio swaps involving off-balance-sheet guarantees. Most participants in the financial sector considered supervision to be weak and corrupt. But issues of the performance of regulation and supervision are not confined to developing countries. Perhaps the best-known case is the U.S. savings and loan crisis. The U.K. Financial Service Authority has recently come under criticism both for failing to prevent some problems and for engaging in overly heavy-handed regulation. Shadow financial regulatory committees of the United States, Japan, and Europe have criticized Basel II for its complexity, emphasis on supervision, and lack of emphasis on market discipline.

Issues of weak supervision and regulatory forbearance, particularly for public sector banks, have been major issues in many countries, not only before but even after crises.[61] In most developing countries, private banks have been intervened only after they were unable to meet their obligations in the payments system, not when supervisors found them insolvent, although the usual rule is that banks become insolvent well before they become illiquid. The recent crisis in the Dominican Republic was triggered by a bank collapse related to a diversion of deposit fraud (commonly called a "bank within a bank") that had gone undiscovered for many years. It remains to be seen whether prompt corrective action procedures have been strengthened enough to change such outcomes.[62]

---

60. Cole and Slade (1996).

61. Lindgren and others (1999).

62. In the United States, after the banking and savings and loan debacles of the 1980s and early 1990s, the deposit insurance agency is legally required to intervene in banks well before estimated capital is lost. Although there are still complaints that intervention is too slow, the change in procedure probably reduces losses to the deposit insurance agency (Benston and Kaufman 1997). Similar procedures have been introduced in some developing countries, but the legal requirement for intervention is often missing.

The question is whether the recent strengthening of prudential regulation and supervision can deal with the increasing complexities of banking and the real obstacles that faced prudential regulation and supervision in developing countries in the past and continue to face them today. Prudential regulation and supervision are technically difficult. Banks are inherently complex organizations. These complexities are complicated by weak auditing and accounting standards in many countries. Moreover, the technical difficulties of supervision are continually increasing with the growth of industrial financial conglomerates, complex hedging transactions, and the opening of capital accounts that allow funding and even capital to be shifted offshore at electronic speed. In this regard, despite improvements in supervision, most countries still face well-known difficulties in the supervision of conglomerates' consolidated activities and intermediaries' offshore activities. And supervisors' salaries are usually far below salaries paid by private sector firms for mastering the technicalities of complex transactions and the risk management systems that are supposed to be supervised now and under Basel II.

The political dimension is probably an even bigger obstacle to strong prudential regulation and supervision. In many developing countries, the owners of private banks are politically powerful; in small countries, bank owners and large borrowers are often one and the same. A good supervision of bank activities, particularly prompt corrective action, requires substantial political backing, which often does not exist. Hence there is a tendency for forbearance, particularly given the costs of resolving a large bank.

Attempts to avoid this problem by making supervisors independent or protecting them legally have many problems. Legal protection for supervisors has often been difficult to achieve.[63] Even if it were achieved, the protection would be subject to the judicial problems that exist in many countries. Moreover, empirical evidence suggests that supervisory independence and greater supervisory authority have had little effect on reducing the negative influences of corruption on banking and may even be associated with greater corruption.[64]

The supervision of public banks faces additional problems. Such supervision need not protect the public against the adoption of risky, high-return lending strategies by the managers—unlike private bank owners, public

63. An important issue with legal protection is that it could protect supervisors who seek bribes. To reduce this problem, legal protection would need to be supplemented by alternatives to the legal system under which supervisors can be charged with such malfeasance.

64. Barth, Caprio, and Levine (2001a, 2001b, 2006).

bank managers would not benefit from such strategies. However, a major role of public banks is to carry out government-directed programs to borrowers that often do not repay, using their deposits and borrowings that effectively have a government guarantee. Public sector banks also may lend to well-connected parties. The costs of these policies are often hidden by the complexity and intertemporal nature of banks' accounts. Good supervision of public sector banks could bring out the costs of these programs to the government and the public. However, pressures within the government are likely to be against such disclosure, particularly if the press and political opposition to the government are weak.[65] Intervention in public banks, which tend to have far worse portfolios than private banks, is usually politically impossible. Nonetheless, there are some signs of improvement in the area of public sector banks. For example, in both Indonesia and Thailand recently, supervisory authorities have publicly taken action to require reclassification and additional provisioning of loans held by public sector banks. In Brazilian states and Mexico, shifting government programs from banks to government agencies that are financed through the budget not only avoids contingent liabilities for the government but also requires a review of the programs during the annual budget debate.

Market discipline is another, complementary approach to reduce the risk of crises that governments in East Asia and Latin America have begun to use. The idea is that depositors will avoid weak banks and thus limit their expansion, which otherwise might turn into a crisis. Some arguments and evidence exist that market discipline can work in developing countries.[66]

The efforts to improve market discipline include requiring banks to make information more frequently available on portfolios and performance. Accounting standards and auditing are also being improved gradually. Basel II includes reference to improving market discipline as a complement to regulation and supervision.

Market discipline faces significant problems under the current financial framework, however. Banks' balance sheets and the contracts that are increasingly part of their business are inherently complex, as experience in industrial countries shows. The average depositor in a developing country would certainly have trouble evaluating risks in a bank balance sheet, and given the limited role of stock markets in many developing countries, there are few market analysts to assist in the process.

---

65. Barth, Caprio, and Levine (2001a, 2001b, 2006) provide some evidence supporting this view.
66. Caprio and Honohan (2004); Martínez-Peria and Schmukler (2001).

Large, savvy depositors can exert market discipline, but their role is often blunted by deposit guarantees and public sector banks—depositors are likely to pay little attention to a bank's performance if their deposits are protected by deposit insurance or the government. In most countries, deposit insurance covers individual deposits up to large multiples of per capita income, and in most cases the blanket guarantees offered in crises are still in place. One might expect that in such circumstances there would be high capital requirements, strong supervision, and strong prompt corrective action in order to limit moral hazard, but there is no evidence of such relationships.[67] Some attempts have been made to limit deposit insurance on large deposits or on deposits paying excessive interest rates, such as might be offered by weak banks. However, in crises, deposit insurance or blanket guarantees have usually been extended, ex post, to deposits that were uncovered. The increased coverage reflects both the political power of large depositors and a more general government concern that a large bailout will be needed if the large depositors initiate a run on a bank. Some governments have attempted to cope with the deposit insurance issues and to increase discipline by charging risk-based fees for deposit insurance. The theory is that differential fees would slow deposit mobilization and lending by weaker banks. However, although a differential in fees is better than a single fee for all banks, in practice the actual differences in fees are far less than the differences in bank risk.[68] The limited differences in fees probably reflect the political influence of private domestic bankers, who benefit the most from deposit insurance. Thus the actual, small differences in fees for deposit insurance are likely to have only a limited effect on deterring deposit mobilization and lending by weak banks.

In sum, governments are attempting to use both stronger prudential regulation and supervision and market discipline to limit crises before they start by encouraging banks to improve their balance sheets and risk management and by limiting the growth of weak banks. However, technical and, more important, political issues represent major challenges to these approaches and are likely to limit their impact on crisis prevention.

Summary and Conclusions

Rapid world growth and a low-interest-rate environment have made the postcrisis recovery easier, particularly in Latin America. Nonetheless, the

---

67. Barth, Caprio, and Levine (2001a, 2001b, 2006).
68. Laeven (2002a, 2002b, 2002c).

crises of the 1990s have left major challenges, risks, and vulnerabilities in the countries of East Asia and Latin America:

—High external debt ratios still represent a source of vulnerability in some countries, particularly in Latin America. Countries often have not taken sufficient advantage of their savings on debt service in today's low-interest environment to reduce their excessive debt. Slowing growth and rising interest rates could create problems.

—High ratios of government and central bank debt to deposits represent a major challenge to growth. Government and central bank debt absorbs much of the small volume of bank deposits in most Latin American economies and is also an issue in Indonesia; in most cases, the debt arose from the crises and has not been reduced much by tight fiscal policy. The debt is a challenge because it, not banks' unwillingness to lend, limits credit to the private sector—a key factor in growth—and access of small borrowers to credit.

—The high government debt in the banking system represents new risks, not just default risk (which is less than on private credit) but market risk as well.

—Credit risk remains a source of vulnerability, from dollarization, from banks' entry into new lines of business, such as consumer credit, mortgages, and small business lending, and from financial industrial conglomerates.

—A potentially costly risk exists in the resurgence of public sector banks. These banks' expansion reflects an attempt to satisfy political demands for faster credit growth and loans to particular groups, but costs of this expansion are already appearing.

—A potential vulnerability exists in the expansion of regional banks; the expansion of well-known international banks is likely to be limited, except in a few countries.

—Another vulnerability exists in the increasing links between onshore and offshore banks, which allow funds and even capital to move back and forth in split seconds.

Governments have attempted to meet these risks in a variety of ways:

—Countries, particularly in East Asia, have built up their international reserves and reduced their short-term international debts to reduce the risks of sudden shocks.

—Countries have taken advantage of the low-interest-rate environment to refinance high-interest-rate external debt and lengthen the maturities of international debt.

—Governments have developed domestic government debt markets and taken advantage of them to reduce their reliance on foreign currency–

denominated debt. While this has contributed to crowding out, it also has reduced currency risk for the government and provided banks with liquid assets that generally will be serviced.

—Government debt markets and low inflation have also contributed to development of the domestic bond market, but equity markets remain stagnant in most Latin American countries.

—Banks are improving their risk management.

—Risks of bank expansion into new areas are being reduced, and credit access is being improved by development of credit bureaus that provide improved information on borrowers. Credit bureaus help to reduce risks and provide an incentive for prompt debt service: the development of the intangible asset of a good credit record.

—Credit risks are also being reduced, albeit slowly, by improvements in the legal system, titling, definition and execution of collateral, and the setup of special courts to handle debt issues.

—Government agencies are replacing public sector banks in a few countries, such as Brazil and Mexico, which reduces the contingent liabilities facing government and forces annual performance review as part of the annual budget debate.

—Governments are attempting to improve prudential regulation and supervision, but this may not help much. Technical problems, such as offshore banking and conglomerates, not only remain but may be increasing. More important, political issues related to politically influential businessmen and the role of public sector banks in financing them and government programs will continue to hinder bank regulation and supervision. This is particularly true in countries that have not taken advantage of the recent crises to undertake reform.

—Governments are also attempting to improve the market discipline of weak banks, but this is blunted by high levels of deposit insurance and government guarantees. Attempts to use risk-based deposit insurance that charges domestic banks fees reflecting their high risks face political difficulties.

The balance of these challenges and vulnerabilities remains unclear. It seems likely that some new crises are likely to occur in Latin America, when countries that have remained highly indebted, internally and externally, and still have high fiscal deficits face a higher-interest-rate environment, a slowing world economy, and deteriorating commodity prices, as in the past. Domestically, banking systems seem to have improved somewhat in most of the larger countries. However, they continue to face challenges to expand private credit, particularly to small borrowers, that will be hard to overcome given the high government debt in many Latin American countries and Indonesia. The banks also face numerous credit risks, and these have increased in some cases. Perhaps most vulnerable are small countries, like the Dominican Republic, where the links among government, banks, and industry are strong, and well-known international banks have lost interest in expanding.

References

Baliño, Tomás J. T., and V. Sundarajan. 1991. "Issues in Recent Banking Crises." In *Banking Crises: Cases and Issues,* edited by V. Sundarajan and Tomás J. T. Baliño, pp. 1–57. Washington: International Monetary Fund.

Barro, Robert J. 2001. "Economic Growth in East Asia before and after the Crisis." NBER Working Paper 8330. Cambridge, Mass.: National Bureau of Economic Research.

Barth, James, Gerard Caprio, and Ross Levine. 2001a. *Bank Regulation and Supervision: What Works Best.* Policy Research Paper 2725. Washington: World Bank.

———. 2001b. *The Regulation and Supervision of Banks around the World: A New Data Base.* Policy Research Paper 2588. Washington: World Bank (updated in 2004).

———. 2006 (forthcoming). *Rethinking Bank Regulation: Till Angels Govern.* Cambridge University Press.

Benston, George, and George Kaufman. 1997. "FDICA after Five Years." *Journal of Economic Perspectives* 11, no. 3: 139–58.

Caprio, Gerard, and Patrick Honohan. 2004. "Can the Unsophisticated Market Provide Discipline?" Policy Research Working Paper 3364. Washington: World Bank.

Cerra, Valerie, and Sweta Saxena. 2003. "Did Output Recover from the Asian Crisis?" Working Paper WP/03/48. Washington: International Monetary Fund.

Clarke, George, and Robert Cull. 1999. "Why Privatize? The Case of Argentina's Public Provincial Banks." *World Development* 27, no. 5: 865–88.

———. 2002. "Political and Economic Determinants of the Likelihood of Privatizing Argentine Banks." *Journal of Law and Economics* 45, no. 1: 165–89.

Clarke, George, Robert Cull, María Soledad Martínez Peria, and Susana Sánchez. 2005. "Bank Lending to Small Businesses in Latin America: Does Bank Origin Matter?" *Journal of Money, Credit, and Banking* 37, no. 1: 83–118.

Coe, David, and Se-Jik Kim, eds. 2002. *Korean Crisis and Recovery.* Washington: IMF and Korea Institute for International Economic Policy.

Cole, David, and Betty F. Slade. 1996. *Building a Modern Financial System: The Indonesian Experience.* Cambridge University Press.

Dooley, Michael. 2000. "A Model of Crises in Emerging Markets." *Economic Journal* 110, no. 460: 256–73.

Edwards, Sebastian. 1999. "How Effective Are Capital Controls?" *Journal of Economic Perspectives* 13, no. 4: 65–84.

Eichengreen, Barry, and Ricardo Hausmann. 2004. *Other People's Money: Debt Denomination and Financial Instability in Emerging Market Economies.* University of Chicago.

Hanson, James. 2002. "Dollarization, Private and Official: Issues, Benefits, and Costs." In *Financial Sector Policy for Developing Countries: A Reader,* edited by Gerard Caprio, Patrick Honohan, and Dimitri Vittas, pp. 129–70. Oxford University Press.

———. 2003. *Banking in Developing Countries in the 1990s.* Policy Research Paper 3168. Washington: World Bank.

———. 2004. "The Transformation of State-Owned Banks." In *The Future of State-Owned Financial Institutions,* edited by Gerard Caprio, Jonathan Fiechter, Robert Litan, and Michael Pomerleano, pp. 13–50. Brookings.

Honohan, Patrick. 2005 (forthcoming). "Fiscal, Monetary, and Incentive Implications of Bank Recapitalization." In *Systemic Financial Distress: Containment and Resolution,* edited by Patrick Honohan and Luc Laeven. Cambridge University Press.

Honohan, Patrick, and Anqing Shi. 2003. "Deposit Dollarization and the Financial Sector." In *Globalization and National Financial Systems,* edited by James Hanson, Patrick Honohan, and Giovanni Majnoni. Oxford University Press for the World Bank.

IMF (International Monetary Fund). Various years. *International Finance Statistics.* Washington.

Kaminsky, Graciela, and Carmen Reinhart. 1999. "The Twin Crises: The Causes of Banking and Balance of Payments Problems." *American Economic Review* 89, no. 3: 473–500.

Kenward, Lloyd. 2002. *From the Trenches, The First Year of Indonesia's Crisis 1997/98 as Seen from the World Bank's Office in Jakarta.* Jakarta: Center for International and Strategic Studies.

Kindleberger, Charles P. 2000. *Manias, Panics, and Crashes: A History of Financial Crises.* New York: John Wiley.

King, Robert G., and Ross Levine. 1993. "Finance and Growth: Schumpeter Might Be Right." *Quarterly Journal of Economics* 108, no. 3: 717–37.

Krugman, Paul. 1979. "A Model of Balance of Payments Crises." *Journal of Money, Credit, and Banking* 11, no. 3: 311–25.

Laeven, Luc. 2002a. "Bank Risk and Deposit Insurance." *World Bank Economic Review* 16, no. 1: 109–37.

———. 2002b. "International Evidence on the Cost of Deposit Insurance." *Quarterly Review of Economics and Finance* 42, no. 4: 721–73.

———. 2002c. "Pricing of Deposit Insurance." Working Paper 2871. Washington: World Bank.

Levine, Ross. 1998. "Financial Development and Economic Growth: Views and Agenda." *Journal of Economic Literature* 35, no. 2: 688–726.

———. 2003. "More on Finance and Growth: More Finance, More Growth?" *Federal Reserve Bank of St. Louis Review* 85: 31–46.

Levine, Ross, Norman Loayza, and Thorsten Beck. 2000. "Financial Intermediation and Growth: Causality and Causes." *Journal of Monetary Economics* 46, no. 1: 31–77.

Lindgren, Carl-John, Tomás J. T. Baliño, Charles Enoch, Anne-Marie Gulde, Marc Quintyn, and Leslie Teo. 1999. *Financial Crisis and Restructuring: Lessons from Asia.* Occasional Paper 188. Washington: International Monetary Fund.

Martínez-Peria, María Soledad, and Sergio Schmukler. 2001. "Do Depositors Punish Banks for Bad Behavior? Market Discipline, Deposit Insurance, and Banking Crises." *Journal of Finance* 56, no. 3: 1029–51.

Minsky, Hyman. 1992. "The Financial Instability Hypothesis: Capitalistic Processes and the Behavior of the Economy." In *Financial Crises: Theory, History, and Policy,* edited by Charles Kindleberger and Jean-Pierre Laffargue. Cambridge University Press.

Savastano, M. A. 1992. "The Pattern of Currency Substitution in Latin America: An Overview." *Revista de Análisis Económico* 7, no. 1: 29–72.

———. 1996. "Dollarization in Latin America." In *The Macroeconomics of International Currencies: Theory, Policy, and Evidence,* edited by Paul Mizen and Eric Pentacost. Cheltenham, U.K.: Edward Elgar.

World Bank. 2000. *East Asia: Recovery and Beyond.* Washington.

———. 2004. *Global Development Finance.* Washington.

———. 2005a. "Financial Liberalization: What Went Right, What Went Wrong?" In *Economic Growth in the 1990s: Learning from a Decade of Reform,* ch. 7. Washington.

———. 2005b. *Global Development Finance.* Washington.

———. Various years. *Global Development Finance.* Washington.

FERNANDO MONTES-NEGRET
THOMAS MULLER

3

Banking System Crises and Recovery in the Transition Economies of Europe and Central Asia

An Overview

Over the past fifteen years, the transition countries in the Balkans, the Baltics, Central and Eastern Europe, and the Commonwealth of Independent States (CIS) experienced nothing short of a paradigmatic change in all political, economic, and social dimensions. This chapter provides a brief overview of financial sector developments in this increasingly heterogeneous region, following the chaotic, prolonged, and costly crises of the 1990s.

After the fall of the Berlin Wall, all transition countries experienced more or less severe systemic financial crises, and most of them went through several phases of reform, usually starting with severe defaults, followed by lax bank entry and a second wave of bank failures. Through restructuring, consolidation, and privatization—often through opening to Western financial intermediaries—conditions in many of the countries (in particular in Central and Eastern Europe) stabilized, and well-functioning financial intermediaries were established. However, a significant number of countries in the Balkans and the CIS still are left with severe vulnerabilities in their financial systems, often rooted in weak legal and institutional arrangements, as well as limited political will to adopt the necessary reforms.

The authors want to thank and acknowledge Steen Byskov's contributions to various parts of the paper, which also benefited greatly from comments by Stijn Claessens and James Hanson. Any remaining errors, misinterpretations, and shortcomings remain the sole responsibility of the authors.

All financial systems in the transition countries are still dominated by banks. Only a few countries have developed some form of capital market–based financial intermediation.[1] Most of the analysis in the chapter therefore concentrates on crises and the development of banking institutions. The first part outlines the background and specific departure point of the transition countries that are transforming themselves from state-planned to market-based economies. The second part gives a brief summary of the current state of and differences in financial sector development in the different countries. The third part concludes and outlines some current issues and challenges ahead.

Transition and Financial Crisis

The transition countries entered the 1990s as centrally planned economies structured along socialist principles of economic organization. The specific crisis experiences and the characteristics of postcrisis financial development were framed by the process of transition from state-planned to market-driven economies that most of the countries embarked on following the fall of the Berlin Wall.

It is important to distinguish the crisis experiences in the transition countries from other financial crises around the world in the 1990s. The process of transition implied a crisis of the entire social and economic model of organization. Crises in the financial sector were a direct result of—and should not be separated from—these more fundamental crises of the centrally planned economic model, which all transition countries faced and, in some cases, have not yet fully overcome. In the centrally planned economies, "banks" had functioned as administrative agencies of the state, collecting deposits and allocating funds according to the decision of the central planning agencies. The concept of "financial intermediation," in which banks and other financial institutions competed for funds and allocated them to their most productive uses, did not exist. Typically, the central bank function and commercial banking functions were performed by the same institution within a "monobanking system." Banking systems were more or less simply "accounting control and

1. The persistent underdevelopment of capital markets is surprising, especially if one considers the widespread use of voucher privatizations in transition countries that were partially relying on capital markets to achieve efficient allocations of ownership rights. The reasons for the limited development of capital markets in the transition countries are not sufficiently understood and require further attention.

cash disbursement vehicles" for the state, which simultaneously provided deposit-holding and payment services to companies and individuals.

As illustrated in figure 3-1, the monobank was responsible for both monetary policy and commercial banking in a centrally planned economy. However, the monobank was not responsible for screening applicants, monitoring projects, or enforcing the repayment of loans; instead its allocative role was limited to channeling funds to state-owned enterprises according to physical and credit plans.[2] Peachey and Roe summarize the implications of this form of organization for the functioning of the financial system:

> Paradoxically the socialist banks of the pre-1989 era were quite safe. . . . Since they were owned by the state, as were their major clients and borrowers, failures on loan repayment were contained within the budgetary sphere. Many banks have been technically insolvent, but the implicit guarantees of the state diluted the importance of that fact. Concepts such as capital adequacy, the creditworthiness of borrowers, portfolio concentration, and insider lending were of only peripheral relevance to the financial durability of banks—their "failure," in any case, was not a possibility to be entertained.[3]

The fall of the Berlin Wall, symbolizing the beginning of political and economic reform in the socialist countries, also marked the beginning of the transformation of the monobank system into decentralized financial institutions, which separated central banking and commercial banking activities,[4] created multiple, smaller, banking units, and allowed the entry of new banks.[5]

The central banks were charged with two new tasks: (a) initiating a semblance of an autonomous monetary policy, through the imposition of credit ceilings and the allocation of credit to the new "spin-off" banks through their refinancing windows, and (b) regulating and supervising the newly established commercial banks. Unfortunately, the central banks were totally unprepared to implement these tasks, lacking the necessary expertise and experience and being, generally, politically weak.

In the first phase of transition, reform efforts focused on strengthening the regulatory regime and establishing a legal framework "following OECD

2. Borish and Montes-Negret (1998).

3. Peachey and Roe (2001: 189).

4. The creation of a two-tier bank system began in 1987 in Hungary, in 1989 in Poland, and in 1990 in the Czech Republic. See McDermott (2004).

5. See Berglof and Bolton (2002).

Figure 3-1. *Monobanking Systems in Centrally Planned Economies*

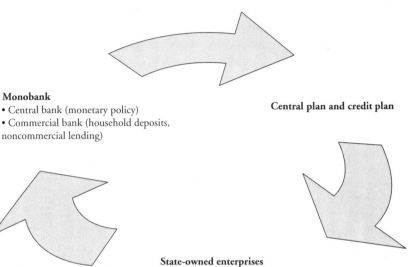

Monobank
• Central bank (monetary policy)
• Commercial bank (household deposits,
noncommercial lending)

Central plan and credit plan

State-owned enterprises

[Organization for Economic Cooperation and Development] standards."
The general thinking presumed that economic reforms and market dynamics would eventually force banks to adjust to the new economic reality, and,
given sound supervision and regulation, they would start allocating resources
in an efficient manner and stop lending to failing enterprises. However,
although the legal and supervisory frameworks were quickly adapted to
international best practice, the actual capacity of the banks and the supervisors to monitor, evaluate, and manage risks was not sufficient to transform
the existing institutions into efficient financial intermediaries overnight.
More important, in most cases there was not sufficient political will to
enforce the newly minted rules.

Since the new state-owned commercial banks were formed out of the
monobanks, they initially remained little more than accounting units that
inherited the old bureaucratic network, staff, and low-quality assets in the
form of "loans" granted to state-owned enterprises. Being state-owned
banks that placed loan portfolios with state-owned enterprises, there were
no incentives or mechanisms to effectively enforce debt service. The large
nonperforming loans were generally rolled over, often through new loans
funded by the central banks.

Shortly after the breakup of the monobanks, governments encouraged
the establishment of new private banks by lowering the minimum entry

requirements for management capacity and capitalization. In Russia, where the increase was largest, this led to the establishment of more than 2,500 banks when the process peaked in 1997. Many of these new banks did little more than provide loans and other services to industrial holdings that typically had the same owners ("pocket banks").

Generally, there was an inverted "U" pattern in the number of banks in the banking systems in many transition countries (see figure 3-2). Early breakup of state banks and entry of new private banks increased the total number of banks. Subsequently, many individual banks failed, and systemic crises significantly reduced the number of banks toward the end of the 1990s. From 1993 to 2000, the number of banks decreased from 62 to 22 in Latvia, from 164 to 59 in Azerbaijan, from 179 to 33 in Georgia, and from 204 to 48 in Kazakhstan.

Crises in Transition Economies

During the period of abandonment of central planning in 1991–98, most countries in the region faced banking sector crises. Zoli identifies five factors that contributed to these crises:[6]

—*External shocks,* resulting from the disruption of the trade system and cross-border financial arrangements in the "socialist block,"

—*Macroeconomic shocks,* reflected in severe output contraction and high inflation, followed by tough stabilization programs, which resulted in high real interest rates that affected the debt service capacity of corporate borrowers,[7]

—*Model change shocks,* in the form of lost enterprise subsidies, difficulties in adjusting to increased external competition, lack of informational and financial tools, and poor-quality bank portfolios (as former quasi-fiscal allocations were converted into loans),

—*Institutional weaknesses,* both in the banking organizations and in the supervisory framework and institutions, and

—*Poor internal governance* in banks and companies, in the form of corruption, fraud, insider lending, and asset stripping.

---

6. Zoli (2001).

7. Households had accumulated large liquid deposits as a consequence of shortages of consumption goods. This massive "monetary overhang" fueled inflationary processes. When central banks attempted to introduce some monetary discipline, reinforced by hard-budget constraints on the fiscal side, a credit crunch followed. The result was enterprise defaults and bank failures, leading to the first wave of banking crises in the region.

Figure 3-2. *Inverted "U" Pattern: Number of Banks in the Russian Banking System, 1991–2004*

Number of banks

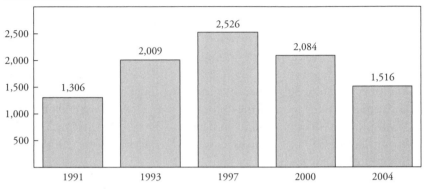

Sources: Standard & Poor's (2004); World Bank (2003).

Stalled reform efforts and lack of political will to restructure the banking sector caused many of the banking systems in the transition countries to retain characteristics of the pre-1989 period, in particular, the predominant role of the state through bank ownership, management of the majority share of household deposits in the largest retail financial intermediaries, and protection of inefficient and even some failed banks. The sharp increase in new entrants of small, undercapitalized, and undermanaged domestic banks also contributed to banking crises in many of the transition countries. Weak supervisory capacity, governance problems, and insider lending prevailed, and the banking systems in Russia, Ukraine, many Central Asian, and some Southeastern European countries practically collapsed. Notable exceptions were the new European Union (EU) member and accession countries, which, following early crises, transformed their banking systems quickly and—often relying on foreign investors—upgraded the capacity and management of the sector.

Given the starting point from which most transition countries departed in the early 1990s, it is not surprising that almost all countries experienced some form of financial crisis within the past fifteen years. Bank failures—and therefore the appearance of a "crisis"—continued to be absorbed in many countries in the state budget through constant life support to "zombie" banks by means of regulatory forbearance, capital support, and so forth. However, the fiscal costs and impact on economic output in the tran-

Table 3-1. *Cost of Crises in Transition Economies and Other Financial Crises in the 1990s*

Country	Crisis period	Fiscal outlay (percent of GDP)	Output loss (IMF)[a]	Output loss (Barro)[a]
Transition economies				
Czech Republic	1989–91	12.0	0.0	n.a.
Hungary	1991–95	10.0	14.0	36.4
Poland	1992–95	3.5	0.0	0.1
Slovenia	1992–94	14.6	0.0	6.2
Market economies				
Turkey	2000–01	26.6	0.0	12.9
Japan	1991–present	24.0	48.0	4.5
Mexico	1994–2000	19.3	10.0	14.5
Indonesia	1997–2002	55.0	39.0	35.0
Thailand	1997–2002	34.8	40.0	26.7
Korea	1997–2002	28.0	17.0	10.0

Sources: Claessens, Klingebiel, and Laeven (2004); authors' calculations.

n.a. Not available.

a. Output loss (IMF) and output loss (Barro) are quoted from Claessens, Klingebiel, and Laeven (2004), who calculate output loss as the sum of the differences between the actual and trend growth rates for the period t until the year in which the trend growth is reached, where trend GDP growth is calculated as the average of GDP growth rates from $t-3$ to $t-1$, and t is the starting year of the crisis.

sition countries were less severe than in the more prominent, recent crises in Asia, Latin America, and Turkey (see table 3-1). The smaller size of the crises in transition countries primarily reflects the low levels of financial depth with which the transition countries entered the 1990s. In the early stages of transition, the economic costs of financial crises were much lower than in countries that relied to a much greater extent on extensive financial intermediation in allocating resources. Low levels of deposits limited the need to put up fiscal resources to bail out depositors.[8] Moreover, the large extent of alternative financing and frequent use of barter exchange and trade credit provided alternative access to funding, which limited the impact of output losses in the real economy.[9]

8. See Peachey and Roe (2001).

9. In the case of Russia, observers even argue that the financial crises promoted output growth, because banks reacted by reallocating credit from government bonds to the private sector, thereby enhancing available funding for investment and growth. See, for example, Huang, Marin, and Xu (2004) or Peachey and Roe (2001).

Although the relative effects of the early financial crises in transition countries appear lower, the cost of a banking crisis is not a "given," and poor incentives, instruments, and crisis management skills often produce very different outcomes in terms of the costs passed to the public sector and ultimately to taxpayers. Typically, the costlier crises in the transition countries were characterized by repeated recapitalizations and several waves of purchases of nonperforming loans, significant central banking support, poorly structured restructurings of banks and corporations, and multiple restructuring agencies.

Differences in costs across the transition countries reflected differences in the approach to bank restructuring and cleanup of the banks' balance sheets at various points during the transition process.[10] Invariably, the process began with the inescapable reality that most countries needed to inject substantial financial resources into their banking system and to address the high level of nonperforming loans at the start of transition. Nonperforming loans skyrocketed, reflecting, to a large extent, the collapse of the production system, with cuts in output as domestic and international markets collapsed. To the extent that accounting figures were credible, the share of nonperforming loans in total bank loans was estimated to be as high as 29 percent in the Czech Republic, 9 percent in Hungary, and more than 33 percent in Poland in 1991.[11] According to Borish and Montes-Negret, "Many of these loans were to large industrial companies that were overstaffed, uncompetitive, and unlikely to emerge as sound credit risks even with the introduction of some operational changes."[12] The fragmented and specialized way in which the banking system had been organized meant that the newly established, now commercially oriented, banks often had to support large concentration risks in sectors, geographic regions, and individual state-owned enterprises for the first time outside of the "protected fiscal cocoon."

Cleaning up the banks' balance sheets was approached both directly and indirectly in different countries, complemented with different strategies for privatizing state-owned enterprises and state-owned banks. Governments resorted to a broad range of instruments for the banks, primarily recapitalizations through consolidation bonds, cash transfers, and purchase of or public guarantees for nonperforming loans.[13] However, regulatory and supervisory capacity and banking skills were lacking, and the legal frame-

10. Matousek (2004).
11. Borish and Montes-Negret (1998: 80).
12. Borish and Montes-Negret (1998: 79).
13. For an overview of instruments applied in select transition economies, see Zoli (2001).

work (for example, banking and central banking laws, bank resolution and company bankruptcy laws, creditors' protection, and collateral recovery) and enforcement capacity (supervisors and courts) were seriously inadequate. Differences in these areas contributed to differences in the fiscal costs of the various crises; in many transition countries, the deficiencies were so severe that they stalled the restructuring process.

The success of financial system reform and bank restructuring varied dramatically in the region. The various waves of bank recapitalizations and the purchase of nonperforming loans were usually done in a nontransparent and ad hoc way and often created perverse incentives to create more nonperforming loans. Corporate governance shortcomings and conflicts of interest among state-owned enterprises, which often were simultaneously owners and borrowers, were not resolved until bank foreign entry became more widespread, at least in the countries of Central and Eastern Europe. Figure 3-3 illustrates the large discrepancies in progress toward transition, as classified by the European Bank for Reconstruction and Development (EBRD) transition indicator scores for 2004, of the new EU member states and the two accession candidates, Bulgaria and Romania, when compared with the remaining transition countries.

Some of the most successful countries in Central and Eastern Europe— like Hungary, Poland, and the Baltics—developed successful banks early in the transition.[14] For example, in Poland and the Baltics, governments initiated wide-ranging and painful restructuring very early in the process. Hungary pursued a successful restructuring strategy by focusing on the entry of foreign strategic investors that brought capital and know-how to the newly privatized state banks. Today, foreign ownership of the banking system is high in all of the new EU member states (table 3-2). Undoubtedly, there has been a positive feedback between the reform efforts driven by the EU accession and the willingness of strategic investors to enter these markets.

In contrast, Russia, Ukraine, and most of the other CIS countries have seen only limited progress in bank restructuring. State-owned banks and banks with political and corporate connections still dominate the system. Politically weak central banks lacking enforcement capabilities have retarded the necessary restructuring, undermining the potential for market forces to promote consolidation and improve efficiency in the banking sector.

In Russia, the 1998 crisis did not trigger a sufficiently broad and deep bank restructuring, in spite of the failure of many banks. Moreover, the state

14. See Bonin and Wachtel (2002).

Figure 3-3. *EBRD Transition Indicator Scores, 2004: Progress in Corporate Restructuring and Banking Reform*[a]

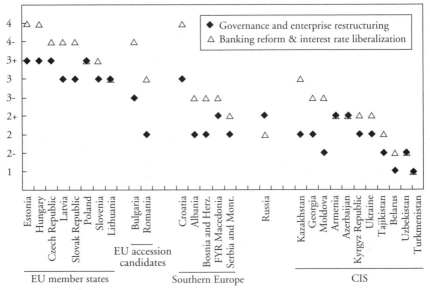

EBRD transition indicator score, 2004

Source: EBRD (2004).
a. The EBRD transition indicators range from 1 to 4+, with 1 representing little or no change from a rigid, centrally planned economy and 4+ representing the standards of an industrial market economy.

banks used the crises to consolidate their dominance in the sector, as they attracted depositors based on implicit and explicit state guarantees. A World Bank study finds that "Policymakers displayed little apparent interest in actively encouraging consolidation of the type that is common sequel to disruptive financial crisis: in their eyes this would have only delayed the return to the pre-1998 status quo stability."[15]

Figure 3-3 also hints at possible feedback mechanisms between enterprise restructuring and banking reform. Theoretically, banks play an important role in setting incentives for enterprises to restructure and enhance performance through their decision to invest in or lend to an enterprise and monitor enterprise performance. However, in most transition countries, banks played only a very small role in the early restructuring of the manufactur-

15. World Bank (2003: 63).

Table 3-2. *Foreign Ownership of the Banking System in
New EU Member States*

Percent

Country	Foreign ownership of the banking system
Poland	52
Hungary	75
Czech Republic	75
Slovak Republic	90
Slovenia	36
Baltic states	68

Source: Data from Bank Austria Creditanstalt.

ing sector. Banks often were too risk averse after the crises and lacked the required know-how to lead restructuring efforts, opting to lend more to their governments than to enterprises. This is reflected in the low level of credit extended to the private sector, as discussed later in this chapter. Banks clearly failed to promote restructuring where the ownership structures favored insider lending and stifled the banks' capacity to push for restructuring.[16] In the case of the transition countries, it is more likely that progress in enterprise reform helped banking sector reform to succeed where privatization, restructuring, and competition enhanced the performance of enterprises, reduced connected lending, and freed the banks' balance sheets of bad assets. In any case, the power of the EU accession agenda in the most advanced countries in the sample is not to be underestimated in setting incentives for a synchronized push for parallel restructuring of the enterprise and banking sector.

Lessons Learned

Some important lessons can be drawn from the crisis experience in the transition countries.

The transition from a centrally planned to a market-oriented economy invariably led to financial crises for the reasons explained in this section, including the legacy of bad credit portfolios, distorted incentives, lack of banking skills, monetary overhang, political pressures to maintain the pattern of connected lending, and soft-budget constraints. Financial institutions are key elements of the organization of an economy, and their modus

16. See Commander, Dutz, and Stern (1999).

operandi and the incentives under which they operate are intrinsically linked to the structure of the economic system as a whole. An economic transformation of the magnitude and speed observed in the early 1990s in the transition economies made it very difficult to address the issues arising from the public ownership of banks and enterprises, the lack of experience of banks and supervisors, the absence of informational capital to screen borrowers, as well as the lack of an enabling legal framework, let alone to address them in an appropriate sequence.

In the Central and Eastern European countries and the Baltic states, painful restructuring and the acceptance of bank failure at the early stages of economic transformation allowed a relatively less costly "creative destruction" than in other regions, because financial systems were typically smaller, and the costs of the almost inevitable crises were lower. Simultaneously, early intervention provided more lead time for the development of sustainable financial intermediation as a driver of economic change. Hungary was likely the country that best managed the transition, and this partly reflected a better starting point in view of reforms adopted under the socialist model. Delaying adjustment uniformly increased costs and required stronger responses. Non-reformers or incomplete reformers (like Russia and Ukraine) still are saddled with rather dysfunctional financial systems and possibly "hidden" insolvent banks based on low capitalization and pervasive insider lending.

The various resolution models adopted confirm the view that multiple waves of recapitalizations and purchases of nonperforming loans are detrimental and only increase the cost of crises. De facto, the willingness to provide continuous bailouts is a form of soft-budget constraint.

Simply granting licenses for new private financial institutions is not enough to transform the financial sector and make it more competitive. A successful approach to transformation needs to manage the restructuring of existing institutions, including the privatization of state-owned banks, and to focus on the entry of first-rate foreign banks bringing financial, reputational, and human capital.

Supervisory know-how and enforcement capacity, beyond laws and regulations, combined with the necessary political backing, are critical to enforce and promote the right incentives for the development of sustainable prudential behavior in the financial system.[17]

17. See McDermott (2004) for an analysis of the politics of supervisory reform in the Czech Republic, Hungary, and Poland; see Tang, Zoli, and Klytchnikova (2000) for an analysis of fiscal implications of the transformation of banking in transition economies.

Corporate restructuring and bank restructuring was necessary, but, over-all, banks' initial contribution to corporate restructuring was very limited, perhaps with the exception of Poland.

Last but not least, monetary and fiscal discipline was crucial to create an environment conducive to successful financial transitions. The entry of foreign banks could be seen as the importation of one additional tool for the enforcement of economywide hard-budget constraints.

Financial Sector Development in Transition Economies Today

Today, the transition economies vary substantially in their level of economic and financial sector development. While the perception of the transition countries is often dominated by middle-income countries like Russia and the new members of the European Union, it also includes a host of low-income countries, in particular in Central Asia and Southeast Europe. In addition, there are enormous regional disparities within countries (particularly in Russia). It is impossible to look at financial sector development in the transition countries without making clear distinctions between different groups. However, there are also important commonalities.

Output

Most transition countries suffered substantial output losses in the early stages of transition (see figure 3-4).[18] The weakness of the real sector put substantial pressure on the financial systems. Many countries have only managed to recoup real output losses in the past couple of years. However, the current favorable environment forms a good basis for sustained growth of financial sectors across the region.

Structure of the Financial System

The legacy of state planning and limited capital ownership by individuals is still mirrored in the structure of the financial systems in transition countries today. The systems are dominated by banks, and the development of capital markets and non-bank financial institutions is one of the key challenges remaining. Even in the most advanced financial systems in the region, banks account for almost the entire assets in the sector (see figure 3-5).

18. World Bank (2002).

Figure 3-4. *Output Recovery in Select Transition Countries, 1987–2003*

Percent of GDP in constant local currency units (1993 = 100)

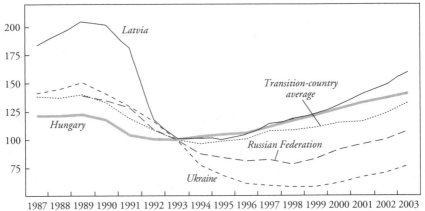

Source: IMF (various years).

In the new EU member states (EU8), the significant increases in the number of non-bank financial institutions have not translated into a significant increase in their share of total financial assets. A recent World Bank study points out,

> Most EU8 countries have initially focused on stabilizing and developing their banking systems, with stock market development to date largely a by-product of privatization, and pension and insurance systems as well as other non-bank financial institutions remaining small and underdeveloped. As the EU8 enter the EU, they are well placed to reap the benefits of financial system deepening and widening in the years ahead, provided they follow financial sector policies that are conducive to the further development of both bank and non-bank forms of financial intermediation.[19]

It is true that equity market capitalization as a percentage of GDP across the region has grown more dynamically than bank credit, accounting for more than 20 percent of GDP in 2003, almost the same share as bank credit to the private sector (see figure 3-6). However, this stage of development largely reflects the situation in some of the larger transition countries and cannot be

19. Bakker and Gross (2004: 8).

Figure 3-5. *Financial Sector Assets and Number of Non-Bank Financial Institutions in New EU Member States, 1996–2003*

Financial sector assets (millions of U.S. dollars)

Banking sector ☐   Insurance sector ⊠   Pension funds ▨
Mutual funds ▨   Leasing companies ■   Factoring companies ⊟
Private equity ■   Stock market capitalization ■   Domestic, nonfinancial corporate debt ☐

Number of financial institutions, excluding banks

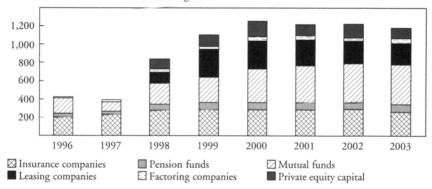

⊠ Insurance companies   ▨ Pension funds   ▨ Mutual funds
■ Leasing companies   ⊟ Factoring companies   ■ Private equity capital

Sources: Bakker and Gross (2004); World Bank, European Central Bank, and European Private Equity and Venture Capital Association.

taken as a general indication of improved access to finance through stock markets in the region. In particular, Russia and Poland drive the volatile growth of stock market valuations. However, stock markets in many other transition countries display a much less dynamic, but also less volatile, growth path.

Financial Depth

One of the most prominent and persistent features of financial systems in transition countries is the low level of financial depth resulting from the

Figure 3-6. *Growth of Market Capitalization and Domestic Credit in Transition Countries, 1992–2003*

Percent of GDP

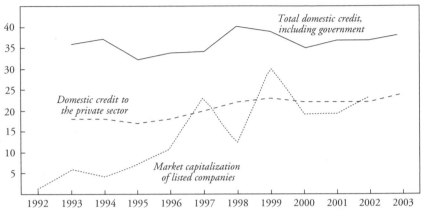

Source: IMF (various years.)

limited role that financial intermediation played in the pre-1989 period. Financial depth is generally lower than in the more advanced countries, where deposits as a percentage of GDP usually are significantly above 70 percent (see figure 3-7). Central and Eastern European countries like the Czech Republic, Hungary, Poland, and the Slovak Republic started with much higher levels of financial depth (around 50–60 percent) than the other countries, but they have not managed to deepen financial intermediation significantly. Croatia and Slovenia display significant growth, in line with growing public confidence in the banking system. Russia and Ukraine have low levels of financial depth. In both countries, trust in the safety of banks is still a significant issue.

Improved Cost-Efficiency in Banking

Fries and Taci find in a sample of 289 banks in fifteen transition economies that "an average size bank in the sample operates at a point that is close to constant returns to scale, while the smaller banks in the sample operate with significant unrealized economies of scale. This suggests that consolidation of smaller banks in the region would contribute to greater cost efficiency in banking."[20] This finding is of relevance especially in Russia, which is still

20. Fries and Taci (2004: 18).

Figure 3-7. *Demand, Time, and Savings Deposits as a Share of GDP in Select Transition Countries, 1993–2004*

Percent of GDP

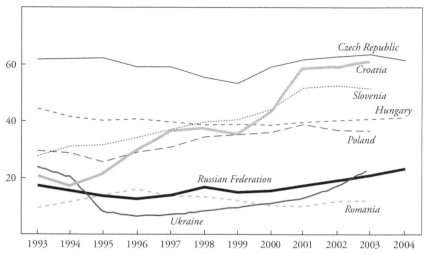

Source: IMF (various years).

characterized by a large number of small banks. Overall, they find that higher cost-efficiency at a country level is correlated with lower interest rates, greater share of foreign-owned banks, and a higher intermediation ratio. Their analysis confirms the positive effects of privatization and entry of foreign strategic investors on profitability at the bank level, as shown in table 3-3. On average, newly established domestically owned banks have a higher return on average assets (ROAA) than newly established foreign banks, although not a higher return on average equity (ROAE). Somewhat surprising, foreign-owned privatized banks perform as poorly as state-owned banks, which, as might be expected, are the least profitable.

Private Sector Access to Finance

Only a few transition countries have reached the point where their financial institutions effectively fulfill their important role as financial intermediaries, collecting deposits and allocating funds to the private sector. Many banking systems not only are too small when compared to the size of their economies but also fail to intermediate funds efficiently to fund the private

Table 3-3. *Profitability of Banks in Transition*

Percent

| Indicator | Foreign ownership | | Domestic ownership | | State-owned |
	Newly established	Privatized	Newly established	Privatized	
Return on average assets (ROAA)	1.33	1.1	1.98	1.02	1.09
Return of average equity (ROAE)	10.13	8.5	6.11	9.78	8.5

Source: Fries and Taci (2004).

sector. In many of the countries, banks still collect deposits mainly for on-lending to the government (see figure 3-8). Average private sector credit in the region—just below 25 percent of GDP—is insufficient to provide the funds needed to fuel economic activity. Generally, the provision of private sector credit is improving,[21] but the growth rates are not sufficient to generate pronounced growth in output, and access to finance for productive use in the private sector remains a key bottleneck in the region.

Lack of private sector credit is confirmed by firm-level survey data:[22] companies are still heavily reliant on internally generated funds to finance new investments (see figure 3-9). Survey results indicate that in Russia and many former CIS countries, more than 70 percent of new investments are financed out of internal funds. Companies in the new EU member states benefit from the more advanced financial sectors, with internal funds financing 40–55 percent of investments. Foreign direct investment and cross-border borrowing are growing in importance.

Against the background of these general themes of financial sector development in the transition countries, a number of distinct country experiences are evident across the region:

—*New EU member states and accession candidates.* The eight countries that joined the European Union in 2004 (Czech Republic, Estonia, Hungary, Latvia, Lithuania, Poland, Slovak Republic, and Slovenia) clearly outperformed their other transition-country peers in restructuring their

21. Slovakia and the Czech Republic registered a marked decline in the measurement of private sector credit as a percentage of GDP, which is largely a result of the delayed removal of substantial amounts of nonperforming loans from the balance sheets of the banks that stem from the pretransition period and were not replaced by new lending to the private sector.

22. EBRD and World Bank (various years).

Figure 3-8. *Private Sector Credit as a Percentage of GDP in Select Transition Countries, 1992–2004*

Percent of GDP

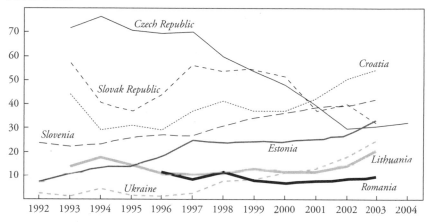

Source: IMF (various years).

financial systems, stabilizing the macroeconomic environment, and implementing sound supervisory regimes. The prospect of EU accession provided necessary political capital and substantial technical and financial assistance for reforming institutions. Subsequently, the countries attracted foreign capital and promoted market entry of foreign banks and financial institutions, which contributed substantially to enhance institutional capacity and strengthen financial intermediation. Nonetheless, the depth and scope of financial sector development remain significantly below those in the more developed EU and other OECD countries. The remaining accession candidates—in particular, Bulgaria and Romania—started from a lower level and still face a challenging agenda of restructuring and privatization in the banking and corporate sectors, as well as low depth and poor access of the population to banking services.[23]

—*Russia.* Russia has benefited greatly from a favorable macroeconomic environment in recent years, with fiscal and monetary discipline and a huge commodity boom (mostly petroleum). However, its small and fragmented

23. Bulgaria experienced a late (1996–97) and severe banking crisis. A currency board was adopted in 1997 to impose monetary discipline after reaching a rate of inflation of 300 percent in 1996. Lending to nonfinancial enterprises as a share of GDP reached only 14 percent in 2001. Only one in three Bulgarians has a bank account (Hackethal, Marinov, and Schmidt 2003).

Figure 3-9. *Internal Funds as a Share of Total New Investment in Select Transition Countries, 2002–03*

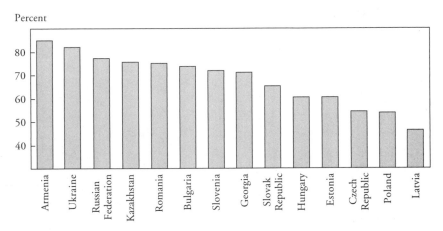

Percent

Source: EBRD and World Bank (various years).

banking system is the Achilles' heel of the development and diversification of its private sector. The banking sector has not developed sufficiently, and reform efforts have had only limited success. The banking system is still dominated by a few state banks that hold a substantial and growing share of household deposits and assets, while the rest of the banking system consists of a vast number of small banks. Out of roughly 1,500 banks, only 220 banks have capital of more than $10 million, and 490 banks have a capitalization level below $1 million. The Russian financial system continues to suffer from a lack of confidence, insider lending, opaque ownership, and the potential for self-fulfilling bank runs. The recent introduction of a deposit insurance scheme was intended to mitigate the risk of such runs. Supervision has made progress, but it still has a long way to go, particularly in getting the autonomy and political support to enforce all the regulations impartially, to promote the orderly exit of insolvent banks, and to promote further orderly consolidation. There may also be problems in the sequencing of reforms, as the deposit insurance regime was adopted prior to having a strong supervisory regime and an efficient bank resolution regime.

—*Central Asia and the Caucasus.* Broadly speaking, the countries in the Caucasus and Central Asian region (Armenia, Azerbaijan, Georgia, Kyrgyz Republic, Tajikistan, Turkmenistan, and Uzbekistan) all have low levels of monetization, high levels of cash transactions, and large informal economies;

credit growth is hampered by widespread enterprise distress and very high real interest rates, although there are some differences in financial sector development between the countries. Financial intermediation remains low even by transition-country standards, and financial sector reform is stuck at a much less advanced stage of transition than in the EU accession states. The banking system suffers from underdeveloped regulatory and legal systems and the failure to resist political pressures to make imprudent loans. Kazakhstan stands out from other countries in the Central Asian region, having adopted sound reforms early. However, the banking system is still highly concentrated, with limited competition, significant insider lending, and lack of transparency in the ultimate shareholder control over the banks.

—Southeastern Europe. Financial sector development experience in Southeastern Europe is very heterogeneous. Bosnia, Serbia and Montenegro, and, to a lesser extent, Croatia experienced significant delays in financial sector reforms in the wake of the civil conflict of the 1990s. Recently, Croatia has undertaken significant reform efforts and is displaying very positive trends in financial sector growth. However, regulatory regimes and legal frameworks still require substantial reforms and strengthening in most of the other countries. In the medium term, all of these countries are expected to benefit from stronger affiliations with the EU and the entry of major European commercial banks, particularly from Austria and Italy. Financial systems in Albania and Macedonia are shallow and display characteristics similar to those in the Central Asian countries, including poor governance and underdeveloped regulatory oversight.

Conclusion and Challenges Ahead

Some authors have argued that crises can bring beneficial consequences, claiming "that many inefficiencies in prevailing institutions arise to serve organized special interests, and the entrenched political power of these groups prevents reforms that would be beneficial in the aggregate. Crises weaken or dissolve these special interests and allow a fresh start," albeit at a large cost.[24] These "useful crises" did indeed happen in many transition countries in Europe and the Central Asian region. However, there were also "indecisive or useless crises" that did not result in a serious revamping of the banking system and the hoped-for start of financial depth–enhancing

24. Dixit (2005: 19).

reforms. Yet even in cases like Russia, where crisis "opportunities" were not realized, some benefits resulted from loosening the tight grip of governments on the capture of domestic credit.

Going forward, there are still unfinished tasks, and strengthening institutional development is the key to developing a framework for growth and sustainable financial intermediation.

Broadly defined, institutional development remains the main challenge (again with various degrees of severity), specifically in the area of banking supervision. The countries of Central and Eastern Europe have made remarkable progress in developing all the institutions and capabilities for a market economy, with the incentives generated by the process of accession and the need to comply with the EU's Acquis. Other countries like Bulgaria, Croatia, and Romania are also making considerable progress. Nonetheless, as indicators of the limited degree of compliance with the Basel core principles show, further progress is required in many areas. In our view, there is significant scope for making progress in four key areas:

—Consolidated supervision, granting adequate powers to supervisors to investigate the composition and cross-shareholdings inside of financial, nonfinancial, and mixed complex conglomerates,

—Autonomy, funding, and adequate remuneration and staffing of supervisory agencies and legal protection for bank supervisors,

—Better risk management systems in financial institutions, while supervisors move to risk-based supervision (in view of the EU decision to adopt Basel II within the proposed timetable, the challenges are going to be more pressing for the EU subset of countries, but all countries are well advised to prepare realistic "road maps" to better risk management systems),

—Contingency plans, including adequate legislative frameworks and institutional capacity, which should be in place to respond effectively to less frequent and less severe banking crises,

—Migration to a single, consolidated supervisory agency model a la the Financial Services Authority of the United Kingdom. (However, it will probably be more important to ensure a continued strong focus on the need to discharge regulatory and supervisory tasks efficiently. Merging agencies with different cultures and interests—supervision and promotion of, for example, capital markets—are difficult tasks and require years to implement and resolve potential conflicts of interest. This could easily lead to a deterioration of regulatory and supervisory capacity.)

The development of financial intermediation is not an end in itself, but financial institutions and markets play an important role in promoting a better allocation of resources in the economy, including facilitating access to underserved segments, particularly small and medium enterprises, which, it is hoped, will lead to faster sustainable growth and poverty reduction. In general, and in spite of tremendous recent progress, indicators of financial intermediation in the transition economies of Eastern Europe and Central Asia remain low in a broader international perspective. Against such a high benchmark, countries still have a long way to go in the development of financial intermediaries, markets, and institutional capabilities.

References

Bakker, Marie-Renee, and Alexandra Gross. 2004. "Development of Non-Bank Financial Institutions and Capital Markets in European Union Accession Countries." Working Paper 28. Washington: World Bank.

Berglof, Erik, and Patrick Bolton. 2002. "The Great Divide and Beyond: Financial Architecture in Transition." *Journal of Economic Perspectives* (U.S.) 16, no. 1 (Winter): 77–100.

Bonin, John, and Paul Wachtel. 2002. "Financial Sector Development in Transition Economies: Lessons from the First Decade." BOFIT Discussion Paper 9/2002. Bank of Finland, Institute for Economies in Transition (www.bof.fi).

Borish, Michael, and Fernando Montes-Negret. 1998. "Restructuring Distressed Banks in Transition Economies: Lessons from Central Europe and Ukraine." In *Preventing Bank Crises: Lessons from Recent Global Bank Failures,* edited by Gerard Caprio, William Hunter, George Kaufman, and Danny Lepziger. Federal Reserve Bank of Chicago and the Economic Development Institute, World Bank.

Claessens, Stijn, Daniela Klingebiel, and Luc Laeven. 2004. "Resolving Systemic Financial Crises: Policies and Institutions." Policy Research Paper. Washington: World Bank.

Commander, Simon, Mark Dutz, and Nicholas Stern. 1999. "Restructuring in Transition Economies: Ownership, Competition, and Regulation." Paper prepared for the Annual World Bank Conference on Development Economics, Washington.

Dixit, Avinash. 2005. "Evaluating Recipes for Development." Paper prepared for the Annual World Bank Conference on Development Economics, Washington.

EBRD (European Bank for Reconstruction and Development). 2004. *EBRD Transition Report 2004: Infrastructure.* London.

EBRD and World Bank. Various years. Investment Climate Surveys (rru.worldbank.org/InvestmentClimate/).

Fries, Steven, and Anita Taci. 2004. "Cost Efficiency of Banks in Transition: Evidence from 289 Banks in 15 Post-communist Countries." EBRD Working Paper. London: European Bank for Reconstruction and Development.

Hackethal, Andreas, Valentin Marinov, and Reinhard H. Schmidt. 2003. "Banking Markets in Central and Eastern Europe (VI): Bulgaria; Emerging Stronger from a Crisis." *Die Bank,* August.

Huang, Haizhou, Dalia Marin, and Chenggang Xu. 2004. "Financial Crisis, Economic Recovery, and Banking Development in Russia, Ukraine, and Other FSU Countries." IMF Working Paper. Washington: International Monetary Fund.

IMF (International Monetary Fund). Various years. *International Financial Statistics.* Washington.

Matousek, Roman. 2004. "Banking Crises Resolution in Central and Eastern Europe: Cross Country Experience." Discussion Paper. London: London Metropolitan University, Center for International Capital Markets.

McDermott, Gerald A. 2004. "The Politics of Institutional Learning and Creation: Bank Crises and Supervision in East Central Europe." Working Paper WP 2004-04. University of Pennsylvania, Wharton School, Reginald H. Jones Center, November.

Peachey, Stephen, and Alan R. Roe. 2001. "Financial Deepening and the Role of Financial Crises." In *Financial Transition in Europe and Central Asia: Challenges of the New Decade,* edited by Lajos Bokros, Alexander Fleming, and Cari Votava. Washington: World Bank.

Standard & Poor's. 2004. "Russia: Banking System Analysis" (www.ratingsdirect.com).

Tang, Helena, Edda Zoli, and Irina Klytchnikova. 2000. "Banking in Transition Economies: Fiscal Costs and Related Issues." Policy Research Working Paper 2484. Washington: World Bank, November.

World Bank. 2002. "Transition: The First Ten Years; Analysis and Lessons for Eastern Europe and the Former Soviet Union." Washington.

———. 2003. "Bank Consolidation in the ECA Region: A Multicountry Study." Mimeo. Washington.

Zoli, Edda. 2001. "Cost and Effectiveness of Banking Sector Restructuring in Transition Economies." IMF Working Paper. Washington: International Monetary Fund.

INDERMIT GILL
BRIAN PINTO

4

Sovereign Debt in Developing Countries with Market Access

Help or Hindrance?

Sovereign debt can help developing countries. It enables their governments to facilitate growth take-offs by investing in a critical mass of infrastructure projects and in the social sectors when taxation capacity is limited or the alternative would be to print money and compromise macroeconomic stability. Debt also facilitates tax smoothing and countercyclical fiscal policies, essential for reducing the volatility of output, and it permits an equitable alignment of benefits and costs for long-gestation projects by shifting taxation away from current generations.

This is what theory tells us. There is every reason to believe that governments that borrow and spend prudently will reap these benefits in practice, but we also know that there was a profusion of costly macroeconomic crises during the 1990s, with public debt either being a central cause (for example, Russia in 1998 and Argentina in 2001) or else absorbing the brunt of the impact (for example, Indonesia, Korea, Malaysia, and Thailand during 1997–98). Moreover, the external debt crisis of the 1980s and the now-

The authors thank Joshua Aizenman, Amar Bhattacharya, Nina Budina, Craig Burnside, Christophe Chamley, Ajay Chhibber, Gautam Datta, Norbert Fiess, Olivier Jeanne, Himmat Kalsi, Homi Kharas, Gobind Nankani, Vikram Nehru, Anand Rajaram, Luis Serven, John Williamson, Holger Wolf, and many others for useful comments or contributions. They are particularly indebted to James Hanson for encouraging them to write this paper and making numerous suggestions for improvement.

controversial financial liberalization of the early 1990s have raised questions about the benefits of market-based external finance for developing countries with access to the international capital markets, called market access countries. These are the countries we look at in this chapter.

Table 4-1 lists the top ten market access countries in terms of public debt (external plus domestic)—Argentina, Brazil, China, India, Indonesia, Korea, Mexico, Poland, Russia, and Turkey. In 2002 their combined public debt was $2.2 trillion, or more than two-thirds of total market-access-country public debt. These countries also accounted for about $1.4 trillion in external debt—that is, public plus private debt held by external creditors. When public debt is expressed as a ratio of GDP, the top eleven market-access-country debtors in 2002 were Argentina, India, Indonesia, Jamaica, Jordan, Lebanon, Morocco, Pakistan, the Philippines, Turkey, and Uruguay, with ratios ranging between 90 and 180 percent.[1] All but three countries had higher ratios of public debt to GDP than a decade earlier in 1992, the year by which the Brady Plan resolution of the 1980s debt crisis had been implemented for the major participating countries. In the three exceptions— Jamaica, Jordan, and Morocco—the ratio of public debt to GDP was exceptionally high in 1992 and had declined only modestly by 2002. Of the seventeen countries in table 4-1, China was the only one not to experience a debt or balance-of-payments crisis during the 1980s or later.[2] This chapter pays special attention to many of the countries listed in the table.

In the face of concern that access to the international capital markets and high and rising public debt are enhancing vulnerability rather than growth, this chapter attempts to answer three questions:

—What are the chances of a new debt crisis?

—Is public debt constraining economic growth?

—What should be done about public debt in developing countries?

---

1. There are varying definitions of both numerator and denominator across countries. Turkey reports debt ratios as a share of GNP, and Brazil and Turkey both report public debt net of central bank assets.

2. Lebanon remains an enigma. In spite of being an outlier in its ratio of public debt to GDP, it did not suffer a debt default or financial system crisis, but its exchange rate collapsed during 1986–87 and 1992 as a result of domestic credit–financed expansions in government spending, which depleted reserves, akin to a first-generation crisis (see box 4-1). It also benefited from a pubic debt reprofiling under the auspices of the Paris II conference held in November 2002 (Ministry of Finance, Republic of Lebanon, 2003).

Table 4-1. *Major Market Access Countries by Total Amount of Public Debt and Ratio of Public Debt to GDP, 1992 and 2002* [a]

Top ten countries	Total public debt (billions of U.S. dollars)		Top eleven countries	Ratio of public debt to GDP (percent)	
	1992	2002		1992	2002
India	156	380	Lebanon	70	177
China	68	366	Jamaica	181	149
Brazil	165	284	Argentina	26	126
Mexico	118	280	Uruguay	48	109
Korea	61	232[b]	Jordan	167	100
Turkey	65	173	Turkey	40	94
Indonesia	56	149	India	74	81
Russia	12	118	Pakistan	81	90
Argentina	59	117	Morocco	102	90
Poland	44	72	Philippines	81	89
			Indonesia	40	86

Sources: World Bank (various years); IMF (2003b); staff estimates.

a. Public debt is defined as public and publicly guaranteed external debt plus domestic public debt.

b. Data for 2001.

What Is the Likelihood of Another Debt Crisis?

What are the risks of another debt crisis as in the early 1980s or in the latter half of the 1990s? This chapter offers the following answer: Such risks have receded since the late 1990s, but this does not mean that such a crisis will not appear in the future. One would be at odds with history for saying otherwise; as Easterly, Islam, and Stiglitz note, "Crises have been a constant of market capitalism," including not just financial shocks but also wars, pestilence, and natural disasters.[3] One might add that crises rarely tend to be similar, making them difficult to predict—witness the successive generations of crisis models (presented in box 4-1).[4] This section explains the answer by discussing the causes of past crises, current attempts by countries to lower their vulnerability, and the market's interpretation of the likelihood of a crisis.

3. Easterly, Islam, and Stiglitz (2000).
4. The three generations of crisis models presented in box 4-1 draw on Frankel and Wei (forthcoming).

Box 4-1. *Crisis Models and the Government's Intertemporal Budget Constraint*

Three generations of crisis models have been identified.

Krugman's first-generation crisis model attributes balance-of-payments crises to budget deficits financed by domestic credit in a fixed-exchange-rate regime with perfect capital mobility (Krugman 1979). This leads to current account deficits and a steady loss of reserves, with a speculative attack exhausting reserves before they would otherwise have been used up. A float is then forced. Such macroeconomic overexpansion and overvaluation were the standard diagnoses of balance-of-payments crises in developing countries before 1993 and were the basis of most adjustment programs administered by the International Monetary Fund. The international debt crisis of the 1980s is an example. Some of the crises in the late 1990s also reflected budget deficits, sometimes related to debt service of excessive debt obligations.

The second-generation model argues that there are "crisis" and "no-crisis" multiple equilibria consistent with unchanged fundamentals. This approach was inspired by the European exchange rate mechanism (ERM) crisis of 1992–93. The speculative attack on France in 1993 was puzzling because its macroeconomic discipline had been comparable to that of Germany, its partner in the ERM. Moreover, after the bands were widened, the crisis passed without a substantial further depreciation of the franc, even though macroeconomic policy seemed unchanged. How then could the fundamentals have been responsible for the earlier speculative pressure? The second-generation argument is illustrated most simply by a "prisoner's dilemma." Consider two speculators. Each realizes that if the other sells, the resulting depreciation will reduce the value of his holdings of domestic currency. Neither wants to stand pat if the other might sell. One equilibrium is for both to sell. Of course, an alternative explanation for the attack on the franc is that currency traders lost faith in the ERM after Danish voters rejected the Maastricht Treaty, speculators forced the United Kingdom and Italy to withdraw from the ERM, and Germany eventually declined to support the franc, as had been feared.

The third-generation model arose from the East Asian crisis of 1997–98, where macroeconomic policy was not a problem but a different kind of weakness in fundamentals appeared: structural distortions in the financial system combined with currency mismatches reflecting implicit exchange rate guarantees. Well-connected banks and businessmen borrow in foreign currency to finance risky projects, including real estate development or construction of new factories in glutted industries. They are aware of the risk but are reasonably confident they will be bailed out by the govern-

(continued)

Box 4-1. *Crisis Models and the Government's Intertemporal Budget Constraint* (continued)

ment if things go badly. The timing of the attack again stems from the calculations of speculators who worry that if they wait too long, there will not be enough foreign exchange reserves to go around, as discussed by Dooley (2000). But there is a key difference from the first-generation model, where reserves fall in the run-up to crisis. In this case, liabilities, artificially encouraged by moral hazard, rise to a point at which investors start to cash in their investments, fearful that if they wait any longer, they might not be able to get their money out. The speculative attack forces the central bank to abandon the exchange rate.

All three models—referred to as model I, model II, and model III—may be triggered by an event, either economic or political. Obviously, it is difficult to predict exactly why and when the next crisis will occur and what shape it will assume.

In all three models, the GIBC plays an important role. The debt crisis in the 1980s, Russia in 1998, and Argentina in 2001 all involved overtly expansionary macroeconomic policies, unsustainable public debt dynamics, or both. In East Asia in 1997–98, public debt rose in connection with the fiscal costs associated with financial sector bailouts. These contingent liabilities became actual liabilities once the implicitly fixed exchange rate pegs were abandoned, leading to distress in the enterprise and financial sectors as a result of currency mismatches on their balance sheet and capital flight, particularly in the context of political change in Indonesia. Thus, in predicting crises, it is not enough to look at fiscal deficits and the dynamics of explicit public debt (which were benign in the East Asian countries). Contingent liabilities, broadly defined, can also be a factor.

Interpretations of Past Crises

The recent analysis of financial crises by Kaminsky, Reinhart, and Vegh provides a useful approach to applying the crisis models, particularly for explaining where an exchange rate collapse or sovereign default in one country led to widespread cross-border contagion and generalized crises and where it did not.[5] In their view, the recent generalized crises were distinguished by three key factors: (a) a rapid buildup of capital flows in the period preceding the

5. Kaminsky, Reinhart, and Vegh (2003). The explanation of past crises does not imply that future crises are predictable, because both the causes and the channels through which they operate may be different.

currency collapse or default announcement, an obvious prerequisite for a sudden stop; (b) a surprise announcement of a float or default, reflecting model I, II, or III in box 4-1; and (c) the presence of a common leveraged creditor that would transmit the crisis across borders. Two points are worth noting here. In many cases, sudden stops are not that sudden. Frankel and Wei prefer to think of a sudden stop interval as opposed to an instant stop and compute an interval of between six and thirteen months in the context of recent crises.[6] Second, sudden stops are a combination of lower reserves, lower inflows, and increased capital outflows.

The Kaminsky, Reinhart, and Vegh combination of factors applies to most of the crises in the early 1980s.[7] The rise in oil prices led to large current account surpluses in petroleum-producing countries. These petrodollars were sent to the money center banks, which recycled them to market access countries, those in Latin America in particular. The shock was a decline in commodity prices and a big rise in U.S. interest rates over 1980–85, which created fiscal stress, as in model I. The Mexican default in August 1982 was the "surprise" announcement, although capital flight had been increasing in Mexico for some time. The U.S. banks, which were heavily exposed to Mexico, withdrew from emerging markets, and many Latin American countries defaulted.

The East Asian crisis of 1997–98 was preceded by substantial capital flows into the affected countries. The common external shock identified by Kaminsky, Reinhart, and Vegh was the large depreciation of the yen against the dollar, to which most of the East Asian currencies were implicitly pegged, between April 1995 and April 1997. The sudden country shock was Thailand's float of the baht in July 1997, after its reserves were exhausted in defending the currency peg during a period of capital flight and relatively easy credit. Afterward, Japanese banks, already under pressure from low profits at home, retreated from East Asia; the Korean crisis prompted European banks to do so as well.[8] Goldstein (chapter 5 in this volume) also suggests the presence of a "wake-up" factor following a reevaluation of risks in the region.

It can be argued that the Russian default and devaluation of August 17, 1998, led to ripple effects in Brazil and eventually in Argentina and, possibly, Turkey. The Russian crisis precipitated the bailout of Long-Term

6. Frankel and Wei (forthcoming).

7. Chile's crisis was something of an exception (World Bank 2005).

8. In early 1998, a concerted effort by the banks to roll over Korea's outstanding external bank debt was a major factor in easing the pressure from the crisis.

Capital Management, a heavily leveraged hedge fund with systemic links to large banks.[9]

More recent crises seem to have been isolated. According to Kaminsky, Reinhart, and Vegh, the Brazilian devaluation of January 1999, the Turkish crisis of late 2000 and float of the lira in February 2001, and the Argentine meltdown and default of 2001 did not have widespread repercussions because these crises were widely anticipated, the asset bubble had been pricked earlier, and the common creditor was less leveraged.

In projecting future crises and their intensity, recent history suggests that it is important to look at the government's intertemporal budget constraint (GIBC) and at balance sheet currency and maturity mismatches in banks and enterprises, which have been an amplifying factor (box 4-1). The GIBC, broadly interpreted, has played an important role in crises among market access countries in the last two decades, either ex ante or ex post. Argentina and Russia have been at one extreme, with adverse public debt dynamics in the lead-up to the crisis in the context of a fixed exchange rate, a variant of model I. In the case of Russia, financial sector linkages with the real sector were small, as were balance sheet currency and maturity mismatches, compared with those in Argentina and East Asia. Argentina's situation was further complicated by the transition costs of its pension reform. These raised fiscal deficits at a time of considerable vulnerability stemming from financial sector fragility and an overvalued real exchange rate that was difficult to address because of the hard peg to the dollar.[10] In the East Asian case, the big fiscal impact came ex post from the bailout of financial sector institutions, as outlined in model III, but concerns about the impact of the potential crisis on monetary and fiscal policy probably played a role in the outflow of capital.

The point going forward is that even if the next crisis assumes a completely unexpected shape, it would affect the GIBC in some way—even though the manner might not be obvious, for example, as a result of hidden liabilities as opposed to large primary fiscal deficits and a large differential between the interest rate and the growth rate[11]—and would have an adverse

9. For a discussion of the bailout of Long-Term Capital Management, see Rubin and Weisberg (2003: 284–88).

10. Perry and Serven (2003) attribute much of the deterioration in the Argentine debt position over 1994–2001 to the widening of the social security system's effective deficit following pension reforms in 1994.

11. In the absence of corrective action, a combination of primary fiscal deficits and interest rates that exceed growth rates means a visible and unbounded rise in the ratio of public debt to GDP.

impact on the real and financial sectors. Reducing vulnerability would thus involve running larger primary fiscal surpluses, building up foreign exchange reserves, and shifting toward domestic currency debt. Some of these issues are discussed in the context of countries that experienced a serious crisis in the 1980s, 1990s, or both. The following questions are addressed in this section: Are public debt levels sustainable, and what are countries doing to lower their vulnerability? What does the market say?

Debt Sustainability: What Are Countries Doing to Lower Their Vulnerability?

For market access countries, a public debt sustainability problem usually means that the prevailing combination of primary fiscal balances, real interest, and growth rates places the ratio of public debt to GDP on a path that makes the market nervous and increases the chances of a sudden stop and exchange rate collapse. It could also mean rising bond spreads on hard currency debt issued by the government if the market senses that a default may be in the cards because the projected present value of primary fiscal surpluses is less than the outstanding public debt—in other words, the debt trajectory is likely to create a solvency problem.[12] In these circumstances, creditors are unlikely to attach a high probability to the possibility that the country will grow out of its debt problem—otherwise, they would not be concerned about debt sustainability to begin with. Such a situation could result in rising real interest rates, while also generating uncertainty about future inflation and taxation, and thereby deter private investment. Thus market concerns about the sustainability and solvency of public debt could slow growth and increase the vulnerability to a crisis.

   Ratios of public debt to GDP for the major market access countries were high and rose significantly after the mid-1990s, as shown in table 4-2. The pertinent issues are whether these high ratios are sustainable and what countries are doing to reduce their vulnerability to crises. There is a sharp contrast between the experience of the East Asian countries and the other big market access countries that experienced a crisis during the 1990s. While the postcrisis response—increase primary fiscal surpluses, move to flexible exchange rates, and build up reserves—is similar, the strength of the government's balance sheet and its ability to act as a shock absorber have been much greater in the East Asian countries (with the exception of the Philippines).

---

12. High interest rates on domestic currency debt could connote a combination of default and devaluation (inflation) risks.

Table 4-2. *Key Macroeconomic Variables in the East Asian Crisis Countries,*
1995–2002

Country	Total public debt as a percent of GDP			Net foreign assets as a percent of GDP[a]			Short-term external debt as a percent of reserves[b]		
	1995–97	*1998*	*2002*	*1995–97*	*1998*	*2002*	*1995–97*	*1998*	*2002*
Indonesia	34.5	94.0	91.3	9.5	11.8	15.2	188.1	88.6	75.26
Korea	12.8	43.0	42.4	4.6	10.4	19.4	200.7	54.1	34.13[c]
Malaysia	46.7	57.2	62.8	20.0	30.2	35.4	47.8	33.1	24.46
Thailand	21.2	57.7	45.3	−3.5	1.5	31.1	131.2	102.9	31.33

Sources: Staff estimates; Global Development Finance, World Bank (various issues).

a. Net foreign assets are the sum of foreign assets held by monetary authorities and deposit money banks less their foreign liabilities.

b. Short-term external debt is debt with an original maturity of one year or less. Reserves are total reserves minus gold.

c. Data for 2001.

Concerns about the sustainability of public debt are consequently more muted in these countries, notwithstanding the sizable jump in public debt following the 1997–98 crisis, mainly as a result of issuing government bonds to recapitalize banks or taking over private external debt. Subsequently, net foreign assets have been built up, and international liquidity has been strengthened considerably, with the ratio of short-term external debt to reserves falling far below 1. This helps to protect these countries from sudden stops. To some degree, all have made efforts to address the structural distortions in the corporate and financial sectors, which, combined with implicit exchange rate guarantees and the bailout of well-connected business groups, led to the crisis in the first place, as noted in box 4-1. The three countries that had International Monetary Fund (IMF) programs after the crisis— Indonesia, Korea, and Thailand—have all completed these, and Korea and Thailand have paid off their IMF obligations. All four economies have been growing for the past five years and are expected to grow about 5 percent annually in the coming years.

No doubt, a sudden rise in world interest rates or a sudden slowdown in world export demand would create problems for the four countries. However, the countries have made major efforts to protect themselves. In contrast, the Philippines has also experienced rising public debt, but this has occurred because of rising off-budget liabilities and an increase in the fiscal deficit due to a falloff in tax revenues, not because of bank recapitalization. Here, fiscal consolidation is a clear priority.

Argentina, Brazil, Russia, and Turkey also experienced crises that began in the second half of the 1990s. In contrast to the East Asian countries, these market access countries suffered from unsustainable public debt dynamics stemming from large fiscal deficits, high interest rates, and slow growth in the lead-up to their crises. Fiscal reforms were incomplete or not credible, or else fiscal policy was procyclical, as in Argentina. To varying degrees—severe in Argentina, mild in Russia—they also suffered from currency mismatches. As a result, when the sudden stop in capital flows and consequent collapse in real exchange rates occurred, the public debt problem was compounded by the collapse of banks and enterprises that needed to be bailed out. Once countries get into this kind of situation, there seem to be only two ways out: restructure public debt to lower its present value, as Russia did and as Argentina did unilaterally, to the consternation of its creditors, or adopt flexible exchange rates and run large primary fiscal surpluses. The prospects of simply "growing out" of such a problem while maintaining existing policies should be considered bleak.

Rather than restructure their public debt, Brazil and Turkey have been running primary fiscal surpluses of unprecedented size. Table 4-3 presents averages of key variables for Argentina, Brazil, Russia, and Turkey for the three years before and three years after the crisis. Apart from Argentina, primary fiscal surpluses have been significantly ramped up. Interest payments have risen from already high levels, except for Russia, which successfully restructured its debt. Net resource transfers shrank significantly in all the countries after the crisis. In Russia, which elected to prepay debt when oil prices rose and benefited from a significant write-down on London Club debt, this was deliberate. The postcrisis bilateral U.S. dollar real exchange rate has depreciated significantly, except in Turkey, where by the end of the "after" period, the real exchange rate had reverted to its precrisis level.

One more development is noteworthy: a shift toward domestic currency debt in many of the major countries that experienced a crisis during the 1990s. Such a shift is most likely to yield dividends in concert with more basic fiscal and institutional reform but is unlikely to make a big difference in isolation, as box 4-2 discusses in the Brazilian context.

Notwithstanding their attempts to improve debt dynamics, the ratio of public debt to GDP in Brazil and Turkey is too high. Moreover, interest payments in both countries remain in excess of even the ramped-up primary surpluses, so that an overall fiscal deficit still exists that needs to be financed by additional debt issue. And the primary surpluses could have negative consequences for long-run growth to the extent that they have been achieved by

Table 4-3. *Economic Indicators before and after Crisis in Four Important Market Access Countries, Annual Averages*

Country	Primary surplus as a percent of GDP		Interest payment as a percent of GDP		Net resource transfers (billions of U.S. dollars)[a]		Real exchange rate (first year = 100)[b]	
	Before	After	Before	After	Before	After	Before	After
Argentina[c]	0.1	0.8	3.4	7.3	7.0	−8.1	97.5	57.5
Brazil[d]	0.5	3.8	7.0	8.1	19.4	4.7	89.2	54.8
Russia[e]	−3.2	4.6	5.0	3.8	6.3	−3.6	111.0	72.4
Turkey[f]	0.1	5.2	18.7	19.8	2.8	−0.4	98.1	84.9

Sources: Staff estimates; World Bank (various issues).

a. Net resource transfers are calculated as net resource flows minus interest on long-term debt and profit remittances on foreign direct investment.

b. The real exchange rate is bilateral with respect to the U.S. dollar, period average.

c. For Argentina, before represents 1998–2000; after represents 2001–03.

d. For Brazil, before represents 1996–99; after represents 2000–03.

e. For Russia, before represents 1995–98; after represents 1999–2000.

f. For Turkey, GNP is used instead of GDP; before represents 1998–2000; after represents 2001–03. Data are not available for 2003.

cutting public investment and social spending, an issue discussed further below. It would be reasonable to assert that debt continues to be excessive and needs to be reduced. The key issues in Brazil and Turkey, regarding potential crises, are whether international interest rates will remain low and whether the market, convinced by these countries' persistent primary surpluses, will lower their sovereign bond spreads. In addition, for Turkey, the return of the real exchange rate to its precrisis level raises a question about the sustainability of the country's high postcrisis growth rate, unless microeconomic efficiency and productivity have risen. Box 4-2 illustrates, with Brazil's experience, the challenges of managing public debt that crosses thresholds that the market deems excessive.

In sum, vulnerable countries such as Brazil, Jamaica, and Turkey are running primary fiscal surpluses of unprecedented magnitude, and these have persisted for lengths of time that would have been considered politically impossible only a few years ago. This "revealed policy preference" may be the outcome of a realization that debt levels are too high and are hurting development and that repeated defaults and restructurings are too costly in a long-term development sense. Bolstering the soundness of public finances and lowering indebtedness in a lasting and credible manner depend on

Box 4-2. *Lessons from Brazil's Macroeconomic Adjustment, 1999–2003*

For market access countries that have debt sustainability problems and rule out default, the GIBC is most likely to be helped by fiscal effort, flexible exchange rates (to weaken incentives for currency mismatches), and institutional reform, as Brazil's experience illustrates.

Brazil's high primary surpluses since 1999, the year in which it switched from a crawling peg to a flexible exchange rate regime, have been both surprising and controversial: surprising because the market, judging by the default-level bond spreads in 2002, did not expect the new administration elected that year to persevere with these and controversial because of concerns about long-run growth and welfare based on "fiscal space." While there has been some good news related to rising growth and private investment in recent months, the EMBI Global spread on March 11, 2005, while much lower at 388 basis points than a year ago, is still much higher than in Chile (58 basis points) and Mexico (156 basis points). Although it is too early to assess the long-run impacts, this box (based in part on a note contributed by Gautam Datta) summarizes key points from Brazil's experience over 1999–2003:

—*The shift toward domestic debt.* By end-2003, net public debt had reached 58 percent of GDP compared with 49 percent in 2000. At the margin, new public borrowing was largely in the domestic market: the rise in the ratio of external debt to GDP was due mainly to the large devaluations in 1999 and 2002. This shift toward domestic borrowing did not, by itself, improve the sustainability of debt because domestic debt tended to be indexed to short-run interest rates, the exchange rate, or the price level. Thus the proportion of nominal (unindexed) bonds fell from 60 percent in 1996 (when credibility following the successful stabilization in 1994 was high) to less than 3 percent in 2002 as a result of economic and political uncertainty.

—*Contingent liabilities and exchange rate losses.* The growth of domestic public debt was driven not just by the fiscal deficit but also by the recognition of contingent liabilities, financial sector bailouts, the restructuring of subnational debt, and indexation. Without contingent liabilities and at 1999 nominal exchange rates, net public debt to GDP would have been 37 percent instead of 58 percent in 2003, even excluding privatization. However, interest rate and exchange rate dynamics would have been much worse without the fiscal adjustment implemented in 1999.

—*Fiscal effort.* The crucial policy response was to raise the primary surplus, which has been at least 3 percent of GDP since 1999. The ratio of revenue to GDP reached 35 percent in 2003, 10 percentage points higher than ten years earlier. But high inter-

(continued)

Box 4-2. *Lessons from Brazil's Macroeconomic Adjustment, 1999–2003* (continued)

est payments and the exchange rate losses on external debt have kept the fiscal deficit at least as high as 8 percent of GDP since 1999. With the shift toward domestic debt not having tangibly improved debt dynamics so far, it is safe to say that Brazil would have been in a worse situation without its fiscal effort. Of course, higher primary fiscal surpluses alone are not enough; how to increase public savings by eliminating waste and how to align the composition of spending more closely with growth objectives remain key topics.

—*Moral hazard.* Private, nonguaranteed debt rose by $59 billion over 1997–98, approximately 7 percent of GDP at the time, as a result of high domestic interest rates, the high fiscal deficit, and a quasi-fixed exchange rate. This created a problem, especially in 2002, when the domestic political situation led to difficulties of debt rollover. However, the authorities refused to accept responsibility for servicing this debt, instead letting the exchange rate float and relying on private debtors and creditors to work out their own arrangements. Fortunately, Brazilian corporates were not highly leveraged, unlike their counterparts in Asia at the time of the 1997–98 crisis. The domestic banking system also proved resilient, partly because it had undergone a major restructuring prior to the 1998–99 crisis, and there were no bankruptcies.

The first lesson is that financial engineering, be it a shift toward domestic debt or indexation, is secondary to fiscal adjustment. By itself, it could even backfire, as Russia's GKO-eurobond swap of July 1998 or Argentina's mega swap of June 2001 showed (Aizenman, Kletzer, and Pinto 2005). Second, the Brazilian experience lends support to the debt-intolerance argument (that weak economic fundamentals predispose countries to crises even at relatively low debt levels) and weakens the original-sin hypothesis (that the problem lies not with the countries themselves but with the absence of long-term external debt instruments denominated in domestic currency). This is because if a country cannot even issue domestic debt that is unindexed, in long maturities, and in domestic currency, it would be unreasonable to expect nonresidents to hold such debt. Third, the major challenges for which market access countries need to prepare include dealing with domestic moral hazard and private external debt, balance sheet mismatches, and contingent liabilities.

improving fiscal management institutions, as Turkey has been trying to do (see box 4-3).[13]

What Does the Market Say?

No matter its flaws—and allegations of these are numerous, including myopia, greed, herding behavior, and excessive risk-taking driven by moral hazard—the market remains the ultimate arbiter of the destiny of market-access-country debt. Markets today are different than in the 1980s. The large money center banks have been largely replaced by emerging-market bond markets. Sovereign external debt is held in diversified portfolios; moreover, even the nature of the investor base for market-access-country debt has changed in a way that could lead to greater stability.[14] There is greater awareness of individual-country fundamentals, and more information is readily available. At the same time, portfolio investors in search of higher yields have recently increased their exposure to market access countries, given historically low interest rates in the United States and European Monetary Union (EMU) countries and the rising credit upgrades of market access countries over the past two years.[15]

The incentives are also different on two counts: during the 1980s, at the political level, the fears of a systemic international financial crisis—because of the concentration of debt in a few large money center banks—played a decisive role in galvanizing high-level support in the creditor countries for a resolution.[16] In spite of the high-level coordination facilitated by the concentration of country debt in a few large banks under the umbrella of the Baker and Brady plans, the resolution and workouts took several years. More recently, expectations that Argentina or Russia would be bailed out were proven wrong. As individual investors have incurred or will incur substantial losses, the moral hazard problem associated with expected bailouts should diminish. All this means that debt problems are likely to

13. Box 4-3 was contributed by Anand Rajaram.

14. World Bank (2005).

15. World Bank (2005: 71, fig. 4) depicts the rise in the credit ratings of market access countries starting in 2003. This report also discusses the rising stability of debt markets in market access countries as a result of stronger domestic macro policy, lower susceptibility to shocks, and improvements in the international financial architecture.

16. The exposure of U.S. money center banks to countries restructuring debt was 215 percent of bank capital and 260 percent of bank equity at end-1982; that of U.K. and Canadian banks was 275 and 195 percent of their respective equity; Chuhan and Sturzenegger (2004).

Box 4-3. *Strengthening Institutions for Fiscal Management in Turkey*

Turkey's volatile economic performance in the 1990s may be attributed, in part, to its coalition politics, which were compounded by weaknesses in the institutional arrangements for aggregate fiscal management. The seeming inability of a number of governments to restrain fiscal commitments within a sustainable policy framework created a credibility problem with domestic and international debt markets.

The weaknesses included (a) an incomplete budget and lack of transparency in fiscal reporting, (b) fragmented responsibility and poor coordination of fiscal management among the three central agencies of government (finance, planning, and treasury), and (c) a failure to control and to incorporate the effect on fiscal risk of quasi-fiscal policies and guarantees that created unrecorded "hidden" liabilities, both explicit and contingent. Differences in the perspectives of coalition partners exacerbated these problems.

As a result, fiscal risk was underestimated. In 1999 the consolidated central government budget reported expenditure equivalent to 36 percent of GDP, but a comprehensive assessment would have revealed general government expenditure closer to 46 percent of GDP. Including the costs of quasi-fiscal policies, such as directed credit programs, would have increased this further. For much of the period up to 1999, such costs were disguised as growing liabilities of the government to the banking sector (the so-called duty losses) that were not explicitly recognized. While estimates of these costs vary, in 1999 the public sector's financing requirement (including the costs of quasi-fiscal programs) of almost 24 percent of GDP was double the reported consolidated budget deficit of 12 percent.

The government has taken steps to address these institutional weaknesses. The Public Finance Management and Control Law that was passed by Parliament in December 2003 put in place a comprehensive fiscal framework encompassing the general government. The new law sharply reduced the scope for extrabudgetary and revolving funds, which are being eliminated or integrated into the budget. Explicit appropriations were provided to compensate for "duty" obligations of state enterprises and banks, and this is now accounted for in the budget. Thus while quasi-fiscal policies still exist, their costs are now provided for in the budget. Longer-term reforms that will modernize the financial control arrangements and allow greater scope for managerial authority to improve public sector performance are also being initiated.

Looking forward, the law provides for the preparation of a medium-term fiscal strategy that will be endorsed by the Council of Ministers and will inform the preparation of a medium-term budget. This will start with preparation of the 2006 budget. Defining and adhering to the medium-term fiscal strategy will be a key in building the credibility of government.

be addressed on a case-by-case basis, with the onus for resolution falling on the countries themselves.

A last critical consideration for market access countries is how the market perceives the sustainability of their debt levels, which can be inferred from the EMBI (Emerging Markets Bond Index) Global spread for a particular country.[17] This spread is an index of default risk relative to advanced benchmark countries, typically the United States, and is usually computed as the arithmetic difference between the yield on a bond in the market access country and that on a bond of comparable maturity in the benchmark country.[18] In general, a lower EMBI spread can be interpreted as connoting a lower probability of default, although this is not automatically the case. This is because a lower spread can be the result, for example, of a sharp decline in the benchmark yield (the case in recent years) even if the probability of default and the default recovery value as assessed by the market do not change. A drop in spreads can also occur if the benchmark yield declines while the assumed default recovery value rises with an unchanged probability of default.[19] In order to deal with this ambiguity, the figures here report spreads for selected countries that experienced a crisis during the 1990s, together with the corporate high-yield spread.

Figure 4-1 contains the EMBI Global spreads for Brazil, Chile, Turkey, and developed-country high-yield debt, or junk bonds, for the period 1996–2003. For much of the time, Brazil's EMBI spread was above the junk bond spread, significantly so during crisis periods, such as the Russian crisis and its aftermath and the confidence crisis that erupted in May 2002 in connection with the presidential elections. It is therefore encouraging that, by the end of the period shown in figure 4-1, Brazilian spreads had dropped to the level of the junk bond spread. In contrast, Turkey's EMBI spread hovered near the junk bond spread and was much less volatile than that of Brazil, while Chile's was consistently lower and on a declining trend. Figure 4-2 shows the spreads for selected East Asian countries. While spreads for Korea,

17. J. P. Morgan's EMBI Global is regarded as the most comprehensive market-access-country debt index. It was introduced in 1999. The EMBI spread is a weighted average of the spreads of U.S. dollar bonds issued by a particular market access country. For details, see J. P. Morgan (1999).

18. It is sometimes analytically more convenient to compute the spread geometrically. Thus letting s denote the spread, Y the bond yield in the market access country, and y the bond yield in the benchmark country, the spread is defined implicitly by $(1 + s)(1 + y) = 1 + Y$. However, the convention is to report the spread simply as $Y - y$.

19. It is easy to construct numerical examples under risk neutrality to show this. All we observe is the price of the bond and its spread; the probability of default and implied recovery value must be extracted. A complete discussion is contained in Merrick (2004).

Figure 4-1. *EMBI Spreads for Brazil, Chile, and Turkey, 1996–2003*

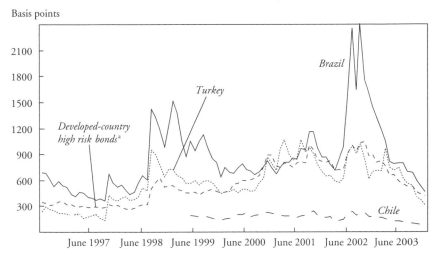

Basis points

Sources: Bloomberg; J.P.Morgan Chase; Global Development Finance,World Bank.
a. An average for the global junk bond market.

Malaysia, and Thailand jumped to exceed the junk bond spread during the 1997–98 crisis period, these dropped to substantially lower levels by mid-1999 and have been on a downtrend since. The Philippines is an exception, with a spread close to the junk bond spread. Overall, therefore, the picture on spreads is mixed. Chile, Korea, Malaysia, and Thailand have clearly strengthened their creditworthiness, but Brazil, the Philippines, and Turkey are vulnerable, although the trends for Brazil and Turkey are encouraging.

To conclude, the initiatives being taken by indebted countries, the changed nature of the markets and incentives, and the signals embedded in EMBI spreads all suggest that the risks of a generalized debt crisis in market access countries have receded since the late 1990s. Vulnerable market access countries have been taking steps to improve the dynamics of public debt and bolster international liquidity, while adopting flexible exchange rates and launching institutional reforms. This does not mean that a crisis will not occur, only that the risks of the type we are now acquainted with have diminished.

In sum, long-term bank loans have been substantially replaced by the international bond markets, and portfolio investors have diversified and seem

Figure 4-2. *EMBI Spreads for Select East Asian Countries, 1997–2003*

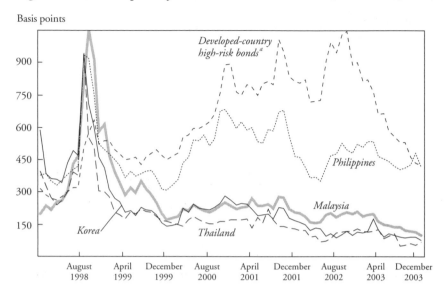

Basis points

Sources Bloomberg; J. P. Morgan Chase; Global Development Finance, World Bank.
a. An average for the global junk bond market.

better able to differentiate between the causes of crises in one country and
another. Nonetheless, concerns remain about shifts in industrial-country
financial systems, the possibility of any large losses they might incur, such
as from hedge funds, and the possible spillover of these problems into developing countries. Concerns also remain regarding the implications of a sudden correction of the large U.S. current account deficit and of the "no" vote
by French and Dutch voters on the European constitution amid the growing controversy about (and diminished chances of adherence to) the EMU
Stability and Growth Pact. Paradoxically, either higher interest rates or
crashes in industrial countries could lead to a flight of capital from developing countries.

Is Public Debt Constraining Growth?

The most obvious way that high public debt can constrain growth relates to
crises, but high public debt can slow growth even without a crisis. Further-

more, high external debt (public plus private) can also be a source of vulnerability and macroeconomic uncertainty that reduce investment and growth. This section discusses these possible constraints.

Debt Intolerance and Crises

Theoretically, public borrowing, both external and internal, can be used to develop investment opportunities with long gestation periods; in a growing economy, it is more equitable to have the richer generations bear the costs. Public borrowing also can be used to smooth government spending and income, in theory, more effectively than varying the tax rates. Likewise, external borrowing (public plus private) by developing countries should augment national savings and thereby contribute to growth and higher output by facilitating more investment. Succinctly,

> The classic case for international capital mobility is well known but worth restating. Flows from capital-abundant to capital-scarce countries raise welfare in the sending and receiving countries alike on the assumption that the marginal product of capital is higher in the latter than in the former. Free capital movements thus permit a more efficient global allocation of savings and direct resources toward their most productive uses.[20]

In practice, however, the results of external borrowing (public and private) have not met expectations—most obviously because recurrent debt crises in market access countries with substantial external borrowing have led to a loss of output and growth. Additionally, market access countries have been unable or unwilling to make good use of public debt. As a result, the recent literature tends to be negative on debt. Expressions like "debt intolerance" and "original sin" have found their way into the titles of recent papers on external debt.[21] Countries with "debt intolerance" tend to suffer repeated crises once they exceed threshold ratios of debt to GDP that are substantially below

20. Eichengreen and Mussa (1998: ch. 3, p. 12). Sturzenegger and Wolf (2004) survey the reasons why the "classic case" might break down, including factors such as human capital, policies, and institutions that reduce risk-adjusted returns in poor countries, the default problem, and the paucity of suitable financial instruments.

21. Reinhart, Rogoff, and Savastano (2003); Eichengreen, Hausmann, and Panizza (2002), respectively. IMF (2003b: ch. 3) also asks whether public debt is too high in market access countries.

current levels.[22] This does not mean that debt is bad per se, however. An analogy that may be uncomfortably familiar will illustrate the point: Doctors counsel patients to lose weight to live longer; this doesn't mean that food is bad, only that patients need to eat less.

According to "original-sin" proponents, the crisis problem emanates from the inability of market access countries to borrow long term in their home currency, which leads to a currency mismatch that enhances the volatility of output and vulnerability to crisis.[23] When the exchange rate collapses, this mismatch generates a large increase in the ratio of debt to GDP and tends to create a financial crisis for local borrowers and lenders in foreign currency. The proponents of original sin further argue that the inability to issue long-term debt in the home currency is unrelated to domestic policies and institutions; this missing market stems instead from capital market imperfections, network externalities, and transaction costs. Others agree that currency mismatches are a threat to stability but argue that much of the problem is related to country situations.[24]

Whatever the fundamental source of the problem, public (external plus domestic) debt and total external (public plus private) debt seem to exceed tolerance levels in a number of prominent market access countries. By the debt tolerance yardstick, public debt is constraining growth in countries like Argentina, Brazil, Jamaica, Lebanon, and Turkey.

Debt Levels and Investment

High public debt may also constrain growth, even without generating a crisis, by reducing public and private investment. The reduction in investment may occur through three channels:

—Crowding out of private investment,

—Debt overhang that reduces incentives for private investment, and

22. Reinhart, Rogoff, and Savastano (2003). Using a sample of fifty-three high-, middle-, and low-income countries over 1970–2001, they find country-specific thresholds of external debt (public plus private) in the range of 15–20 percent of GDP for countries with a history of default and high inflation. IMF (2003a: 130) computes a sustainable level of public debt for the median market access countries to be 25 percent of GDP based on a sample of twenty-one countries. The actual median level of public debt to GDP in these countries was two-and-a-half times the benchmark median level of 25 percent, indicating substantial overborrowing. Pattillo, Poirson, and Ricci (2004) find that external debt (public plus private) may exert a negative effect on growth at levels as low as 18 percent of GDP or 65 percent of exports, based on a sample of sixty-one developing countries from Africa, Asia, Latin America, and the Middle East over the 1969–98 period, with the sample tilted toward market access countries.

23. For example, see Eichengreen, Hausmann, and Panizza (2002).

24. For example, see Goldstein and Turner (2004).

—Limits on fiscal space that reduce public investment and social spending.

Crowding out is a standard macroeconomic issue associated with high public debt and fiscal deficits. The financing of high public debt and fiscal deficits could raise real interest rates and dampen, or crowd out, private investment. Within a closed economy, the extent of crowding out will depend on the interest elasticity of saving and investment and the impact of the higher fiscal deficit on private saving rates.[25] Selling public debt to finance interest and maturing principal, in the context of interest-inelastic saving, will raise interest rates sufficiently to reduce private investment, according to standard macroeconomic arguments. To the extent that governments and private investors raise funds offshore, this effect will be mitigated, but not disappear.

A large debt overhang may deter private investment. In a highly indebted economy, private investors expect future output to be taxed to repay the debt. The expected return to private investment is reduced; hence investment and growth fall.[26] Private investment may also be discouraged by the macroeconomic uncertainty and unpredictable taxation engendered by high debt.[27] And the incentives for governments to carry out policy reform may be lower since successful reforms would result in greater pressure to repay creditors.[28]

The fiscal space argument relates to the possibility of high debt service leading to crowding out within the government budget. Pressure to cover debt service may lead to a reduction in public investment and social spending, which in turn would reduce economic growth and hurt the government's net worth and long-run solvency. The idea has arisen because of the fiscal adjustment programs in Latin American countries that suffered debt crises over the past two decades and discussions of EMU fiscal targets.[29]

Public debt could also be a constraint on growth and development even when vulnerability to a crisis is low, as in India. This claim may appear surprising in view of India's stellar record of growth in the past twenty-five years and the absence of major crises. But beyond a point, public debt and

---

25. The impact on saving rates relates to the question of Ricardian equivalence, an idea resurrected in Barro (1974).

26. The classic papers on debt overhang are by Krugman (1988) and Sachs (1986). The debt overhang argument is related to the first and third models of crises.

27. Serven (1997).

28. Corden (1989).

29. Blanchard and Giavazzi (2004); Calderón, Easterly, and Serven (2004); Easterly and Serven (2004).

the lack of fiscal space become a constraint on the composition of government spending, as interest payments consume a growing fraction of revenues (see box 4-4). They could also constrain financial sector reform and development—because the government relies on a captive financial system to buy its debt—and therefore could affect the allocation of resources and reduce private investment to the extent that it exploits complementarities with public investment.

In sum, once a country crosses a certain threshold of debt to GDP, debt can easily become a dominant factor going forward as well as the biggest constraint on policies and growth; how it was accumulated becomes secondary, and dealing with the indebtedness itself becomes a primary task.[30] And countries that choose to generate large primary surpluses in pursuit of debt tolerance can run into fiscal space problems. Moreover, their ability to run large primary surpluses will be convincing only if these efforts are accompanied by institutional reform, as noted in box 4-3 on Turkey's reforms.

The good news is that policies and institutions in market access countries may mature over time, but the process is time-consuming and prone to setbacks. Some setbacks may enhance welfare, forcing fundamental institutional, political, and social reform. For example, Mexico in the early 1990s and Korea in the mid-1990s followed policies that were not sustainable. Both countries experienced a crisis and deep recessions but rebounded quickly, with output exhibiting a V-shaped path. This pattern of recovery was facilitated by adopting more flexible exchange rates, relying on export orientation, and undertaking major internal restructuring. The process induced important changes in the political economy, reducing the ability of incumbents—political or business elites—to block reforms. A number of countries, including Chile, Israel, Mexico, and Poland, have moved toward debt tolerance in spite of "bad" histories.[31]

What Is Being Done about Market-Access-Country Debt?

Given the evidence presented above, market access countries should, in general, aim to lower permanently the level of public debt to GDP in order to reduce vulnerability and create a better platform for growth. This applies

---

30. Fiscal dominance associated with high sovereign risk and unsustainable public debt dynamics, for example, becomes a severe constraint on monetary policy and the achievement of inflation targets, as argued in Blanchard (2004).

31. IMF (2004b).

Box 4-4. *High Deficits, Debt, and Reserves in India, but High Growth?*

India's growth performance during the 1980s and 1990s was exceeded by only a handful of countries; so was the size of its fiscal deficits. But India is not vulnerable to a repeat of its 1991 fiscal and balance-of-payments crisis because of the buildup of foreign exchange reserves, capital controls, a flexible exchange rate system, and widespread public ownership of banks. Nevertheless, a fiscal adjustment is needed to bolster the chances of sustained high growth over the long run. The growth rate was more than 8 percent in 2003–04, but this followed 4 percent growth the previous year. (The trend rate of growth is closer to 6 percent—below the 8 percent target mandated for the Tenth Plan, 2002/03 to 2006/07.) The composition of spending deteriorated as a result of an inefficient fiscal adjustment during the ten years following the 1991 balance-of-payments crisis. The following table illustrates this by presenting changes in key fiscal variables for the general government during the precrisis (1985/86 to 1989/90), the Eighth Plan (1992/93 to 1996/97), and the Ninth Plan (1997/98 to 2001/02) periods.

The Dynamics of Fiscal Adjustment in India, 1985/86–2001/02
Percent of GDP, based on period averages

Indicator	Eighth Plan versus precrisis period	Ninth Plan versus Eighth Plan
Revenues	−1.5	−0.9
Primary deficit	−3.2	+1.4
Debt	+8.0	+0.0
Interest	+1.3	+0.7
Capital expenditure	−2.8	−0.4
Fiscal deficit	−1.8	+2.1

Source: Pinto and Zahir (2004).

During the Eighth Plan period, revenues fell and interest payments rose relative to the precrisis period, "compensated" by a big reduction in capital expenditure. This happened even though growth was at its highest level for the past two decades, and the primary deficit was reduced substantially. The fall in revenues and rise in interest rates both stemmed from reforms—cuts in customs and excise duty rates to stimulate efficiency and a reduction in domestic financial repression. The net result was that capital expenditure fell by more than 3 percentage points of GDP by the Ninth

(continued)

Box 4-4. *High Deficits, Debt, and Reserves in India, but*
High Growth? (continued)

Plan period. And the sum of interest, administration, and pensions rose by 3 percentage points of GDP and a huge 22 percentage points of revenue, while developmental spending on health and education stagnated and that on irrigation, power, and transport declined (not shown in table).

Crisis proofing by accumulating foreign exchange reserves and switching toward long-term rupee debt for deficit funding in this milieu meant high real interest rates for the private sector for much of the second half of the 1990s. The key to reversing the fiscal slide and eventually raising public savings to a level consistent with Tenth Plan macroeconomic targets is to mobilize revenue by completing direct and indirect tax reforms and to alter the composition of spending by reducing and redirecting subsidies toward rural infrastructure and agricultural research and experimentation—most of the poor live in rural areas. Power sector reform is also important for fiscal reasons and for manufacturing, one of the most tax-buoyant sectors in the economy.

General government grew from less than 60 percent of GDP in 1985/86 to 87 percent by 2002/03, not including debt of central public enterprises and guarantees. This growth risks an uncontrolled upward trajectory if interest rates rise and growth slows. This is a good time to begin implementing a phased reform given high reserves and low interest rates. The Ministry of Finance's Economic Survey 2003–04 (released July 7, 2004) notes the seriousness of the situation: "Growing deficits and public debt and the concomitant declining share of the private sector in total credit have been preventing the economy from realizing its growth potential. The unobserved cost of fiscal deterioration is the growth forgone." The challenge is to implement the Fiscal Responsibility and Budget Management Act of 2003, which mandates the central government to eliminate, by 2008, its revenue deficit (the difference between total revenues and current spending; eliminating it is tantamount to requiring that borrowing be used only for public investment), reform the borrowing regime for states, expand center-to-state transfers linked to reform and performance, and simplify expenditure management. In short, the government will have to strengthen fiscal institutions and improve the quality of the fiscal stance.

to countries such as Brazil, Jamaica, and Turkey, which are already committed to reducing public indebtedness by running primary surpluses of unprecedented magnitude. Even countries such as India, which are not under any imminent threat of a crisis, are concerned about the impact of public debt and the adverse composition of public spending on long-run growth. Even success stories like Chile, Korea, and Russia are attempting to lower public indebtedness. The discussion in this section focuses on the two extremes: where there is a clear public debt overhang and public indebtedness is hurting growth (for example, Brazil, Jamaica, and Turkey) and where public debt is not a constraint on growth but is being paid down nevertheless (for example, Chile, Korea, and Thailand).

Debt Sustainability Problems

In this group, the priority is to lower public indebtedness. To a large extent, the question "How?" is being answered by the countries themselves: run large primary fiscal surpluses in an attempt to improve creditworthiness and lower spreads and thereby signal the country's determination not to inflate away its debt or default.[32] Countries choosing this course have displayed unexpected political stamina and commitment. Two concerns have arisen during this process. The first is that political commitment might falter. The second is that the quality of the fiscal adjustment leaves a lot to be desired, as public investment programs have been cut to the bone, creating infrastructure gaps that could hurt growth and thereby compromise the process of attaining debt sustainability, as discussed in the context of fiscal space.

Both concerns are well founded; we focus on the second one. Controversy about the fiscal adjustment in countries like Brazil and Turkey, with the claimed adverse implications for fiscal space and hence for long-run growth and solvent public finances, tends to pay insufficient attention to the role of the market, politics, and the quality of public investments. If the market is unforgiving (as manifested in high borrowing spreads), a country decides not to default, and public infrastructure projects lose money, then cutting public investment might be the optimal way to reduce indebtedness; indeed, if public investments lose money, they should be cut back whether there is a debt problem or not. Efforts to create fiscal space for

32. We cannot rule out the possibility that this attitude has been endogenous to the historically low interest rates since September 11, 2001.

high-return public infrastructure (or any other) investments thus need to consider several factors:

—How does the return on infrastructure investments compare with the marginal cost of borrowing? If the return on infrastructure investments is lower than the marginal cost of borrowing (which is likely to be the case for debt-intolerant countries), increasing infrastructure investments could actually lower net worth. The efficiency and pricing of infrastructure service provision become priority issues.

—How can governments ensure a high return on new infrastructure investments without first addressing the existing portfolio? For example, the Tamil Nadu Electricity Board in India lost almost one rupee on each unit of power sold in 2001, and it sold more than 3 billion units a month.[33] Can it feasibly price power differently for the marginal project without first reforming the whole power sector? If the inherited portfolio of infrastructure investments (pricing, regulation, and so forth) is fixed, such reform will expand fiscal space and net worth.

—Have other possibilities to enhance fiscal space been explored? Two alternatives are to mobilize revenue, which is a prime consideration in the Philippines, and to improve the composition and efficiency of non-interest current spending, a consideration in Brazil, which has an exceptionally high ratio of revenue to GDP.

—Have structural reforms to encourage growth been implemented?

Creditworthy Yet Paying Down Public Debt

Are countries like Chile, Korea, Russia, and Thailand making a mistake by paying down debt in spite of enjoying investment-grade status? The following factors can help to answer this complex question:

—What is the primary role of the state, and how is it being redefined? It may be more than a coincidence that countries regarded as successful are paying off debt and self-insuring by building up net foreign assets. The government becomes the shock absorber and provider of insurance, while the private sector becomes the engine of growth. This pattern is illustrated by the experience of East Asian countries such as Indonesia, Korea, Malaysia, and Thailand, in the aftermath of the 1997–98 crisis, as summed up in table 4-3. The emphasis in these countries—and also in Chile—has shifted to policies, institutions, and governance to minimize domestic moral hazard and financial sector vulnerabilities, which were at the heart of the 1997–98 crisis.

---

33. Government of Tamil Nadu (2001: 32).

—Are there high-return investment opportunities in infrastructure or the social sectors that are not being exploited? If the economic rate of return is higher than the cost of borrowing, but the financial rate of return is lower, a case can be made for subsidies financed by taxes, not by borrowing. Borrowing under these circumstances would adversely affect debt dynamics.

Without knowing more about these two factors as well as the political economy and social compact in these countries, it is difficult to take a position on whether or not these countries should cease paying down public debt and building up reserves.

International Development Community

Three areas have received attention in recent years: (a) strengthening the international financial architecture, (b) creating new lending instruments, and (c) upgrading debt sustainability analysis to better anticipate looming problems. Notwithstanding numerous initiatives, tangible progress has been limited.

On the international financial architecture related to crisis resolution, the only proposal to take root is the inclusion of collective action clauses in new sovereign bond issues. Collective action clauses attempt to overcome the "collective action problem" epitomized by *Elliott Associates* v. *Peru* and thereby speed up debt restructuring agreements in the aftermath of a crisis.[34] Another attempt to speed up debt restructuring is contained in the sovereign debt restructuring mechanism (SDRM), put forward by the IMF.[35] So far, it has not gained support among either debtor countries or their creditors.

On new instruments, areas that have received wide attention are GDP-indexed bonds and proposals for overcoming "original sin" through development of domestic and international bond markets in developing-country

34. The collective action problem refers to a situation in which a small minority of creditors stay out of an agreement reached with the majority: they hold out in the hope of securing a better deal for themselves. Elliott Associates sued Peru for full payment on the original terms after Peru reached an agreement with 180 creditors, obtaining a restraining order on restructured payments in the process. Rather than default on its restructured debt, Peru settled out of court, paying Elliott $56 million in 2000 for unrestructured debt that had been purchased on the secondary market for $11 million in 1996. More recently, in spite of the absence of collective action clauses, Argentina was able to complete its restructuring of $100 billion of bonds it had defaulted on in December 2001 at 34 cents on the dollar when a New York court of appeals struck down the attempt of a small group of holdout investors to scuttle the restructuring deal, which had earlier been accepted by investors holding 76 percent of the debt (Thomson 2005).

35. For a description of the proposal, see Krueger (2002).

currencies. Both proposals provoke the question of why such instruments have not been introduced spontaneously by the market: Is it because of barriers to financial innovation and the need for the international financial institutions to play a catalytic role in generating a critical mass? Or is it that fundamental economic problems need to be addressed in policies, institutions, and governance, which take time to address and will not be solved by such instruments—the debt intolerance argument? Whatever the reason, we appear to be far from new external debt instruments for market access countries that have equity-type features or are long term and denominated in domestic currency.[36]

In sum, the main breakthrough so far in the field of market-access-country debt is at the country level. The evident willingness of some countries to address unsustainable public debt by reestablishing creditworthiness through fiscal effort is worth encouraging. The extent to which international financial institutions can encourage such efforts is a matter of some debate. What should not be debated is that stronger fiscal fundamentals are a necessary condition for success; for most countries, this implies lowering the level of public debt.

Conclusions

The macroeconomic crises of the 1980s and 1990s have spurred concerns about sovereign debt and capital account openness. We find that sovereign debt may be constraining growth in prominent market access countries at current levels of indebtedness. However, the chances of another 1980s-type crisis seem to have receded since the turbulence of the late 1990s. On what is being done, the willingness of countries facing debt sustainability problems to run persistently large primary fiscal surpluses, while adopting flexible exchange rates and strengthening fiscal institutions, stands out. Based on the relatively low thresholds for debt sustainability identified in the lit-

36. Kleiman (2005: 22) suggests that market access countries may no longer need to "borrow in dollars, at higher interest rates, to entice foreign investors." Russia also was able to entice foreign investors into the ruble debt market before its 1998 crash. Besides, many of the countries cited in the article are addressing debt intolerance through fiscal and institutional reform. Without knowing more about the maturities, yields, and foreign exchange derivatives involved, it is difficult to say whether the increasing participation of foreign mutual and pension funds, which have joined private banks and hedge funds in these local currency bond markets, spells a new era of stability or of opportunism driven by low G-7 yields.

erature and the even lower thresholds at which public debt seems to hurt growth, this response is justified.

For market access countries, a major lesson of the crises of the 1980s and 1990s is that paying attention to the GIBC is vital. Crises, no matter their origin in the public or private sector, tend to affect the GIBC adversely. It is not enough to achieve single-digit inflation, as Russia did just six months before its 1998 meltdown; it is not enough to ensure that macroeconomic policy is conservative and that public finances are in good order, as Korea did before 1997–98. The channels through which the GIBC is affected are varied and not always obvious. In addition to the standard variables—primary fiscal balances, real interest rates, and growth rates—these include whether or not the enterprise and financial sectors are efficient and competitive, with well-structured balance sheets; the existence of contingent liabilities, whether explicit (guaranteeing bonds issued by loss-making state enterprises) or implicit (bailing out banks even when there is no explicit deposit insurance); the presence of overvalued real exchange rates; and the costs of pension reform. Also included is the potential impact of exogenous shocks, when the government may be called on to play the role of shock absorber. Assessing debt sustainability thus requires looking at a range of complex factors, including contingent liabilities, the micro foundations for sustainable economic growth, and the vulnerability to exogenous shocks.

If a country is experiencing public debt sustainability problems, it would be prudent to assume that the impact on growth is negative—from the growth perspective, optimal debt levels are likely to be lower than sustainable debt. Moreover, the causality is more likely to flow from unsustainable public debt dynamics to slow growth than vice versa; a country with limited growth potential is unlikely to attract market financing to begin with. The channels through which public debt affects growth include uncertainty about future inflation and taxation created by the debt overhang, crowding out, and fiscal space problems, whereby high interest payments squeeze out public investment and social spending.

Concerns about fiscal space have led to the argument that countries that cut public infrastructure investments as part of fiscal adjustment could hurt the GIBC by reducing long-run growth. This argument raises at least four questions: How do the economic and financial rates of return on infrastructure projects compare with the government's borrowing cost? Is there scope for reducing wastage in government spending, thereby increasing public saving, and can the composition of expenditures be better aligned with growth? Can the microeconomic foundation for growth be strengthened through structural reform? What are the market signals on default and devaluation risk?

There are a priori reasons to believe that countries for which the markets are signaling an unsustainable debt situation and hence overborrowing need to address this situation first, even if the short-run impact on growth is negative. This view is reinforced by the debt-intolerance argument: if fiscal deficits are shaped by weak fiscal and financial institutions, a presumption of wasteful spending and poor selection of public investment projects would be reasonable. In this case, fiscal and institutional reform would need to precede any expansion of public investment spending.

A puzzling question remains: Why does the market allow overborrowing, especially by debt-intolerant countries? To the extent that moral hazard fueled by expectations of an international financial institution bailout is a possible explanation, this is likely to have diminished after the Russian crisis of 1998 and the Argentine crisis that began in 2001. In the Russian case, only about a fourth of the rescue package of $22.6 billion was disbursed before being halted less than a month after being approved, notwithstanding expectations that Russia was too nuclear to be allowed to fail. Nonresident investors suffered an estimated 70 percent loss of the face value of their holdings of ruble-denominated treasury bills and bonds as a result of the devaluation and default. And the agreement reached with the London Club in August 2000 involved a 50 percent write-off in present value terms of the $31.8 billion Russia owed. More recently, the conclusion in June 2005 of the Argentine debt restructuring deal—at 34 cents on the dollar in present value terms, involving $100 billion in bonds defaulted on in December 2001—inflicted a loss of $67 billion on the bondholders.[37]

If the experience with financial liberalization had been in line with the predictions of neoclassical growth theory, and if the experience with sovereign debt during the 1990s had been more positive, the chances are that this chapter would not have been written. But with capital market liberalization and access to external finance having more likely increased vulnerability than spurred growth, some hard issues need to be confronted. The evidence and arguments advanced in this chapter indicate that market access countries should, in general, aim to lower their public indebtedness. Their debt tolerance would improve with better policies, institutions, and governance. But becoming debt tolerant is a time-consuming process. Can international financial institutions help to speed it up? For example, for countries that are developing a track record of fiscal credibility, can international financial

---

37. Thomson (2005).

Table 4-4. *Select Countries with Large Exposure to the IMF and World Bank, 2003*

Country	Outstanding credit and loans (billions of U.S. dollars)		Share in total external debt (percent)		Share in public sector debt (percent)		Share in GDP (percent)	
	World Bank	IMF	World Bank	IMF	World Bank	IMF	World Bank	IMF
Argentina	7.92	10.69	5.61	11.24	4.17	8.35	6.09	12.20
Brazil	8.66	19.06	4.15	13.46	2.98	9.66	1.75	5.67
Indonesia	10.27	6.92	7.64	7.60	6.85	6.81	4.95	4.92
Russia	6.43	3.25	3.63	2.73	4.24	3.18	1.42	1.06
Turkey	5.27	16.06	3.71	16.64	3.15	14.15	2.21	9.92
Uruguay	0.75	1.63	5.95	19.17	5.49	17.67	6.68	21.50

Sources: World Bank (2003); IMF (2004a).

institutions help to speed up the attainment of permanently lower ratios of debt to GDP by buying out private debt to lengthen maturities and lower borrowing costs? Given the magnitude of outstanding public external debt for countries like Turkey and Brazil ($53 billion and $60 billion, respectively, at end-2003) and high World Bank–IMF exposure levels ($21 billion and $28 billion, respectively, see table 4-4), such a course does not seem feasible given the current resource base of the international financial institutions.

In the absence of a fundamental shift in thinking about market-based development finance, market access countries have little option but to adjust to their market-determined external financing constraint and reduce public indebtedness through fiscal restraint and institutional reform. This general conclusion follows from the evidence pointing to low thresholds at which public debt risks becoming fiscally unsustainable and the even lower thresholds at which debt begins to harm economic growth.

References

Aizenman, Joshua, Kenneth M. Kletzer, and Brian Pinto. 2005. "Sargent-Wallace Meets Krugman-Flood-Garber, or: Why Sovereign Debt Swaps Don't Avert Macroeconomic Crisis." *Economic Journal* 115, no. 503: 343–67.

Barro, Robert J. 1974. "Are Government Bonds Net Wealth?" *Journal of Political Economy* 82, no. 6: 1095–117.

Blanchard, Olivier. 2004. "Fiscal Dominance and Inflation Targeting: Lessons from Brazil." Mimeo. Massachusetts Institute of Technology.

Blanchard, Olivier, and Francesco Giavazzi. 2004. *Improving the SGP through Proper Accounting of Public Investment.* Discussion Paper 4220. London: Center for Economic Policy Research (www.cepr.org/pubs/dps/DP4220.asp).

Calderón, Cesar, William Easterly, and Luis Serven. 2004. "Infrastructure Compression and Public Sector Solvency in Latin America." In *The Macroeconomics of Infrastructure,* edited by William Easterly and Luis Serven. Regional Study. Washington: World Bank, Latin America and Caribbean Region.

Chuhan, Punam, and Federico Sturzenegger. 2004. "Default Episodes in the 1990s: What Have We Learned?" In *Managing Economic Volatility and Crises: A Practitioner's Guide,* edited by Joshua Aizenman and Brian Pinto. Washington: World Bank.

Corden, W. Max. 1989. "Debt Relief and Adjustment Incentives." In *Analytical Issues in Debt,* edited by Jacob Frenkel, Michael Dooley, and Peter Wickham. Washington: International Monetary Fund.

Dooley, Michael. 2000. "A Model of Crises in Emerging Markets." *Economic Journal* 110, no. 460: 256–73.

Easterly, William, Roumeen Islam, and Joseph E. Stiglitz. 2000. "Shaken and Stirred: Explaining Growth Volatility." In *Annual World Bank Conference on Development Economics 2000,* edited by Boris Pleskovic and Joseph E. Stiglitz. Washington: World Bank.

Easterly, William, and Luis Serven, eds. 2004. *The Macroeconomics of Infrastructure.* Regional Study. Washington: World Bank, Latin America and Caribbean Region.

Eichengreen, Barry, Ricardo Hausmann, and Ugo Panizza. 2002. "Original Sin: The Pain, the Mystery, and the Road to Redemption." Paper prepared for the conference "Currency and Maturity Matchmaking: Redeeming Debt from Original Sin," Inter-American Development Bank, Washington.

Eichengreen, Barry, and Michael Mussa. 1998. *Capital Account Liberalization: Theoretical and Practical Aspects.* IMF Occasional Paper 172. Washington: International Monetary Fund.

Frankel, Jeffrey, and Shang-Jin Wei. Forthcoming. "Managing Macroeconomic Crises: Policy Lessons." In *Managing Economic Volatility and Crises: A Practitioner's Guide,* edited by Joshua Aizenman and Brian Pinto. Cambridge University Press.

Goldstein, Morris, and Philip Turner. 2004. *Controlling Currency Mismatches in Emerging Markets.* Washington: Institute for International Economics.

IMF (International Monetary Fund). 2003a. "Sustainability Assessments: Review of Application and Methodological Refinements." Mimeo. Washington, June 10.

———. 2003b. *World Economic Outlook: Public Debt in Emerging Markets.* Washington, September.

———. 2004a. "Financial Statements." Washington.

———. 2004b. "Sovereign Debt Structure for Crisis Prevention." Washington: IMF Research Department, July 2.

J. P. Morgan. 1999. "Introducing the J. P. Morgan Emerging Markets Bond Index Global (EMBI Global)." Methodology Brief. New York.

Kaminsky, Graciela L., Carmen M. Reinhart, and Carlos A. Vegh. 2003. "The Unholy Trinity of Financial Contagion." NBER Working Paper 10061. Cambridge, Mass.: National Bureau of Economic Research.

Kleiman, Gary. 2005. "Emerging Economies' Local Currency Bonds Come of Age." *Financial Times,* February 7, p. 22.

Krueger, Anne. 2002. "New Approaches to Sovereign Debt Restructuring: An Update on Our Thinking." Paper prepared for the conference "Sovereign Debt Workouts: Hopes and Hazards," Institute for International Economics, Washington, April 1.

Krugman, Paul. 1979. "A Model of Balance of Payments Crises." *Journal of Money, Credit, and Banking* 11, no. 3: 311–25.

———. 1988. "Financing versus Forgiving a Debt Overhang." *Journal of Development Economics* 29 (November): 253–68.

Merrick, John. 2004. "Evaluating Price Signals from the Bond Markets." In *Managing Economic Volatility and Crises: A Practitioner's Guide,* edited by Joshua Aizenman and Brian Pinto. Washington: World Bank.

Ministry of Finance, Republic of Lebanon. 2003. "One-Year Progress after Paris II." Special Report. Beirut, December.

Pattillo, Catherine, Helene Poirson, and Luca Ricci. 2004. "What Are the Channels through Which External Debt Affects Growth?" Working Paper WP/04/15. Washington: International Monetary Fund, January.

Perry, Guillermo, and Luis Serven. 2003. "The Anatomy of a Multiple Crisis: Why Was Argentina Special and What Can We Learn from It?" Mimeo. Washington: World Bank.

Pinto, Brian, and Farah Zahir. 2004. "Why Fiscal Adjustment Now." *Economic and Political Weekly,* March 6, pp. 1039–48.

Reinhart, Carmen, Kenneth Rogoff, and Miguel Savastano. 2003. "Debt Intolerance." *BPEA,* no. 1: 1–62.

Rubin, Robert E., and Jacob Weisberg. 2003. *In an Uncertain World: Tough Choices from Wall Street to Washington.* New York: Random House.

Sachs, Jeffrey. 1986. "The Debt Overhang of Developing Countries." Paper presented at the conference in memorial to Carlos Díaz-Alejandro, Helsinki, August.

Serven, Luis. 1997. "Uncertainty, Instability, and Irreversible Investment: Theory, Evidence, and Lessons for Africa." Policy Research Working Paper 1722. Washington: World Bank.

Sturzenegger, Federico, and Holger Wolf. 2004. "Developing Country Debt: An Overview of Theory, Evidence, Options." Mimeo. Washington: World Bank, Economic Policy and Debt Department, PREM Anchor.

Tamil Nadu, Government of. 2001. "White Paper on Tamil Nadu Government's Finances." August 18.

Thomson, Adam. 2005. "Argentina Closes Door on Dollars 100bn Debt Exchange." *Financial Times,* June 3.

World Bank. 2003. *Annual Report.* Washington.

———. 2005. *Global Development Finance: Mobilizing Finance and Managing Vulnerability.* Washington.

———. Various years. *Global Development Finance.* Washington.

MORRIS GOLDSTEIN,
WITH THE ASSISTANCE OF ANNA WONG

5

The Next Emerging-Market Financial Crisis

What Might It Look Like?

This chapter is a speculative exercise in thinking about what the next emerging-economy financial crisis might look like. By a financial crisis, we mean a currency crisis, a banking crisis, a debt crisis, or some combination of the three.[1] The aim of the chapter is neither to identify the one or two emerging economies most vulnerable to a crisis today nor to assess the likelihood that a crisis will occur this year. It is instead to offer some thoughts on the following question: if a crisis affecting a group of emerging economies were

---

1. In the literature, a currency crisis is typically defined as a large deviation in an index of currency market pressure, where such pressure is a weighted average of changes in nominal exchange rates and changes in international reserves. An advantage of defining a currency crisis this way is that it permits crises to occur under both fixed and floating exchange rates. Consensus on what constitutes a crisis is somewhat weaker for banking crises than for currency crises, but a popular treatment of the former is to regard a systemic banking crisis as having occurred if emergency measures were adopted to assist the banking system (for example, bank holidays, deposit freezes, blanket guarantees to depositors or creditors), if nonperforming loans reached at least 10 percent of total bank assets at the peak of the crisis, or if the cost of rescue operations was at least 2 percent of GDP; see Lindgren, Garcia, and Saal (1996) and Caprio and Klingebiel (1996). The definition of a debt crisis also differs across studies. Manasse, Roubini, and Schimmelpfennig (2003) regard a debt crisis as having taken place if the country is classified as being in default on any of its obligations by Standard and Poor's or if the country has had access to non-concessional finance from the IMF in excess of 100 percent of its quota. Episodes where two or more types of crises occur simultaneously are not uncommon and are often referred to as "twin crises"; see, for example, Kaminsky and Reinhart (1999), who coined the term for the simultaneous occurrence of currency and banking crises.

to take place sometime, say, over the next three years, where would the crisis likely originate, how could it be transmitted to other economies, and which economies would likely be most affected by particular transmission or contagion mechanisms? This is a speculative exercise because it strings together a series of "what if" conjectures without much of a handle on the conditional probabilities. Still, even speculative exercises can be useful if they throw light on policies that can improve the prevention and resolution of crisis.

Some might regard this as an odd time to be analyzing the makeup of the next emerging-market crisis. After all, not only was last year's 6 percent (weighted average) growth rate for emerging economies the best performance in twenty years, but this improvement was widely shared across regions, and it came on the heels of strong growth (5 percent plus) in 2003 as well.[2] Equally noteworthy, most analysts believe that the strong growth performance of emerging economies, as well as of developing countries more broadly, will continue at only a modestly reduced pace (5 percent plus) in 2005–06, and this despite anticipations of both some slowdown in growth in the Organization for Economic Cooperation and Development (OECD) area and the continuation of high world oil prices; see the World Bank's forecasts in table 5-1. World trade growth in 2004 (9–10 percent) was considerably above the average of the past twenty years (6.5 percent), and it too is expected to remain buoyant over the next two years, albeit at a slightly reduced level.[3] Global commodity prices are, according to some popular indexes, at their highest level since 1981.[4]

Other positive developments also merit mention.[5] The average interest spread on benchmark emerging-market global bonds, as captured by the

2. Even excluding China and India, the World Bank (2005a) estimates that economic growth in developing countries would have been 5.8 percent in 2004; also, all developing-country regions recorded higher growth rates in 2004 than in 2002, with particularly large increases taking place in Latin America and the Caribbean, Europe and Central Asia, and South Asia.

3. The terms of trade of developing countries improved in 2003–04 (by 2 percent on average)—again, much better than the average over the past two decades—but this improvement is not expected to continue in 2005. See IMF (2004c).

4. See, for example, Deutsche Bank (2005).

5. The focus of attention here is the group of twenty or so larger emerging economies that have relatively heavy involvement with private capital markets. This would include Argentina, Brazil, Chile, China, Colombia, Czech Republic, Hong Kong, Hungary, India, Indonesia, Malaysia, Mexico, Philippines, Poland, Russia, Singapore, South Africa, South Korea, Taiwan, Thailand, Turkey, and Venezuela. This introductory section, however, often refers as well to "developing countries," a group that includes the aforementioned emerging economies but also a much larger, more heterogeneous, and lower-income group of other economies outside the industrial countries.

Table 5-1. *The Global Economic Outlook in Summary, 2003–06*

Percentage change from previous year, except interest rates and oil prices

Indicator	World Bank forecast			
	2003	2004	2005	2006
Global conditions				
World trade volume	5.6	10.3	7.7	7.7
Consumer prices				
G-7 countries[a]	1.6	1.8	1.7	1.6
United States	2.3	2.7	3	3.5
Commodity prices (U.S. dollar terms)				
Non-oil commodities	10.2	17.5	4.7	−5.2
Oil (World Bank average)[b]	28.9	37.7	42	36
Oil price (percent change)	15.9	30.6	11.3	−14.3
Manufactures[c]	7.5	7.0	3.0	2.8
Interest rates (percent)				
Dollars, six-month	1.2	1.6	3.5	4.6
Euro, six-month	2.3	2.1	2.1	2.8
Real GDP growth[d]				
World	2.5	3.8	3.1	3.1
World (purchasing power parity weights)[e]	3.9	5	4.3	4.2
High income	1.9	3.1	2.4	2.6
OECD countries	1.8	3.1	2.3	2.5
Euro area	0.5	1.8	1.2	2.2
Japan	1.4	2.6	0.8	1.9
United States	3.0	4.4	3.9	3
Non-OECD countries	3.2	6.2	4.4	4.4
Developing countries	5.3	6.6	5.7	5.2
East Asia and Pacific	8.0	8.3	7.4	6.9
Europe and Central Asia	5.9	6.8	5.5	4.9
Latin America and the Caribbean	1.7	5.7	4.3	3.7
Middle East and North Africa	5.8	5.1	4.9	4.3
South Asia	7.8	6.6	6.2	6.4
Sub-Saharan Africa	3.4	3.8	4.1	4
Excluding transition countries	5.2	6.7	5.7	5.3
Excluding China and India	3.9	5.8	4.8	4.4

Source: World Bank (2005a).

a. Canada, France, Germany, Italy, Japan, the United Kingdom, and the United States. In local currency, aggregated using 1995 GDP weights.

b. Simple average of Dubai, Brent, and West Texas intermediate crude oils.

c. Unit value index of manufactured exports from major economies, expressed in U.S. dollars.

d. GDP in constant dollars at 1995 prices and market exchange rates.

e. GDP measured at 1995 purchasing power parity weights.

Figure 5-1. *Emerging Market Bond Index Global Spreads,*
December 1997–June 2005

Basis points

Source: IMF.

EMBIG (Emerging Markets Bond Index Global), has recently been hover-
ing around 300 basis points over U.S. treasuries—a record low and about a
third of the level prevailing in the summer and fall of 2002; see figure 5-1.[6]
Such low risk premiums, in concert with very low interest rates in the major
financial centers, have translated into low external financing costs and
reduced debt-servicing burdens for most emerging economies. As the share
of external financing has moved from bank loans to bonds, so too has the
share of fixed-rate instruments in that financing.[7] Although slightly below
the peak years of 1996–97, net private capital flows to emerging economies
in 2003–04 were about double the average of the two preceding years, and
the Institute for International Finance expects them to be high this year as
well; see table 5-2. In 2004 emerging economies as a group ran a current

6. The EMBIG spread has been affected by Argentina's debt restructuring; excluding Argentina,
the EMBIG would not quite be at an all-time low.
7. Borensztein and others (2004) report that floating-rate bonds now make up only about 5 percent of the bonds in the EMBIG.

Table 5-2. *Emerging-Market Economies' External Financing, 2002–05*
Billions of dollars

Indicator	2002	2003	2004[a]	2005[b]
Current account balance	78.8	119.6	169.8	113.3
Net external financing				
Private flows	120.4	207.6	303.4	310.7
Equity investment	118.8	125.1	176.7	184.9
Direct investment	117.7	92.7	138.3	148.2
Portfolio investment	1.1	32.5	38.5	36.7
Private creditors	1.6	82.5	126.7	125.9
Commercial banks	−3.9	30.6	54.2	46.2
Nonbanks	5.4	51.9	72.5	79.7
Official flows	−3.3	−21.0	−27.9	−50.4
International financial institutions	7.8	−6.7	−18.7	−16.9
Bilateral creditors	−11.1	−14.3	−9.1	−33.5
Net resident lending and other[c]	−45.1	11.2	−53.5	−46.3
Reserves[d]	−150.8	−317.4	−391.8	−327.4

Source: Institute for International Finance (2005).
a. Estimate.
b. Institute of International Finance forecast.
c. Including net lending, monetary gold, and errors and omissions.
d. Minus sign indicates an increase.

account surplus for the sixth year in a row, and the aggregate surplus in 2004 was more than twice as high as the average of the four preceding years. And emerging economies, particularly in Asia, have built up a much larger cushion against adverse external shocks by increasing significantly their holdings of international reserves; indeed, as a group, developing countries hold 70 percent more reserves than they did at end-2002.

Continuing the inventory of positive developments, more emerging economies have moved (often not entirely voluntarily) from fragile publicly announced exchange rate targets to less fragile currency regimes of managed floating.[8] Currency mismatches, which have been at the heart of practically all prominent emerging-market crises of the past decade and which have been identified as a key conditioning factor in the size of the ensuing real output losses, have been much reduced on the whole over the past seven

8. See IMF (2004c).

or eight years, particularly in the former Asian crisis countries.[9] The domestically issued part of total public debt in emerging economies, which is denominated in local currency to a much higher degree than the international component and which can act as a spare tire in case of external disruptions, has grown faster than the foreign component over the past dozen years or so.[10] The largest sovereign bond default in history (Argentina) took place with little spillover to other emerging markets (outside Uruguay).

No large emerging economy went into crisis in 2004, and three of those that were in crisis in the preceding five or six years (Brazil, Russia, and Turkey) continued to make progress in building market confidence, in improving fiscal policies and debt profiles, and in achieving healthy rates of economic growth. Argentina and Uruguay too are recovering from the depth of their recent crises. During the latter half of 2004, thirteen countries in the EMBIG obtained ratings upgrades, while none received downgrades.[11]

According to the International Monetary Fund's *Global Financial Stability Report* of September 2004, the global financial system is more resilient now than at any time since the bursting of the equity bubble in 2001.[12] That report argues that banks and non-banks have strengthened their balance sheets to the point where they could, if need be, absorb considerable shocks, that short of a major and devastating geopolitical incident or major terrorist attack, it is hard to see where systemic threats could come from in the short run, and that market players are relatively well prepared to deal with the expected tightening cycle in monetary policy.

Others are less persuaded that the risks of an emerging-market crisis over the next two to three years are quite so low. They point out that excesses during the expansion phase of the business cycle frequently plant the seeds of the subsequent collapse. Such excesses have been no less present in this expansion, including excessively rapid investment growth in China, excessive foreign borrowing essentially to finance consumption and housing in the

---

9. This is true if one looks either at simple indicators of aggregate currency mismatch, like the ratio of short-term external debt to reserves, or more comprehensive measures, like the aggregate effective currency mismatch (AECM) index constructed by Goldstein and Turner (2004); the latter both employs a broad definition of net foreign currency assets and adjusts this for differences across countries and over time in export openness and in the domestic currency share of the total (domestic and international) debt market.

10. See Goldstein and Turner (2004); Borensztein and others (2004).

11. See Institute for International Finance (2005).

12. IMF (2004a).

United States, and excessive compression of spreads on high-risk investments, including emerging-market bonds. It is true that the consensus baseline forecast for OECD growth in 2005–06 is benign, but if the unwinding
of China's investment boom and the financing of the U.S. current account
deficit prove to be more difficult than typically assumed, large-country
growth could be considerably below expectations—to say nothing of the
recent write-downs of 2005 growth forecasts for the European Union and
Japan. Slower growth in China and the OECD, in turn, is apt to weaken
both commodity prices and emerging-market export receipts. Perhaps most
troublesome, if the inevitable correction of the unsustainable U.S. current
account deficit is resolved in a disorderly way, interest rate and exchange rate
developments could be considerably more adverse for emerging economies
than assumed in the baseline, and these, in turn, could feed through to affect
private capital flows, risk premiums, and debt-servicing costs.

Although the average interest spread on emerging-market debt is very
low, much of that decline has been driven mainly, so the pessimists say, by
the greater availability of global liquidity and by strong risk appetites, and
these could change abruptly if the path of monetary tightening in the
United States becomes much steeper than anticipated and if tensions associated with the correction of global payments imbalances worsen investor
confidence. Then, not only would spreads on emerging-market borrowing
rise but also private capital flows could once again experience a sudden stop.
A Bank of England study estimates that each 100-basis-point increase in
U.S. interest rates tends, other things being equal, to be associated with an
80-basis-point increase in the average emerging-market bond spread.[13]
Likewise, rapid rises in U.S. long-term interest rates (for example, April–May
2004) have been associated with significant increases in emerging-market
spreads, especially for the most risky credits.[14] A rise in U.S. long-term
interest rates is also likely to be accompanied by rises in long-term interest
rates in other G-7 countries. Illustrative of the impact of sharp increases in
uncertainty, the Russian default in 1998 was followed by a nearly fourfold
increase in spreads for Latin American countries, along with a decline in
their capital inflows from 5.5 percent of GDP just before the Russian crisis to less than 2 percent of GDP one year later.[15]

13. Bank of England (2004).
14. See also IMF (2004a).
15. See Calvo and Talvi (2005).

The average maturity of emerging-market external debt has declined in recent years (adding to the rollover problem), and the safety cushion provided by much higher levels of international reserves does not look quite as impressive when net reserves substitute for gross reserves and when reserves are measured against total external debt rather than short-term external debt alone.[16] All of this, in turn, could place some emerging markets in liquidity difficulties and under currency pressures, which could feed back into both higher risk premiums and further increases in their still-considerable public debt.[17] In principle, fiscal and monetary policies could be used to counter the effect of adverse external shocks on economic growth, but recent empirical work has shown that, in contrast to industrial countries, macroeconomic policies have tended to be procyclical in emerging markets.[18] Since net private capital flows to emerging economies have also been shown to be procyclical, the capital flow cycle and the macroeconomic cycle reinforce one another, leading to a "when it rains, it pours" outcome.[19] With slower growth and higher interest rates, the inclination to maintain or to increase fiscal discipline could erode, and mounting risk premiums on government bonds could incite concerns in those emerging-market banking systems that hold high shares of government bonds in their portfolios. And weak banking systems could limit the scope to use higher interest rates to defend emerging-market currencies that are under attack.

Developing-country aggregates and averages also conceal considerable cross-country variations. Although the group's aggregate current account position is in surplus, according to World Bank reports, more than fifty developing countries last year had current account deficits equal to 5 percent or more of GDP, including the Czech Republic, Hungary, Turkey, the three Baltic countries, and six Central American economies.[20] Similarly,

16. Borensztein and others (2004) show that the share of emerging-market debt in the EMBIG with remaining maturity of less than five years was higher in 2001–03 than in 1994–96 and that the share with remaining maturity of twenty years or more experienced a much larger deterioration. Various liquidity indicators are analyzed in tables 5-7 through 5-17.

17. The IMF (2003) estimates that the average ratio of public debt to GDP in developing countries rose from roughly 60 percent in the mid-1990s to 70 percent by 2002; even if that ratio has fallen a little over the past two years, it would still be above the ratio prevailing at the beginning of the 1990s.

18. See Kaminsky, Reinhart, and Vegh (2004), who find that both fiscal and monetary policies in emerging economies have been procyclical over the past several decades.

19. See Kaminsky, Reinhart, and Vegh (2004) on the procyclicality of capital flows to emerging economies; the "when it rains, it pours" characterization comes from the title of their paper.

20. World Bank (2005b).

high aggregate reserve holdings and recent favorable terms-of-trade developments can be misleading because they have been concentrated in a relatively small number of emerging economies and in a relatively narrow range of commodities (metals and oil). Over half of the 2002–04 reserve gain for developing countries was accounted for by developing Asia.

Although the risks in emerging economies of overvalued fixed exchange rates being blown out of the water in capital account crises are less now than they used to be, these risks are being replaced, so the argument goes, by growing problems with heavily managed—some would even say "manipulated"—floating exchange rates, especially in parts of emerging Asia. When real exchange rates are significantly undervalued, they contribute to large trade surpluses and to large inflows of portfolio capital (chasing expected gains from projected exchange rate appreciation). If the capital inflows are very large, it becomes increasingly costly to "sterilize" them so that they do not spill over into excess growth of credit and monetary aggregates, lest they increase both inflationary pressures and future nonperforming loans in the banking system. The lion's share of earlier currency and banking crises in emerging economies has been preceded by credit booms, and more than half of these credit booms, in turn, have been linked with large capital inflows.[21] If undervalued exchange rates are maintained by use of large-scale, prolonged exchange market intervention in one direction, they can also induce a protectionist trade response in major-industrial-country markets. Both of these risks are particularly relevant in the current context, where there is an ongoing contentious debate about who is responsible for the unhealthy pattern of global payments imbalances and, in particular, about the role that Asian currency appreciation ought to play in the needed further depreciation of the real, trade-weighted U.S. dollar. And when emerging economies with large reserve holdings do permit a large appreciation of their currency vis-à-vis the dollar and other major reserve currencies, they face a sizable capital loss (expressed in domestic currency) on these reserve positions.[22]

If conflicts over exchange rate and trade policy were to become more frequent and severe and if emerging-market export growth were to slow in response to slower GDP growth in the industrial countries, more emerging

21. See IMF (2004b).
22. See World Bank (2005a). On the positive side of the ledger, appreciation of the local currency increases residents' purchasing power over foreign goods.

economies might be inclined down the road to pursue ambitious programs of domestic financial liberalization in an effort to accelerate the growth of domestic demand. Financial liberalization—at least when implemented without improved financial supervision—has also been shown to be a leading indicator of financial crises in emerging economies as well as a factor associated with credit booms.[23] These are not abstract concerns. During the past two years, real credit to the private sector has grown faster than 20 percent a year in some East Asian and Eastern European economies.[24] A number of emerging economies (including Hungary, Indonesia, Latvia, Poland, and Thailand) have also experienced rapid growth in either consumer or mortgage credit over the past four or five years, some of it driven by the increased presence of foreign banks in these economies.[25] How does one know that recent or future rapid expansions of bank credit or of credit to households will not end in tears, as they did during the unwinding of earlier credit booms and in the 2002–03 collapse of South Korea's credit card boom?

True, Brazil, Turkey, and Russia have all made considerable progress in recent years. But Brazil and Turkey still have both very high real interest rates and relatively high levels of public debt, and it remains to be seen how resilient primary surpluses and broader reform efforts would be to a more generalized pullback of international capital from emerging economies.[26] Similarly, the performance of the Russian economy in a scenario of much lower world oil prices is far from certain. Little comfort should be gotten from today's high sovereign credit ratings, since empirical work has shown that (unlike in industrial countries) such ratings are lowered when growth falls in emerging economies;[27] in addition, empirical work indicates that sovereign credit ratings have done a poor job of anticipating currency and banking crises in emerging economies.[28] The international spillover effects of the Argentine debt default have so far been minimal, but who is to say how the favorable terms that Argentina obtained from its private creditors will tilt both the incentives for imposing fiscal discipline and the market

---

23. See Kaminsky, Lizondo, and Reinhart (1998); IMF (2004b).
24. See IMF (2004c).
25. See Bank for International Settlements (2004).
26. See Stracke (2005) for a pessimistic assessment of Brazil's medium-term prospects, emphasizing the high value of the real exchange rate, the currency risk attached to the still large public sector external debt, the increased amortization burden on the domestic public debt, and the interest rate sensitivity of the domestic public debt.
27. See Kaminsky, Reinhart, and Vegh (2004).
28. See Goldstein, Kaminsky, and Reinhart (2000); Berg, Borensztein, and Pattillo (2004).

behavior of private creditors the next time an emerging economy is in the midst of debt-servicing difficulties. Won't the president of the next emerging market that comes under debt-servicing pressure be pressed by domestic political forces to deliver a "haircut" to investors as large as that achieved by Argentina, and won't the possibility of that event induce crossover investors to run early to avoid holding the losing hand in debt negotiations?[29] Will the role model for emerging-market debtors be President Lula or President Kirchner?

Even if many banks and non-banks have strengthened their risk management systems and even if there is no other player with the leverage and exposure of a 1998 Long-Term Capital Management, couldn't a group of medium-size market participants initiate a major market disruption if they all took sizable, like-minded positions in less liquid financial instruments and then simultaneously sought to liquidate their positions, including those in emerging markets, after the receipt of bad news? Hedge funds have continued to attract large investor inflows in recent years, and the transparency of their operations remains limited. It has been reported that international investment banks obtained as much as $25 billion in 2004 from their hedge fund clients—about an eighth of these banks' total revenues and more than banks earned from such traditional activities as mergers and acquisitions.[30] In an environment where flows into hedge funds are strong, where banks face strong competition from other suppliers of services to hedge funds, and where hedge funds are very important clients of banks, how heavily can we count on a regulatory model where banks are the agents primarily responsible for exercising oversight over the risk management practices of hedge funds? Even if the main players in international financial markets have expanded their use of stress tests against market risk, what if these stress tests do not incorporate adequately the potential feedback effects of many market actors simultaneously reducing their exposure?[31] What if one of the big losers in a particular trade or the offending party in a serious abuse of

29. See Lachman (2005).

30. See "Banks Earned up to $25 Billion from Hedge Funds Last Year," *Financial Times,* March 2004.

31. A recent report on stress testing at major financial institutions by the Committee on the Global Financial System (2005) discusses the results of a survey that covers sixty-four banks and securities firms in sixteen countries. One of its findings is as follows: "The treatment of market liquidity in stress tests varies across firms. Although firms recognize the potential for feedback effects—which measure the second-round impact of firms' own activities on prices—these effects are rarely incorporated in stress tests because they are difficult to measure" (p. 1).

market-integrity guidelines turns out to be one of the ten large commercial or investment banks that together dominate the market for derivatives?[32] Could that big commercial or investment bank unwind its exposure without initiating wider market disruptions that would spill over to emerging markets?

Just as the unexpected outcome of the Danish referendum in 1992 upset a large volume of "convergence plays" predicated on a smooth path to the European Monetary Union (EMU), is there not a danger that bad news on ratification of the European constitution or on a timetable for some transition economies (or Turkey) to qualify for euro-area membership could eventually lead to chaotic unwinding of current convergence trades in Europe?[33] In this connection, a recent International Monetary Fund (IMF) study not only found that the currencies of three new European Union (EU) accession countries (Czech Republic, Hungary, and Poland) were significantly overvalued but also suggested that under current policies these currencies would be unlikely to stay within the ERM2 stability corridor.[34] What would be the outlook for reducing fiscal deficits in these economies if EMU-related incentives were weakened substantially? Or what would happen if the large recent investment in energy funds based on a forecast of continued strong upward movement in energy and other primary commodity prices were undermined by a sharp (downward) revision in the future price of these commodities?

So much for motivating the issues at hand, for proposing that there is more than one kind of risk currently facing emerging economies, and for

32. According to a recent *Bank Derivatives Report* compiled by the U.S. Office of the Comptroller of the Currency (2004), five commercial banks accounted for 96 percent of the total notional amount of derivatives in the commercial banking system; in addition, for four of the top five, credit exposure to derivatives accounted for 230 percent or more of their risk-based capital. And in the bank with the largest exposure to derivatives, such exposure represented almost six times its risk-based capital. New York Federal Reserve president Timothy Geithner highlighted some of the implications of very large, systemically important private financial institutions in a recent speech on key challenges in risk management (Geithner 2005). He noted not only that the failure or perceived risk of failure of one of these institutions would have large negative implications for the financial system but also that "their greater relative size limits their ability to take actions that would reduce their exposure in the event of a shock without creating the risk of magnifying the shock."

33. The French and Dutch "no" votes in referenda on the European constitution (in late May and early June, respectively) have not yet produced any widening in the spread on Turkish benchmark global bonds (in fact, the spread has declined some), but the implications of those no votes may take some time for markets to assess fully.

34. Bulir and Smidkova (2005). Truman (2005a) concludes that one should not be confident that Hungary or Poland will avoid an external financial crisis during the next five years.

defending the view that now is not such a bad time to look a bit deeper into sources of vulnerability for a new emerging-market financial crisis.

It would be beyond the manageable scope of this chapter to try to analyze all the potentially relevant scenarios that could give rise to an emerging-market financial crisis.[35] We have therefore decided to focus on the crisis scenario that we think is the most likely—namely, an overlapping and greater-than-expected slowdown in growth in China and the United States—made more troublesome for emerging economies by a rise in long-term U.S. interest rates linked to a disorderly correction of global payments imbalances. In the following section, we speculate on what factors might bring about such a slowdown in growth in those two countries. The main culprit in China is the unsustainably high share of fixed-asset investment in GDP, while in the United States it is the unsustainable U.S. current account deficit. We explain how a "long" unwinding of China's investment boom could produce a "long landing" for the Chinese economy. For the U.S. case, we tell a story about how various obstacles to achieving the right pattern of exchange rate adjustment and growth in domestic demand across the United States, the European Union, and emerging Asia could degenerate into a "blame game" and a loss of confidence, marked, inter alia, by a sharp rise in long-term interest rates in the United States (and to a lesser degree in other G-7 countries). We then consider the transmission channels by which this growth slowdown in China and the United States—cum higher long-term interest rates—could affect emerging economies. The emphasis here is on bilateral trade links and global commodity prices; the costs and availability of external financing; the effects of exchange rate changes; and the likely pressures operating on fiscal and monetary policies in emerging markets. In each case, we present a set of indicators to infer which emerging economies are likely to be most and least affected by these various transmission channels. In the tables presenting these indicators, economies most (least) vulnerable to that particular transmission channel appear at the top (bottom) of the column.[36] A summary table gives the five most vulnerable economies

---

35. To take perhaps the most obvious exclusion, this chapter does not analyze a scenario in which a large supply shock leads to much higher world oil prices than currently envisaged by either futures markets or most analysts. This would, of course, have the short-term effect of reducing growth in the United States and China beyond what I have assumed in my scenario. But lower growth in China and the United States should, over the medium term, put downward pressure on world oil prices. See IMF (2005) for an analysis of the implications of sustained higher world oil prices.

36. The presentation of vulnerability indicators is a streamlined version of the more comprehensive treatment found in Goldstein (2005a).

under each of five transmission channels. Finally, we offer some brief concluding remarks about what the crisis scenario implies for crisis prevention efforts in both the major industrial countries and emerging markets.

Two themes run through much of the subsequent analysis. The first is that if a growth slowdown in China and the United States were to materialize, it would matter a great deal to emerging economies *how* this slowdown occurs; more specifically, a growth slowdown that is linked to a disorderly correction of global payments imbalances is apt to be considerably more damaging to emerging economies—because of its effects on global financing conditions—than one that is more orderly and affects emerging economies primarily via their bilateral export links to China and the United States. A slowing of emerging-market economic growth would be one thing; an emerging-market financial crisis would be another. The second theme is that there are *multiple channels* by which a slowdown in China and the United States could be transmitted to emerging economies, and each of these transmission channels implies a somewhat different ordering of vulnerability to crises among individual emerging economies; for example, the economies most likely to be adversely affected by a large decline in China's imports are, on the whole, not the same ones apt to be most affected by either a sharp decline in private capital flows to emerging economies or a fall in local currencies that is greater than the assumed fall in the U.S. dollar. Since one does not know in advance what the transmission process will look like, it is sensible to examine a wide enough set of vulnerability indicators to cover the main possibilities.

How Could Economic Growth in China and the United States Slow Down?

The IMF calculates that the United States and China account, respectively, for 21 and 12.5 percent of world GDP, using purchasing-power-parity (PPP) exchange rates. Given 2003 and 2004 growth rates, this implies that the United States was responsible for roughly 16 percent of global GDP growth in 2003 and 17 percent in 2004.[37] The same kind of calculation for China reveals a higher contribution: 30 percent of global GDP growth in 2003 and 24 percent last year. Together, these two locomotives made up more than 40 percent of the 2003–04 global expansion. Their joint contribution to

37. IMF (2004c).

global growth in 2003–04 would be similar if we were to use market exchange rates as weights, but their relative contribution would be reversed; the U.S. contribution would then be on the order of a third, while China's contribution would fall to roughly a tenth. This reflects the facts that the U.S. share of world GDP is somewhat higher with market exchange rates than with PPP exchange rates (29 versus 21 percent), while China's share is much lower with market exchange rates than with PPP exchange rates (4 versus 12.5 percent). If the relevant measuring rod is taken to be growth in domestic demand (at market exchange rates), the U.S. contribution to global growth (in domestic demand) would be slightly higher still, and China's contribution would be slightly lower, since the U.S. has been running an increasing trade deficit, whereas China has been running an increasing trade surplus. Turning to world trade, in 2004 the U.S. share of world trade was 12.5 percent, while China's share was 6 percent (ten times its share in 1977). China alone accounted for more than 10 percent of global trade expansion in 2003–04, while the U.S contribution was 8 percent. Together, China and the United States supplied about one-fifth of global trade expansion during the past two years.

These back-of-the-envelope estimates suggest that if China and the United States were to grow considerably slower over the next three years than they did during the last two, emerging economies would, ceteris paribus, face a less supportive global environment. Hence we turn next to explanations of why and how growth slowdowns might occur in these two large economies.

The Long Landing in China: Unwinding of the Investment Boom

In 2003 and 2004 the Chinese economy grew 9.3 and 9.5 percent, respectively—the highest rates of growth since 1997 (see figure 5-2). This upsurge in growth was driven primarily by very rapid growth of real fixed-asset investment and by a boom in bank lending.

Most analysts characterize the Chinese economy as "overheated" from the last quarter of 2002 through at least the first half of 2004.[38] This overheating had a number of dimensions, including:

—The emergence of bottlenecks in coal, oil, electric power, and transport,

—The breakneck pace of growth in real fixed-asset investment (25 percent in 2003 and 19 percent in 2004), which led the investment share of GDP to hit an all-time high (44 percent of GDP in 2004), with strong indications of overinvestment in steel, aluminum, cement, and real estate,

---

38. Many would argue that the overheating is still ongoing.

Figure 5-2. *Real GDP Growth in China, 1992–2005*[a]

Percent

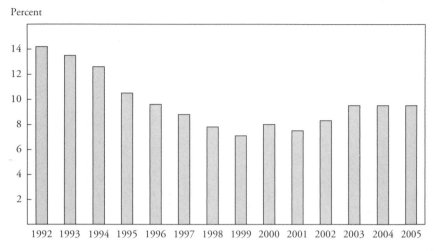

Source: National Bureau of Statistics of China (2004).
a. Data for 2005 are for the first six months.

—Upward pressure on prices, with a switch from deflation in 2002 to peak inflation rates of 5 percent for consumer prices and 9 percent for corporate goods prices in the summer and fall of last year,

—A rapidly declining "real" rate of interest on bank loans, reaching a level of negative 4 percent in the fall of 2004,

—Unsustainably high rates of credit and monetary expansion, with the increase in bank loans relative to GDP reaching a historic high of 24 percent in 2003 and with the growth of both bank lending and broad monetary aggregates attaining peak annual rates near 20 percent,

—Buyers turning increasingly to imports to supplement domestic sources of supply, with the total value of imports rising 40 and 36 percent, respectively, in 2003 and 2004 and with dramatic effects on global prices of some critical raw materials and basic industrial goods,[39]

39. Lardy (2005) notes that China is now the world's largest consumer of copper, tin, zinc, platinum, steel, and iron ore; the second largest consumer of oil, aluminum, lead, and petroleum; and the third largest consumer of nickel. China's steel imports soared in 2002–03, as China became the world's largest importer, driving up global steel prices. It is also a major importer of iron ore to feed the world's largest steel industry. China alone accounted for 45 percent of the increase in global demand for oil in 2002–03, again with strong upward effects on the world price.

—A depreciating, real trade-weighted exchange rate for China's currency, the renminbi, with the level in May 2005 being approximately 8 percent below that in February 2002, and

—A large and rising external imbalance, marked by rapidly increasing exports (up about 35 percent in both 2003 and 2004), a growing current account surplus (3.3 and 4.2 percent of GDP in 2003 and 2004, respectively), huge capital inflows (much of it chasing an expected appreciation of the renminbi), and unprecedented increases in China's international reserves ($162 billion in 2003 and $206 billion more in 2004), representing an astonishing 11–13 percent of GDP.

The Chinese authorities' initial response to signs of overheating in the economy was one of denial. This may have reflected the new leadership's desire for strong growth to bolster their standing with the Chinese public as well as concerns about the slowing effects of the SARS (severe acute respiratory symptom) outbreak in the second quarter of 2003. But as evidence of overheating accumulated, economic officials were gradually given the authorization to implement restraining measures: the 2004 official targets for economic growth, bank lending, and monetary expansion were all lowered, albeit modestly; reserve and capital requirements for banks were increased; most important, strong administrative controls were put in place over bank lending, approval for new investment projects, and land use; and "sterilization" of reserve inflows continued on a large scale to diminish the impact of reserve accumulation on credit aggregates. Increases in interest rates were small and far between.[40]

There are at least three schools of thought on how well the Chinese economy has responded to these restraining measures and on the economy's medium-term growth prospects.

The first view, held by the Chinese authorities and by most China watchers, is that administrative controls and other measures have been quite effective in controlling overheating and that the economy is well on its way to achieving the desired *soft landing*. In support of the soft-landing view, they point out the following:

—The growth of bank lending and monetary aggregates has slowed from an unsustainable annual pace of 20 percent to a more comfortable 13–15 percent.

---

40. Interest rates on bank loans and bank deposits were raised roughly 30 basis points last fall; at the same time, the legal ceiling on the interest rate that banks could charge for loans was eliminated. In March 2005, a small upward adjustment was made in the interest rate for consumer housing loans, and the minimum downpayment for such loans was increased.

—Consumer price inflation has fallen sharply from the peak rates recorded last summer, and other producer and raw materials price indexes are showing moderation as well.

—The fall in inflation has, in turn, begun to reverse the fall in the real interest rate on bank loans, at least bringing it into positive territory.

—The growth of real fixed-asset investment has started to decline, with last year's 19 percent growth down markedly from 2003's 25 percent climb.

—There has been a change in the composition of investment away from sectors with overcapacity toward sectors with bottlenecks.

—Growth of real private consumption has stayed buoyant.

—To judge from the interest rates on bonds used for sterilization, there is little evidence of sterilization fatigue.

—The economy has been able to accomplish all of this while still growing at a healthy 9 percent plus pace. Their expectation is that this progress can be maintained in 2005, while the economy grows at between, say, 8 and 9 percent.

The second school of thought might be called the *no-landing* or *hard-landing* view. It sees the Chinese economy as still in a state of overheating, but one masked by administrative controls and poor price statistics. Xie, for example, argues that the demand effects of rapidly rising investment initially put upward pressure on prices and profitability, drawing large amounts of resources into particular sectors, especially property, automobiles, steel, chemicals, and electronics.[41] But this overinvestment is unsustainable because the demand effects of investment eventually give way to the supply (overcapacity) effects. The hard landing comes when interest rates rise to keep inflation down and when there is no longer enough demand to take up overcapacity. Makin also sees an early hard landing ahead for China, but one driven by the contractionary effect of administrative controls and of capital outflows on credit flows.[42] Yet another variant of the hard-landing view is that, with the real interest rate close to zero and a significantly undervalued exchange rate, there is latent excess demand in the system. Provinces and ministries will continue to press for relaxation of administrative controls on bank lending, project approvals, and conversion of land use. China's central bank is far from having operational independence, and, with capital inflows still booming, it could easily get behind the curve on monetary

41. Xie (2005).
42. Makin (2004).

Figure 5-3. *Investment as a Share of GDP in China, 1979–2004*

Percent

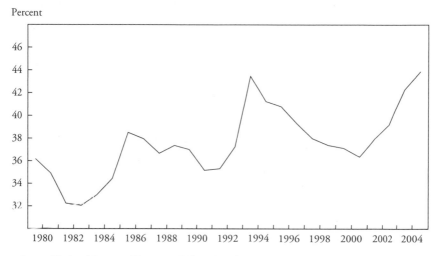

Source: National Bureau of Statistics of China (2004).

policy (as in 2003 and the first part of 2004). That, in turn, would require large increases in interest rates or a more draconian reactivation of administrative controls, either of which would push the economy into a hard landing this year or next. It needs to be acknowledged, however, that thus far there is scant evidence of a significant reacceleration of key credit and monetary aggregates.

Yet a third view is the *long-landing* hypothesis. We argue that at the heart of imbalances in the Chinese economy is an unsustainable investment boom that has been in the making for at least four years and that will probably take at least several years to undo.[43] There is nothing in the last twenty-five years of Chinese growth to indicate that an investment share of GDP above 38–40 percent of GDP is sustainable. As shown in figure 5-3, last year, capital's share of GDP hit 44 percent—an all-time high that exceeded even the peak share (43 percent) reached during the top of the last investment boom in 1993. Because real fixed-asset investment in China today is still growing faster than real GDP, the investment share is still rising.[44] To judge from

43. Put forward in Goldstein and Lardy (2004a, 2004b).
44. Figures based on GDP expenditure accounts indicate lower real investment growth in both 2003 and 2004, but the qualitative implications for the long-landing hypothesis are similar.

the unwinding of China's last investment boom, the most likely outcome is that economic growth will decline during this unwinding period—perhaps as much as 4–5 percentage points from its current rate. The decline in growth may be more gradual than in the hard-landing view, but its cumulative magnitude may not be any less.

A decline in investment growth does not, of course, require economic growth to fall, because other components of GDP could grow faster to offset an investment slowdown. But figure 5-4 indicates that private consumption is the only other component of GDP with a weight equal or close to that of investment. But when investment growth was declining from its peak in 1993, no sustained, large, upward offsetting movement in private consumption occurred. Indeed, over the past decade and longer, growth of real fixed investment and of real household consumption was positively—

Figure 5-4. *Expenditure as a Share of GDP, 2003*

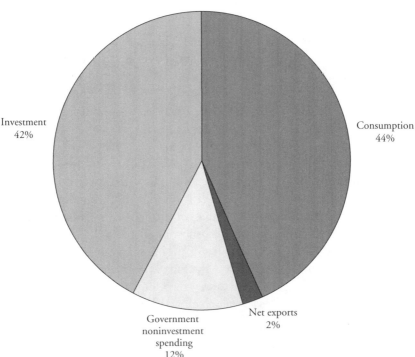

Source: National Bureau of Statistics of China (2004: 65–66).

not negatively—correlated, and the same result holds even for samples restricted to years when investment growth slowed.

Since government consumption has less than one-third the weight of investment, even doubling the growth of government consumption from its recent pattern would add less than 0.75 percentage point to China's GDP growth. Also, China has been quite conservative in its budgetary policy, demonstrating a reluctance to run budget deficits beyond a few percent of GDP.

Net exports have by far the smallest weight in GDP (about 2 percent), but they probably have the most potential for large change among the noninvestment components of GDP. During the unwinding of the last investment boom, net exports of goods and services rose 6 percentage points of GDP, making a substantial contribution to growth. We would expect net exports to strengthen this time too, as the Chinese economy slows and import growth declines faster than export growth; in fact, that process has been under way over the past two quarters, and one prominent specialist on the Chinese economy, Jon Anderson of UBS, has recently suggested that China's trade balance this year could climb to as high as 8 percent of GDP.[45] One difference, however, between this investment cycle and the previous one is that, this time, China is starting from a sizable current account surplus (4 percent of GDP in 2004), not from a modest deficit (in 1993). As explained later in this section, it is hard to believe that the rest of the world would sit passively by while China's current account surplus mushrooms, particularly if China refuses to take any meaningful action on its undervalued exchange rate.

As shown in figure 5-2, growth of China's real GDP declined cumulatively by about 5–6 percentage points from the peak of the last investment cycle in 1993 to its trough in 1997 and 1999. This was a long landing. The landing can, of course, be made shorter by accelerating the fall in the growth rate of real investment, but then the decline in the growth rate of GDP will be sharper each year to eliminate the investment-share overhang more quickly.

Critics of the long-landing view argue that things are likely to be different this time. They maintain that the sustainable rate of investment in China is now much higher than it used to be, reflecting, inter alia, the positive effects of rising urbanization and industrialization on investment. But urbanization and industrialization were also well under way during the

45. See Anderson (2005b).

unwinding of the last investment boom, and they did not prevent it.[46] Trends in the efficiency of investment do not point to a higher sustainable investment rate either, and the 2003 behavior of bank credit, along with investment excesses in steel, aluminum, cement, and real estate, hardly suggest that banking reform has progressed to the point where investment that constitutes 44 percent of GDP can be invested profitably.

In sum, Goldstein and Lardy conclude that the investment share in China will have to fall markedly from its present high levels. Investment will need to grow more slowly than real GDP for several years, and China's growth rate—notwithstanding perhaps some offset from other components of spending—is likely to fall as well from last year's lofty pace (9.5 percent).[47]

The Chinese authorities have indicated that some slowdown in growth this year—perhaps to between 8 and 9 percent—would be desirable; similarly, they concede that there is a need to deal with excessive, wasteful, and inefficient investment. But they have not suggested for how long and how far the growth rate of investment should fall or what they would be prepared to do if the growth rate of GDP were to decline markedly as a result of falling investment. Note that the long-landing view and the soft-landing view are observationally equivalent for 2005 (both predict some fall in growth). Where they differ is on what will happen in 2006 and 2007; the long-landing view predicts that growth will decline in those years as well, whereas the soft-landing view sees growth returning quickly to its long-term path. If the long-landing view is right, China's growth in 2006–07 is apt to be on the order of 3–4 percentage points lower than in 2004.

A Disorderly Adjustment of the U.S. Current Account Deficit

By most yardsticks, the U.S. economy still looks strong. Real GDP growth was 3 percent in 2003 and 4.4 percent last year. The recent (June) blue-chip consensus is that growth will moderate this year and next (3.5 and 3.3 percent, respectively) and will be roughly equal to long-run potential growth (often calculated to be, say, 3.25 percent). Anticipating that the Federal

---

46. Some have argued that the sustainable rate of investment in residential housing is now higher than before because it is increasingly private. But as noted in Goldstein and Lardy (2004b), real estate investment as a share of GDP has risen sharply for six consecutive years and by 2003 was already half again as high as the previous peak in 1993, suggesting that over the next few years, adjustment is more likely to be on the downside rather than the upside.

47. Goldstein and Lardy (2004a, 2004b).

Reserve will continue to raise the federal funds rate toward a neutral stance, the consensus forecast is that inflation will remain under control (about 2.7 percent on consumer prices for 2005–06). Meanwhile, the labor market is firming, and productivity growth remains broadly encouraging. The fly in the ointment is the large U.S. current account deficit.

The U.S. current account deficit hit an all-time high last year of $660 billion—or 5.7 percent of GDP; if the outturn in the fourth quarter of 2004 were put on an annual basis, the current account deficit would be more than $730 billion. Reflecting several decades of current account deficits, the ratio of U.S. net external liabilities to GDP is now about 25 percent, an enormous turnabout from the world's largest net creditor position, with net external assets equal to 25 percent of GDP in the mid-1970s.

Many analysts see the U.S. current account shortfall rising to 6–9 percent of GDP in 2005–07.[48] But even if the current account deficit is maintained at 5 percent of GDP while U.S. GDP grows in nominal terms at 5 percent a year, the U.S. net external liability position will reach 50 percent of GDP in eight years and 100 percent within twenty-five years.[49] Given this unfavorable trajectory, there is a consensus that U.S. current account deficits of recent magnitude are unsustainable. The "unsustainability" results primarily not from the retarding effect on U.S. consumption and investment of rising net interest payments (on the increasingly negative U.S. international investment) but rather from the assumed increasing reluctance of foreign investors to accept a steadily rising share of U.S. assets in their portfolios.[50] Once these foreign investors reach the point of saying "no mas," there will be inevitable adjustments in asset prices and exchange rates to restore portfolio equilibrium.

A popular view is that a sustainable U.S. current account deficit would be a little less than half as large as the present deficit (say, 2.5 to 3 percent of GDP); under reasonable assumptions about U.S. GDP growth, this would stabilize U.S. net external debt at somewhere between 45 and 50 percent of GDP.

---

48. See, for example, Mann (2004), Cline (2005), and Roubini and Setser (2005). These forecasts of a rising U.S. current account deficit in the medium term typically assume that growth is faster in the United States than in partner countries, that the income elasticity of demand for U.S. imports remains substantially higher than income elasticity of demand for U.S. exports, and that rising U.S. interest rates lead to larger income payments to foreigners on their investments in the United States.

49. See Mussa (2005).

50. Because the rate of return on U.S. investments abroad has been higher than the return on foreigners' investments in the United States, net interest flows on the increasingly negative U.S. international investment position have thus far been tiny relative to U.S. GDP.

The key issue at hand is whether this correction of the U.S. current account deficit to a more sustainable level is likely to be accomplished in an orderly way, without recourse to high interest rates, falling asset prices, and much slower growth (maybe even a recession) in the United States and adverse spillovers to other economies, including emerging markets.

Those who champion the "orderly" adjustment view emphasize that whatever the track record for developing countries, earlier episodes of large current account adjustments in industrial countries present little evidence of sustained depreciation of exchange rates, increases in real interest rates, or declines in real stock prices; some episodes showed significant falls in GDP growth after the onset of current account adjustment, but substantial exchange rate depreciations were usually expansionary, not contractionary.[51] They also point to the attractiveness of investment opportunities in the United States as an explanation for observed cross-country differences in savings and investment patterns and to the shared interest of Asian countries and the United States in continuing large-scale, official financing of the U.S. current account deficit under a "revived Bretton Woods" system. In contrast, the disorderly adjustment view emphasizes the potential for delayed adjustment or "blame games" if each of the major players refuses to take painful but necessary policy actions. The disorderly adjustment view also highlights the disruptive role that undisciplined U.S. fiscal policy can and recently has played in thwarting the efforts to correct saving-investment imbalances as well as fragilities and contradictions in the long-term maintenance of any revived Bretton Woods system.

As Mussa has recently pointed out, the inevitable correction of the U.S. external imbalance will necessarily involve three broad and related macroeconomic developments: (a) a real depreciation of the U.S. dollar against the currencies of most other countries, (b) slower growth in domestic demand than in domestic output in the United States to make room for the

---

51. This conclusion comes from a recent Federal Reserve study by Croke, Kamin, and Leduc (2005), which examines twenty-three episodes of current account adjustments in industrial countries since 1980. The Bank for International Settlements (2004) also examines episodes of lasting and substantial current account adjustments in industrial countries since 1973, finding that (a) on average, current account deficits tended to be reversed when deficits approached levels around 4–5 percent of GDP; (b) the adjustment process was generally associated with both a depreciation of the domestic currency and a marked slowdown of growth; (c) the more volatile types of flows generally adjusted the most; (d) the adjustment was driven mainly by the behavior of nonresidents; (e) changes in financing were largely in private flows; and (f) in most cases, the changes in the composition of flows were orderly. On the whole, their conclusions are not quite as optimistic as those in the Federal Reserve study.

expansion of U.S. net exports, and (c) faster growth in domestic demand than in domestic output in the rest of the world so as to reduce net exports.[52] The first development is the expenditure-*switching* channel of adjustment; the second two developments represent the expenditure-*changing* channel of adjustment. Both channels are needed. If only the expenditure-reducing channel is activated, adjustment can be too costly in terms of economic growth for the deficit country; if only the expenditure-switching channel is activated, the result can be excessive inflation in the deficit country and undue contractionary pressure in the surplus countries.

One can also think about the adjustment of the U.S. current account deficit in a saving-investment framework. Here, the inevitable adjustment will involve a decline in the current savings shortfall in the United States and a corresponding diminution of the savings glut (or investment shortage) in the rest of the world.

Suppose we employ a rule of thumb that each 1 percent depreciation in the real trade-weighted value of the dollar improves the U.S. current account deficit by approximately $10 billion. This then generates the conclusion that the real value of the dollar would have to fall about 30–35 percent from its peak in February 2002 to reduce the U.S. current account deficit to 2.5 to 3 percent of GDP. As shown in table 5-3, there have indeed been some sizable appreciations in the currencies of *some* U.S. trading partners since February 2002. More specifically, the euro has appreciated 23 percent, the Canadian dollar 10 percent, and the Australian dollar 27 percent. Most of the currencies that have shown significant appreciation are those whose value is set mainly by market forces. In contrast, with the notable and largely recent exceptions of the Korean won (up more than 18 percent since February 2002) and the Singapore dollar (up 10 percent), there has been very little real exchange rate appreciation in the Asian countries, despite the large current account surpluses in most of these economies. The Chinese renminbi has depreciated in real trade-weighted terms about 8 percent since February 2002, the Malaysian ringgit has depreciated 15 percent, and the Japanese yen and the Taiwanese dollar have shown small depreciations over this period.[53] It has not escaped attention that some of these Asian economies have been engaging in large-scale, protracted, one-way intervention in

52. Mussa (2005).
53. These figures use J. P. Morgan's indexes of real trade-weighted exchange rates. According to this same data series, the U.S. dollar has fallen about 19 percent since February 2002.

Table 5-3. *Sharing the Adjustment of Payment Imbalances*

Percent unless otherwise indicated

Country	Change in the real effective exchange rate, February 2002– May 2005	Fed weight, 2005	Change in international reserves, 2004		Current account as a percent of GDP, 2004	Estimated exchange rate undervaluation, 2004
			Billions of dollars	Percent of GDP		
Select countries and euro area						
China	−8	11	207	13	4	26
Euro area	23	19	211	2	1	...
United Kingdom	−1	5	45	2	−2	...
Canada	10	16	34	4	3	...
Australia	27	1	36	6	−6	...
Mexico	−7	10	8	1	−1	...
Japan	−3	11	171	4	4	37
Emerging Asia						
Hong Kong	−16	2	5	3	10	5
Indonesia	3	1	0	0	3	12
Malaysia	−15	2	22	19	13	14
Korea	18	4	44	7	4	10
Singapore	10	2	16	16	26	14
Taiwan	−2	3	35	11	6	22
Thailand	1	1	7	5	5	9

Source: For the real effective exchange rate, J. P. Morgan; for Fed weights, Federal Reserve Board; for international reserves, IMF, *International Financial Statistics*; for current account as a percent of GDP, IMF, *World Economic Outlook*; for exchange rate undervaluation, Anderson (2004a).

... Not covered.

exchange markets to hold down the value of their currencies.[54] Since Japan plus emerging Asia have a combined weight of approximately 40 percent of the Federal Reserve's trade-weighted index for the dollar, this lack of sizable real appreciation in Asian currencies has weakened the operation of the expenditure-switching channel of adjustment: without Asia's participation, either the overall depreciation of the dollar will be too small to bring the U.S.

54. See Goldstein (2004, 2005a) on why this behavior should be regarded as currency "manipulation."

current account deficit under control or the dollar depreciation will be so skewed toward a few currencies that the adjustment burden on them (especially the effect on their GDP growth rates) will become intolerable. The same line of thinking also explains why revaluation of the Chinese renminbi is typically given such prominence in any discussion of wider Asian currency policy. If China does not appreciate its exchange rate, other countries in the region will be reluctant to allow theirs to do so, lest they lose competitiveness vis-à-vis China. But if none, or few, of the Asian economies takes exchange rate action, then the overall depreciation of the dollar will be too small.

As Mussa argues, there are also obstacles in getting the cross-country pattern of domestic demand growth to accord in a timely way with what theory says needs to happen.[55] In the European Union, a recent string of budget deficits has left the larger countries with little scope for expansionary fiscal policy, and the European Central Bank is reluctant (given its mandate to pursue price stability and maintain the prevailing monetary and inflationary conditions) to lower interest rates below their already low level. Ongoing changes in structural policies may improve European economic growth in the longer term, but not right away. Hence the best that can be expected (as regards raising domestic demand) in the near term is that the European Central Bank will be cautious in raising interest rates and that fiscal consolidation will not occur too rapidly. Meanwhile, Japan has accumulated a very high ratio of public debt to GDP, ran a fiscal deficit of nearly 7 percent of GDP last year, has already reduced interest rates effectively to zero, and is struggling with a lingering deflationary threat and a still fragile recovery. Thus, beyond pledging to refrain from resuming large-scale exchange market intervention to hold down the value of the yen, not much should be anticipated from the Japanese contribution to external adjustment. But all this generates the prospect that growth in domestic demand and overall GDP in the euro area and in Japan will remain slower than in the United States this year (and maybe next year as well). This explains why U.S. officials sometimes argue that the U.S. current account deficit reflects a "growth deficit" in some of our main trading partners.

What about the analysis of current account adjustment as viewed from a saving-investment perspective? Here, the dominant development has been the continuing decline in the U.S. net national saving rate (the resources that Americans are saving net of the amount that the U.S. federal government

55. Mussa (2005).

is borrowing)—from about 12 percent of GDP in the early 1960s to about 5–6 percent in the mid-1980s and to roughly 3 percent last year—the lowest level since the postwar period.[56] As many observers have highlighted, while U.S. net national investment also weakened over the 2000–04 period, more than 100 percent of the widening of the U.S. current account deficit over this period was accounted for by a drop in the level of U.S. national saving, and within the national saving rate, the one component that has shown the most dramatic deterioration was federal government (dis)saving; see figure 5-5.[57] Between 2000 and 2004, the actual federal budget deficit worsened by 6 percentage points of GDP.[58] In fiscal 2004, the U.S. federal budget deficit was just over $400 billion—or 3.6 percent of GDP.

Almost everyone, including the current U.S. administration, views a federal budget deficit of this size as too large; indeed, President Bush has pledged to cut the budget deficit in half (relative to GDP) in four years. But this is anything but a forgone conclusion. A reasonable forecast is that the budget deficit will decline only marginally as a share of GDP until 2010 and then will likely deteriorate further, as the retirement of the baby boom generation and rising entitlement payments (especially health care costs) make their influence felt.[59] This can be seen in figure 5-6, which uses the Congressional Budget Office's January 2005 baseline projection for the federal budget and then adjusts it for likely fiscal policy developments—that is, the extension of expiring tax cuts, reform of the alternative minimum tax, growth of discretionary spending roughly equal to the growth rate of nominal GDP, and a phasedown of activities in Iraq and Afghanistan plus continued spending for the global war on terrorism. We agree with Mussa that a more ambitious program of fiscal consolidation in the United States (that is, reducing the structural U.S. budget deficit to less than 1 percent of GDP by 2010)

56. Bernanke (2005) similarly discusses a decline in the U.S. gross national saving rate—from 18 percent of GDP in 1985 to 16 percent in 1995 and to less than 14 percent last year.

57. For example, Summers (2004). Since U.S. net investment has been falling over most of the 2000–04 period and is just now regaining the 2000 level, it is difficult to argue that foreign savings are merely funding investment opportunities in the United States.

58. The IMF (2004c) estimates that the deterioration in the structural U.S. federal budget deficit over the 2000–04 period was about 5 percentage points.

59. See Mussa (2005), who reports that the budget deficit in 2010 would then be 3.1 percent of GDP and that the ratio of U.S. public debt to GDP would be 44 percent, up from 37 percent now. In February 2005, the Bush administration projected a fiscal deficit of 3.5 percent of GDP for fiscal 2005, but it recently revised that projection down to 2.7 percent of GDP, due primarily to much higher than anticipated tax receipts. It remains to be seen how long-lasting those higher tax receipts will be; see "Revenue Surge Shrinks Deficit," *Washington Post,* July 14, 2005.

Figure 5-5. *U.S. Savings and Investment as a Share of GDP in the United States, 1998–2004*

Percent

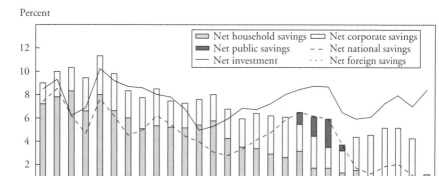

1980   1982   1984   1986   1988   1990   1992   1994   1996   1998   2000   2002   2004[a] 2004[c]
                                                                                              2004[b] 2004[d]

Source: Bureau of Economic Analysis (2005).
a. First quarter.
b. Second quarter.
c. Third quarter.
d. Fourth quarter.

would be much better, both for putting U.S. fiscal policy on a sounder long-term footing and for exerting favorable spillover effects on the U.S. current account deficit.[60] Because no credible fiscal program of this type is currently being proposed by the U.S. administration, our trading partners in Asia and Europe can claim not only that the U.S. current account deficit is "made in America" but also that the United States should put its own house in order before giving policy advice to others.

Bernanke has pointed out that the big swing in current account surpluses in the 1996–2003 period took place not in other industrial countries but rather in developing countries, as these countries moved from their traditional

---

60. Mussa (2005). Erceg, Guerrieri, and Gust (2005) estimate that each one dollar reduction in the federal budget deficit reduces the U.S. current account deficit by less than twenty cents.

Figure 5-6. *Budget Projections as a Share of GDP in the United States, January 2005*

Percent

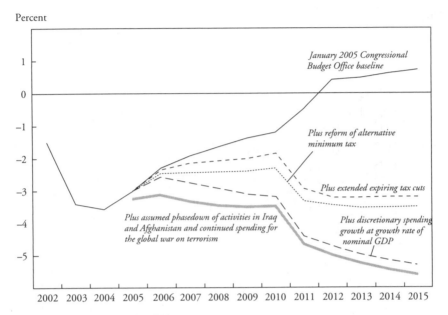

Source: Congressional Budget Office.

role as net capital importers to net capital exporters.[61] He argues that financial crises in Asian emerging economies and a sharp rise in world oil prices contributed strongly to this turnaround and that the United States became the natural destination for the excess savings of developing countries. Bernanke's bottom line is that events in the developing countries had a lot to do with the recent evolution of the U.S. current account position and therefore that purely inward-looking policies are not likely to resolve the U.S. imbalance. Instead, developing countries will have to improve their domestic investment climate sufficiently and accumulate enough reserves such that they feel comfortable once again returning to their natural position as net capital importers. But this will take time, so the United States needs to be patient.

61. Bernanke (2005).

Whether Bernanke is right or wrong about the role that external versus internal influences played in the evolution of the U.S. current account over the past decade, a key question is whether markets and countries have the incentives to allow the U.S. current account to be in large and increasing deficit for an extended period, while developing countries are improving their domestic investment opportunities.[62]

A recent set of papers by three Deutsche Bank economists answers that question in the affirmative by postulating that the United States and the Asian economies have entered into an implicit contract—the so-called "revived Bretton Woods" system—that can comfortably carry on for another decade or two, with significant net benefits to both parties.[63] The United States gets a stable and low-cost source of finance for its large current account deficit as well as access (via a welcoming attitude in Asia toward incoming foreign direct investment) to a low-cost and productive Asian work force. For their part, the Asian creditor economies are permitted to engage in prolonged, large-scale exchange market intervention that limits or prevents their currencies from rising in value against the U.S. dollar. This, in turn, underpins a strategy of export-led development that produces high enough economic and employment growth to keep a lid on social pressures emanating from large pools of surplus labor. And incoming foreign direct investment in the export industries is alleged to contribute toward building a world-class capital stock that would be unattainable due to weaknesses in the domestic financial system.

Others are not persuaded that the revived Bretton Woods can last anywhere near as long as a decade.[64] Their objections span a wide range, including the following points:

—More than three-quarters of the U.S. current account deficit in 2003–04 was financed by foreign central bank purchases of U.S. treasury securities and most of that by just a handful of Asian central banks.

—As the size of the U.S. current account deficit rises in the future, these few Asian central banks will have to undertake larger and larger interven-

---

62. One problem with Bernanke's diagnosis is that real exchange rates play little role in the correction of payments imbalances (Bernanke 2005). Setser (2005) criticizes the Bernanke thesis for getting wrong the timing of Asian reserve accumulation, for underplaying the fall in investment in emerging Asia, and for not giving enough attention to China's exchange rate policies in influencing its balance of payments.

63. Dooley, Folkerts-Landau, and Garber (2003, 2004a, 2004b, 2004c).

64. See Eichengreen (2004); Goldstein and Lardy (2005); Roubini and Setser (2005); Truman (2005b).

tion operations, but their risks will not be adequately compensated by the interest rate on those securities.[65]

—Unlike the original Bretton Woods system (which required the United States to maintain the dollar's parity to gold), the revived Bretton Woods does not impose adequate constraints on the anchor country (that is, the United States) to induce it to act responsibly.

—Similarly, there is much less cohesion among Asian creditor countries today than there was among creditor countries in the original Bretton Woods system (hence it will be harder to limit free riding by smaller central banks or to allocate the burden of adjustment on financing the United States; South Korea already seems to have thrown in the towel, judging by the recent appreciation of the won).

—Europe is unlikely to join the Asian coalition, and private foreign investors will stay in the game only as long as foreign central banks are intervening to limit the currency risk.

—Undervalued real exchange rates attract huge capital inflows chasing expected currency revaluation in some large Asian creditor countries, and the difficulty of sterilizing these inflows exposes them to serious bouts of domestic financial stability (China had just such a bank credit blowout in 2003 and early 2004).

—The costs of sterilization of reserve inflows are poorly captured by domestic interest rates in Asian economies with financial repression.

—When the game ends and Asian creditor countries have to revalue their currencies relative to the dollar and other reserve currencies, they will suffer a large capital loss, which in some cases could run to 10 percent of GDP (realizing this, they will not want to play too long).

—Focusing exclusively on undervaluing the exchange rate against the dollar does not make sense for those Asian economies (like China) where most exports go to markets other than the United States or to countries with currencies not pegged to the dollar.

—The contention that Asian creditor countries always prefer undervalued exchange rates for employment reasons does not stand up to closer

65. The World Bank (2005a) reports that the Reserve Bank of India now faces a dilemma because its inventory of government securities is falling rapidly, but it is not allowed to issue its own securities or sell rupee assets on international markets; as a result of open-market operations, the Bank of Korea came up against the annual limit set by its legislature on sales of government securities; and the People's Bank of China accumulated nearly $100 billion of foreign exchange reserves in the fourth quarter alone and had (as of November 2004) sold the equivalent of nearly $80 billion of central bank bonds domestically, more than tripling the total stock of bonds outstanding.

scrutiny; China allowed its real trade-weighted exchange rate to appreciate by nearly 30 percent between 1994 and early 2002, during a period when there were large employment losses in state-owned industries.

—Foreign direct investment cannot easily substitute for a weak domestic banking system (for example, in China's case, foreign direct investment has financed less than 5 percent of fixed-asset investment over the past few years).

—The benefits of accumulating a large war chest of reserves (to cushion shocks and eliminate the need for turning to the IMF in extremis) are subject to diminishing returns, and several Asian countries are rapidly approaching that point, if they have not reached it already.

—As U.S. bilateral deficits with Asian creditor countries grow in size, pressures for a protectionist response in the United States will also grow (in fact, bills now before the U.S. Congress would place an import surcharge on China's exports to the United States if China does not end its alleged currency manipulation).

—The average maturity of U.S. government bonds has fallen sharply in recent years, increasing rollover risk and vulnerability to sudden shifts in U.S. interest rates.

—As U.S. investors become increasingly concerned about a large prospective fall in the dollar, they will shift more of their portfolio to foreign stocks and foreign currency–denominated assets, further increasing U.S. external financing needs. After all, sending money overseas is not like changing your citizenship: you can send the money back after the dollar depreciation scare is over, and there are plenty of places with decent financial markets (for example, the United Kingdom and euroland) to park the funds in the interim.

Bringing together the factors affecting the sustainability of a growing U.S. current account deficit yields a mixed picture. On the plus side, orderly adjustment of large current account imbalances in industrial countries tends to be more the rule than the exception; the first wave of dollar depreciation, running from February 2002 to the present, fits that mold. The United States also has practically no foreign currency–denominated public debt, nor is its banking system so fragile that an interest rate defense of the dollar, if needed, would induce a crisis. And it may be that the lagged effects of the past three years of dollar depreciation will ultimately make more of a dent in the current account deficit than has been observed thus far.

But there is also the more worrisome, negative side of the U.S. current account imbalance. As noted, each of the main players often suggests that the present pattern of global payments imbalances is primarily the fault of the other players. Thus the United States argues that if Asian countries would only adopt more flexible exchange rate policies, if the European Union would only grow faster, and if developing countries would only improve their domestic investment climates, the correction of the U.S. current account deficit would soon follow. Under this interpretation, the U.S. current account deficit is more a "badge of honor" bestowed on America by the market than a reflection of inadequate U.S. macroeconomic policies; the deficit will shrink once other countries do the right thing. Similarly, Asian economies maintain that the U.S. current account deficit reflects primarily a low and declining U.S. national saving rate and, since 2000, a switch toward large-scale dissaving by the U.S. federal government. Why should Asia have to change its exchange rate policies to correct a U.S. problem that is mainly of the United States' own making, especially if such a change could disrupt their own economies? And Europe can charge not only that U.S. and Asian governments are engaging in misguided fiscal and exchange rate policies, respectively, but also that Europe has been the unlucky victim of those policies, with the blow delivered by a euro exchange rate that has appreciated massively against the dollar in the space of three years. Why should Europe have to change a monetary policy viewed as appropriate for its domestic needs just to compensate for the policy failings of others?

A key reason why it has been convenient to play what IMF managing director De Rato has called "the blame game" is that making wholesale changes in economic policies in each of the three key regions would entail costs, and there has not yet been enough external pressure—either from markets or from other countries—to motivate such policy changes.[66] The market has not signaled—via either a big run-up in long-term U.S. interest rates or a rapid, disorderly fall in the dollar—that it is deeply concerned about U.S. macro policies, and canceling pledges to make tax cuts permanent would have political costs for the current U.S. administration. Likewise, the G-7 countries have not given China and other Asian economies a deadline for moving to more flexible exchange rates; neither the United States nor the IMF (both of which have legal mandates to monitor currency manipulation) has named any of these economies a currency manipulator

66. De Rato (2005).

or imposed other penalties.[67] Meanwhile, Chinese authorities appear to be worried that a large renminbi revaluation would be unduly contractionary for growth and employment. And Europe, while complaining about the effects of such a high euro, is expecting growth this year that is very close to its ten-year average.

The rub is that imbalances are growing and that once the markets decide that prospects for a smooth, cooperative resolution are dim, the resulting adjustment could be disorderly and difficult to control. As noted earlier, the U.S. current account deficit this year will likely be bigger than last year and so too for 2006.[68] The Bush administration and the U.S. Congress are debating social security reform, but no credible plan has yet been put on the table to bring the structural budget deficit close to balance in the next five years.[69] China's current account surplus was 3.3 percent of GDP in 2003 and more than 4 percent last year, and it is likely to be considerably higher this year, as a slowing Chinese economy reduces import demand. The rising share of China in the U.S. trade deficit and the large increase in China's exports of apparel to the United States (now that the Multi-fibre Agreement has expired) will add to the political pressure on U.S. legislators to "do something," but that something could be trade protection, not fiscal reform to increase U.S. national saving. The euro has risen by more than 20 percent in real effective terms during the past three years, and European politicians and legislators too will feel increasingly pressed if the euro continues to rise and if growth in the euro area remains weak. Foreign investors and governments now own almost half of the privately held stock of U.S. treasury securities, almost a third of both agency securities and corporate bonds, and about a

67. In the U.S. Treasury's latest report to Congress on international economic and exchange rate policies, the Treasury offered a considerably more critical evaluation of China's exchange rate policies than in previous reports, emphasizing that China's rigid currency regime has become highly distortionary, poses risks to the health of the Chinese economy, and poses risks to China's neighbors (U.S. Treasury 2005). While the Treasury report does not name China as a currency manipulator, it concludes that if current trends continue without substantial alteration, China will likely meet the technical requirements (of the relevant U.S. statute) for designation as a currency manipulator.

68. Data recently released on the U.S. current account deficit in the first quarter of 2005 are consistent with this projection: the deficit climbed to 6.4 percent of GDP.

69. If one combines loose U.S. fiscal policy with increasingly tighter U.S. monetary policy (the so-called Reagan policy mix), there is the worry that the rise in U.S. interest rates could temporarily suck in more capital flows to the United States and temporarily cause the dollar to appreciate, thereby removing the expenditure-switching channel from U.S. external adjustment and setting the stage for an even larger and more disorderly fall in the dollar once concerns about the current account deficit overwhelm the incentives related to interest rate differentials.

tenth of equities. And some foreign central banks have recently been discussing the advantages of greater "diversification" in their reserve holdings.

Suppose the revived Bretton Woods system manages to hold together until, say, the middle of 2006, by which point (intermittent concerns about a near-term slowdown aside) U.S. economic growth is running close to today's consensus forecast of 3.25 percent of GDP. Suppose, too, that any remaining slack in the U.S. economy has been eliminated, that the federal funds rate is around 4 percent, and that ten-year U.S. treasuries are yielding about 5–5.25 percent.[70] Assume, too, that earlier G-7 meetings have failed to reach any meaningful consensus on how to accelerate the correction of global payments imbalances. Now imagine that several worse-than-expected U.S. monthly trade reports, or a drop in U.S. productivity growth, or a rising U.S.-China trade dispute, or rumors about official reserve diversification out of the dollar prompt both foreign private investors and some foreign central banks not only to slow sharply their acquisition of U.S. treasuries but also to sell some U.S. dollar-denominated securities (for example, equities, agency bonds, corporate bonds).

In this kind of unwelcome scenario, one would expect "confidence effects" to put both strong downward pressure on the U.S. dollar and sharp upward pressure on U.S. interest rates. Faced with this situation, the U.S. Federal Reserve might feel compelled to raise U.S. short-term interest rates to prevent the expenditure switch toward U.S. products (induced by a rapidly falling dollar) and the pass-through from higher import prices that unduly push up aggregate demand and inflation and send a signal to nervous foreign investors that it does not have a "benign neglect" policy toward the dollar. A policy-induced increase in U.S. interest rates might occur even though the Fed recognizes that personal consumption and residential investment might well suffer a sharp reversal after their rapid run-up in recent years. The U.S. Commerce Department's Bureau of Economic Analysis has reported that the most interest-rate-sensitive components of U.S. GDP (namely, consumption of automobiles, furniture and household equipment, home improvements, and new home structures) recently accounted for more than 15 percent of real

---

70. The U.S. Federal Reserve began raising the federal funds rate in June 2004 and has since raised it eight more times by 25 basis points, bringing the rate to 3.25 percent today. The markets seem to expect the federal funds rate to hit about 3.75 percent by the end of this year. Since January 2004, the yield on ten-year U.S. treasuries has fluctuated between 3.7 and 4.7 percent; it now stands at 4.2 percent. Over the past twenty years, the yield on ten-year U.S. treasuries has, on average, exceeded the federal funds rate by about 150 basis points.

GDP, up from 13 percent in 2000. In a similar vein, U.S. personal consumption expenditure as a share of GDP, cash refinancing and home equity loan spending as a share of total consumer spending, mortgage borrowing as a percent of residential investment, household interest payments as a percent of disposable income, and the ratio of house prices to income have all recently reached peak levels. True, home mortgages in the United States tend to be more of the fixed-rate variety than in some European countries, but this alone would not prevent a sharp increase in short- and long-term U.S. interest rates from slowing the U.S. economy.

Three related points. First, even if the Fed does not raise U.S. interest rates, strong downward pressure on the dollar would make it difficult for the Fed to reduce them, thereby taking out of play one of the main policy instruments used to combat earlier slowdowns. Second, if there is a serious confidence problem about the orderly resolution of global payments imbalances, long-term U.S. interest rates would rise even in the absence of further Fed policy tightening; whether long-term rates would rise more with a Fed tightening than without one is not entirely clear. And third, judging from past behavior, if U.S. long-term interest rates rise, one would expect long-term rates to rise in other G-7 countries as well, although probably not as much as in the United States.[71]

Just how sharp and how prolonged would be the rise in U.S. interest rates and the fall in the dollar after a "run" away from dollar assets is a matter on which there is little consensus. Roubini and Setser have surveyed the range of estimated interest rate effects associated with a hypothesized large fall (say, $300 billion) in central bank demand (intervention) for long-term U.S. treasury securities.[72] The estimates range from 40 basis points to 200 basis points (based on the argument that the current conjuncture is less favorable than that in the 1990s on which most estimates are based).[73] In addition to the wide range of estimates themselves, it is not clear how many

---

71. In this connection, it is worth recalling the large and generalized increase in yields on ten-year benchmark government bonds that took place between the beginning of February and the end of March 1994. During that two-month period, such yields increased by 50–70 basis points in Japan, Germany, Switzerland, and Belgium; 70–100 basis points in the United States, the Netherlands, Italy, and France; and 130–167 basis points in the United Kingdom, Canada, Australia, and Sweden; see IMF (1994).

72. Roubini and Setser (2005).

73. Roubini and Setser (2005) argue that the present combination of U.S. fiscal deficits and U.S. growth rates "ought" to produce long-term U.S. interest rates in the 6 percent range and that low real interest rates in the United States and Europe, along with enormous reserve accumulation in emerging economies, are anomalies that will not last.

of these estimates are merely estimates of portfolio effects rather than the combined effect of portfolio shifts and a loss of confidence. Baily has reported some simulation results for the U.S. economy of an assumed rapid decline in the dollar (20 percent over two years) using the macroeconomic model of Macroeconomic Advisors.[74] We interpret his results as relating only to the demand-switching effects of such an exchange rate path rather than the combination of expenditure-switching effects and loss-of-confidence effects. In any case, he finds that (relative to a baseline scenario) the rapid decline in the dollar leads both the federal funds rate and the ten-year treasury note yield to be significantly higher (225 to 250 basis points) than the baseline; growth is not that much lower (just over 1 percent less) because higher net exports provide an import offset to lower consumption and investment.

If confidence effects do turn out to be important in a disorderly adjustment of the U.S. current account deficit, ten-year yields on U.S. treasuries could be 200–300 basis points higher than otherwise expected; that would put them in the 7–8 percent range. Recall that in the six-week period between April 1, 2004 (the day before the U.S. nonfarm payrolls estimate of 308,000 new jobs was released), and May 13, 2004, the yield on ten-year U.S. treasuries increased 96 basis points. With ten-year treasuries paying 7–8 percent, thirty-year, fixed-rate mortgages might well be in the neighborhood of, say, 8–9.5 percent. Residential investment and house prices would then be expected to take a tumble, and this would likely be followed by a fall in consumption and eventually business investment. In this scenario, U.S. economic growth could fall in 2006 from, say, 3.25 percent to 1 percent—or even into a recession. In other words, the eagle would join the dragon in a slowdown.

Moreover, if the slowdown were mainly attributable to fears about the sustainability of the U.S. current account deficit, it is not obvious that the slowdown would be over in a few months. Expansionary fiscal policy would not be available to counteract the slowdown because this would only add to concerns about the U.S. budget deficit and about the low U.S. national saving rate. Presumably, the decision to lower U.S. interest rates would need to await progress in stabilizing expectations about further declines in the dollar. Concerted exchange market intervention by the G-3 in support of the dollar could buy some time but at best would likely be effective only in the short term in the absence of progress on the underlying determinants of current account imbalances. And arranging a Plaza II or Bonn Summit type of policy coordination package would take time to negotiate.

74. Baily (2003).

Impact of an Overlapping China–United States Slowdown on Emerging Economies

If China and the United States do suffer slowdowns along the lines suggested above, the outlook for emerging economies in 2006 and 2007 would be considerably less favorable than it is today: the prospects for emerging-market exports and for their real GDP growth would decline, the costs of their external (and internal) financing would rise, private capital flows to many of them would fall, and the challenges facing exchange rate, fiscal, and monetary policies would become more demanding. This section outlines some of the expected effects and indicates which countries would likely be more vulnerable under each of the main transmission channels.

Bilateral Export Links

If growth in China and the United States slows, so too will their demand for imports.[75] A large depreciation of the U.S. dollar would further decrease the demand for imports in the United States. This means that economies that depend relatively heavily on the Chinese and U.S. markets as destinations for their exports will, ceteris paribus, be most adversely affected. So too will emerging economies in which exports make up a large share of GDP.

Table 5-4 identifies the emerging economies that would fall under these criteria for 2004.[76] Hong Kong, South Korea, and Taiwan head the list of

75. Anderson (2005b) reports that the slowdown in China's import growth has probably already begun, with nominal and real import growth in January and February 2005 considerably below (on a year-over-year basis) the rates in 2004; more recent data through May 2005 suggest that China's import slowdown is continuing.

76. There are, of course, additional yardsticks one could use to draw inferences about the impact of a China–United States import slowdown on emerging-economy exports, including the contribution of the Chinese and U.S. markets to the growth of total exports in 2003–04. Anderson (2004a) reports that Taiwan, South Korea, and Singapore were the Asian emerging economies for which China's contribution to total export growth was largest in 2004. One could also take into account differences in income elasticities for the export products of different economies. For example, it is generally agreed that the income elasticity of demand is higher for manufactures than for primary products. Some authors—for example, Reinhart and Reinhart (2001) and Frankel and Roubini (2000)—interpret these differences as implying that Asian emerging economies (with a high share of manufactures in their exports) would, ceteris paribus, be more adversely affected by a growth slowdown in their export markets than would, say, Latin American countries (with a lower share of manufactures in their exports); others counter that Asian economies can more easily (than Latin American economies) switch either from slow-growing export markets to faster-growing ones or to the domestic market.

Table 5-4. Vulnerability to Import Slowdown in China and the United States, 2004

Exports to China				Exports to the United States				Exports to China plus United States			
Country[a]	Percent of total exports	Country[a]	Percent of GDP	Country[a]	Percent of total exports	Country[a]	Percent of GDP	Country[a]	Percent of total exports	Country[a]	Percent of GDP
Hong Kong	**44**	**Hong Kong**	**69**	**Mexico**	**81**	**Hong Kong**	**26**	**Mexico**	**82**	**Hong Kong**	**95**
Korea	**22**	**Singapore**	**15**	**Venezuela**	**55**	**Singapore**	**22**	**Hong Kong**	**61**	**Singapore**	**37**
Taiwan	**19**	**Taiwan**	**9**	**Ecuador**	**48**	**Venezuela**	**22**	**Venezuela**	**56**	**Malaysia**	**28**
Philippines	**11**	**Korea**	**7**	**Colombia**	**41**	**Mexico**	**21**	**Ecuador**	**49**	**Venezuela**	**23**
Malaysia	**10**	**Malaysia**	**7**	**Peru**	**30**	**Malaysia**	**20**	**Colombia**	**42**	**Mexico**	**21**
Peru	10	Philippines	6	**China**	**23**	Ecuador	14	Korea	40	Taiwan	18
Singapore	9	Thailand	4	Brazil	21	**China**	**9**	Peru	40	Ecuador	14
Argentina	8	Chile	3	Malaysia	19	Philippines	8	Taiwan	36	Philippines	14
Brazil	8	Saudi Arabia	2	Saudi Arabia	18	Taiwan	8	Brazil	29	Korea	13
India	8	Indonesia	2	India	18	Saudi Arabia	8	Philippines	29	Thailand	11
Indonesia	7	Argentina	2	Korea	18	Thailand	8	India	26	Saudi Arabia	11
Thailand	7	Russia	2	Philippines	17	Colombia	7	Malaysia	25	Chile	8

Country		Country		Country		Country		Country		Country	
Malaysia	7	Ukraine	2	Hong Kong	17	Korea	6	Saudi Arabia	24	Peru	7
Russia	7	Peru	2	Taiwan	17	Peru	5	Chile	24	Colombia	7
Saudi Arabia	6	Brazil	1	Thailand	16	Chile	4	Thailand	23	Indonesia	6
United States	**4**	India	1	Chile	14	Indonesia	4	Singapore	22	Argentina	4
Ukraine	4	Venezuela	1	Singapore	13	Brazil	3	Indonesia	20	Brazil	4
South Africa	2	South Africa	1	Indonesia	13	Argentina	2	Argentina	19	Russia	4
Egypt	2	Czech Republic	0	Egypt	12	India	2	Egypt	13	India	3
Venezuela	1	Egypt	0	South Africa	10	South Africa	2	Russia	13	Ukraine	3
Mexico	1	Argentina	0	Argentina	10	Lithuania	2	South Africa	13	South Africa	3
Colombia	1	Turkey	0	Turkey	8	Russia	2	Turkey	8	Lithuania	2
Ecuador	1	Russia	0	Russia	6	Egypt	2	Ukraine	6	Egypt	2
Czech Republic	1	Lithuania	0	Lithuania	5	Czech Republic	2	Lithuania	6	Czech Republic	2
Hungary	1	Czech Republic	0	Czech Republic	3	Turkey	1	Czech Republic	4	Turkey	2
Poland	1	Poland	0	Hungary	3	Ukraine	1	Hungary	4	Hungary	1
Turkey	1	Hungary	0	Poland	3	Hungary	1	Poland	3	Poland	1
Lithuania	0	Ukraine	0	Ukraine	3	Poland	1				

Source: IMF, Direction of Trade Statistics and International Financial Statistics.
a. From top to bottom, ranked from most to least vulnerable.

economies whose total exports in 2004 were most dependent on China.[77] More interesting is the appearance in the top ten of several commodity-producing economies, mostly from Latin America—namely, Chile, Peru, Argentina, and Brazil. Some of China's Asian neighbors—the Philippines and Singapore—also make the top ten. Taken as a group, emerging economies in Eastern Europe have relatively small export exposure to China, as does the United States. The table also shows the ranking of dependence on exports to China (for 2004), but this time using GDP (rather than total exports) as the denominator. Because Asian emerging economies—particularly Hong Kong and Singapore—have, on average, much higher degrees of export openness than economies in Latin America, Asian emerging economies take the top seven positions in GDP-adjusted exports, with only Chile from Latin America slipping into the top ten.

Table 5-4 also presents the same kind of export-concentration calculations for emerging-market exports to the United States. Here, Latin American emerging economies, led by Mexico, show the highest shares of total exports going to the U.S. market. But it is noteworthy that four Asian economies, led by China itself, make it into the top eleven for 2004, along with Saudi Arabia; the rankings using 2003 data are broadly similar.[78] Again, adjusting by the share of exports in GDP vaults the very open economies higher up on the list, with Hong Kong, Singapore, and Venezuela then being the three most dependent on the U.S. market, with Mexico and Malaysia close behind, and with China occupying the number seven spot.

Finally, table 5-4 combines the results for China and the United States to show the economies that would be most affected by a joint import slowdown in the two locomotives. The bottom line is that Hong Kong's exports would be most affected by an overlapping slowdown in Chinese and U.S. imports, followed by Singapore, Malaysia, Venezuela, and Mexico. European emerging economies congregate near the bottom of the list.

---

77. Anderson (2004a) uses a different data source and reports that, excluding Hong Kong, Taiwan had the highest share of exports going to mainland China for the November 2003–November 2004 period.

78. Adjusting for reexports from Hong Kong to the United States would probably raise the share of China's exports going to the United States to about a third; see Goldstein and Lardy (2005). The fact that China has a relatively high export dependence on the United States suggests that there is potential for interactions between a growth slowdown in China and one in the United States; because U.S. dependence on exports to China is relatively low, the effect of economic developments in China on the U.S. economy would have to operate mainly via other channels (for example, the effect of exchange market intervention on U.S. interest rates).

Commodity Price Effects

By focusing on the destination of exports, calculations like those in table 5-4 underestimate the effect of China and the United States on emerging-economy export earnings. This is because some emerging economies—notwithstanding the longer-term switch away from primary products and toward manufactures—depend to a large extent on exports of primary commodities whose prices are set by world supply and demand conditions and because China and the United States are large enough consumers or producers of these goods to affect world demand and supply and, hence, world prices. Since such primary-product exports also go to destinations other than China and the United States, a bilateral calculation underestimates the influence of those two large economies. Figures put together by the IMF indicate that the United States and China together account for roughly a quarter of global consumption of wheat, a third or more of global consumption of petroleum, copper, steel, and aluminum, and two-fifths or more of global consumption of cotton and soybeans.[79] In terms of the increase in global demand for such commodities in recent years, China's influence would be much greater than implied by its share of global consumption.[80] Lardy notes, for example, that China alone accounted for 45 percent of the increase in global oil demand in 2002–03.[81] China's contribution to the 2003–04 increase in global demand for metals would be even larger than its contribution to the increase in global demand for petroleum. Large changes in production of primary commodities in these two economies, particularly when they move in the opposite direction to that of consumption, can also result in large changes in imports, often again with potentially significant implications for global prices. China's steel imports increased 42 percent in 2002 and an additional 52 percent in 2003. But reflecting the effects of both diminished overheating and expanded domestic steel production, steel imports fell 21 percent last year, and the expectation is that China will be a net exporter of steel this year.

Reinhart and Reinhart have surveyed a group of empirical studies suggesting that slower growth in industrial countries, especially the United

---

79. IMF (2004c).

80. Simpfendorfer (2004) estimates that in 2003 China accounted for 121 percent of the increase in global copper demand; the corresponding percentages for steel, iron ore, aluminum, and primary nickel were 90, 66, 51, and 44 percent, respectively.

81. Lardy (2005).

States, has historically been associated with weakness in real commodity prices.[82] More specifically, they report that a 1-percentage-point drop in the growth of industrial production in the industrial countries results in a drop in real commodity prices of roughly 0.77 to 2 percent, depending on the study.

An overlapping slowdown in the United States and China could have a noticeable moderating effect on the path of commodity prices in 2005–07, with mixed results for emerging economies. Net exporters of those commodities would be adversely affected, while net importers would gain.

The IMF has estimated that a 30 percent decrease (increase) in average crude oil prices would reduce (increase) the import bill of emerging and developing countries by about 0.5 percent of GDP, while decreasing (increasing) the oil revenues of oil exporters by just over 3 percent of GDP.[83] Estimates produced by the Bank of England suggest that among a sample group of twelve net oil-importing emerging economies, those that would gain most from a large decrease in world oil prices would be, in descending order, Thailand, the Philippines, Pakistan, South Korea, India, Turkey, the Czech Republic, Poland, South Africa, China, Peru, and Brazil.[84]

To get a further rough picture of which emerging economies would be more vulnerable to a decline in primary commodity prices, table 5-5 identifies those economies that had 5 percent or more of their total exports during the 1990–99 period in any of thirty-five disaggregated product categories within the broader groups of beverages, energy, food, agricultural raw materials, and metals.[85] The highest export concentration seems to be in crude oil. Moving beyond oil exporters that are not in our emerging-economy group (for example, Nigeria, Saudi Arabia, Iran, and so forth), table 5-5 indicates that Venezuela obtained nearly four-fifths of its export revenues from crude oil; Russia, Colombia, Indonesia, Mexico, and Argentina were next in line, all with export concentrations in oil that were 10 percent or higher.[86] The metals group is another category that has made a relatively large contribution to the export earnings of some emerging economies, with Chile having obtained about 40 percent of export earn-

82. Reinhart and Reinhart (2001).

83. IMF (2004c).

84. Bank of England (2004).

85. We are indebted to Kalpana Kochar of the IMF Research Department for sharing these data with us.

86. Refined oil is not regarded as a primary commodity in table 5-5.

Table 5-5. *Specialized Primary Commodities as a Share of Total Exports,*
1990–99

Country and commodity	Percent of total exports
Venezuela (crude oil)	**78**
Chile (copper)	**41**
Russia (crude oil)	**24**
Colombia (crude oil)	**23**
Colombia (coffee)	**18**
Russia (natural gas)	17
Indonesia (crude oil)	15
Mexico (crude oil)	11
Indonesia (natural gas)	10
Argentina (crude oil)	10
Argentina (soybean meal)	8
Colombia (coal)	8
Brazil (iron ore)	7
South Africa (coal)	6
Poland (coal)	6
Argentina (wheat)	5
Argentina (soybean oil)	5
Malaysia (palm oil)	5
Argentina (hides)	5

Source: International Monetary Fund.

ings from copper and Brazil having obtained about 7 percent from iron ore.[87]
Other notable export concentrations occur in coffee (Colombia, 18 percent),
natural gas (Russia, 17 percent; Indonesia, 10 percent), coal (Colombia,
8 percent; South Africa and Poland, 6 percent each), iron ore (Brazil, 7 per-
cent), soybean meal (Argentina, 8 percent), soybean oil (Argentina, 5 per-
cent), wheat (Argentina, 5 percent), palm oil (Malaysia, 5 percent), and hides
(Argentina, 5 percent).[88] A recent World Bank forecast suggests that coal,
soybean meal, soybeans, wheat, and sawn wood are among the primary
commodities expected to suffer price declines in 2005.[89] If one takes the

87. Bank of England (2004) indicates that exports of metals accounted for roughly 11 percent of
Chile's GDP in 2004; the corresponding figures for other metals exporters were South Africa (6 percent), Russia (5 percent), Czech Republic (4 percent), and Brazil (3 percent).
88. If soybeans were regarded as a single commodity rather than as a group of separate products
(soybean meal, soybean oil), Argentina's degree of export concentration would be higher than suggested
in table 5-5.
89. World Bank (2005b).

share of nonmanufactured exports in GDP as a rough indicator of vulnerability to a decline in export earnings from primary commodities, then the emerging economies with the highest vulnerability (using 2002 data) are, in descending order, Venezuela (24 percent), Russia (24 percent), the Philippines (23 percent), and Chile (22 percent);[90] at the other end of the spectrum, Korea, India, China, Taiwan, and Turkey all have shares of nonmanufactured exports in GDP that are 3 percent or lower; see table 5-6.[91]

If a joint China–U.S. growth slowdown leads to a lower medium-term price path for primary commodities than is currently priced into futures markets, there could also be repercussions in financial markets. For example, during the one-year period ending in the spring of 2005, there was a surge of funds ($50 billion to $75 billion) flowing into securitized commodity assets, attracted by the large price rises for primary commodities.[92] The implicit assumption was that strong demand for energy, combined with supply restraints (for example, the influence of the Organization of the Petroleum Exporting Countries), would keep oil and other energy prices high. Verleger argues that swap and futures markets for oil are not large enough to handle a surge of speculative buying like the one that occurred in 2004 without large price increases.[93] Eventually, profit margins will fall as more buyers enter the market, and inventories will increase in response to high prices. Negative shocks to demand or government action to lower prices could then burst the bubble.[94] Although the amount invested in such energy funds is small relative to assets of the world's largest pension funds (more than $6 trillion), it is not clear how positions in other financial markets would be affected by a pullback from such commodity speculation.

To sum up, the available evidence supports the commonsense notion that slower growth in both China and the United States would, on balance,

90. Singapore and Malaysia also appear in table 5-6 with relatively high vulnerability, but the importance of reexports in these economies makes the interpretation of such data ambiguous. If the vulnerability indicator instead is the share of nonmanufactures in total exports, then Venezuela, Chile, Russia, Argentina, and Colombia head the list.

91. Preliminary indications are that the data on primary product concentration for 2004 would be quite similar to those for 2002.

92. According to Verleger (2005).

93. Verleger (2005).

94. Verleger (2005) does not argue that increased investment in securitized energy assets was the primary factor pushing up global oil prices in 2004. Instead, he regards such investment as adding to the price pressure caused by "fundamentals." Among these fundamentals is the rapid growth of oil consumption in China and India (that is, an average growth rate of 7 percent a year over the 1990–2003 period versus a growth rate of 0.8 percent a year for the rest of the world).

Table 5-6. *Nonmanufactured Exports, 2002*

Country[a]	Percent of total merchandise exports	Country[a]	Percent of GDP
Venezuela	87	**Venezuela**	24
Chile	82	**Russia**	24
Russia	78	**Philippines**	23
Argentina	69	**Chile**	22
Colombia	62	**Singapore**	21
Philippines	50	**Malaysia**	21
Brazil	46	Argentina	17
Indonesia	46	Indonesia	15
South Africa	37	Thailand	14
Thailand	26	South Africa	10
India	25	Colombia	9
Malaysia	21	Hungary	7
Poland	18	Hong Kong	6
Mexico	16	Brazil	6
Turkey	16	Czech Republic	6
Singapore	15	Mexico	4
Hungary	14	Poland	4
Czech Republic	11	Turkey	3
China	10	Taiwan	3
Korea	8	China	3
Taiwan	6	India	2
Hong Kong	5	Korea	2

Source: World Bank (2004).

a. From top to bottom, ranked from most to least vulnerable.

be adverse for emerging-market exports and, ceteris paribus, for emerging-market economic growth as well. Several recent studies have attempted to provide somewhat more specific estimates of such trade-induced growth effects.

The September 2004 IMF *World Economic Outlook* considers the likely implications of a one-time 10-percentage-point decline in the growth of China's imports for domestic use, arising from the further slowdown in domestic investment.[95] Such a decline would be consistent with an initial drop of 5.5 percentage points in China's real investment growth and would correspond to an initial drop of 2.5 percentage points in GDP (and eventu-

95. IMF (2004a).

ally a 4-percentage-point decline if multiplier effects are taken into account). The impact (inclusive of multiplier effects) on the rest of Asia is estimated to be a 0.4-percentage-point drop in growth, with the Asian newly industrialized economies being most adversely affected (slowing their GDP growth rate by 0.6 percentage point). These estimates do *not* include second-round growth effects, effects on countries' terms of trade, or offsetting policy adjustments.

A recent scenario exercise conducted by the Asian Development Bank provides more country detail and also considers the effects of a simultaneous slowdown in growth in China, the United States, and Japan.[96] The simulations employ the Asian Development Bank's multiregion, multisector, computable general-equilibrium model. In the first scenario, a cut (relative to the baseline scenario) of 5 percentage points in China's real investment growth reduces China's real GDP growth by 2 percentage points (again relative to the baseline). Such a unilateral slowdown in China is found to have the most pronounced effects on Hong Kong, whose growth would fall almost 1 percentage point; the next most-affected economies would be Taiwan and Singapore (just over 0.4 percentage point), with Indonesia, Malaysia, the Philippines, and Thailand next in line. Growth in Latin America is estimated to fall only 0.2 percent. The sectors in China most affected by the fall in investment would be motor vehicles, ferrous metals, and construction; the least affected sectors would be clothing, electronics, and food. In another scenario, the Asian Development Bank adds growth slowdowns in the United States (to 2 percent) and in Japan (to 1 percent) to the hypothesized growth slowdown in China. This would reduce global economic growth by 1 percentage point and increase the growth slowdown in Asian emerging economies by about 40 percent from the estimated slowdowns in the China-only slowdown scenario (for example, Hong Kong's growth slows by 1.4 percentage points instead of 1 percentage point). As the authors of the exercise acknowledge, one important limitation of their estimates is that they do not include some important transmission channels, such as private capital flows and contagion in financial markets.

On the whole, the message from the bilateral trade figures and from the simulation exercises is that an overlapping growth slowdown in China and the United States would, via the channel of trade interactions, reduce growth in Asian emerging economies by a moderate degree (perhaps on the order of 0.5 to 0.75 percentage point). The induced effects of such a slowdown on

96. Asian Development Bank (2004).

global commodity prices are, we think, harder to pin down, although the direction of influence is certainly clear.

Slower growth in emerging economies would not, by itself, make a crisis. But there are other channels of crisis vulnerability to consider.

Increased Interest Costs and a Fall in Private Capital Flows to Emerging Economies

Between February and June 2005, most forecasters revised downward their expectations about the future path of short-term and long-term U.S. interest rates.[97] Still, the market seems to expect the federal funds rate to rise to about 3.75 percent by the end of this year and to roughly 4 percent by the middle of 2006; this would be close to what is regarded as a "neutral" level, often taken to be 4 to 4.5 percent. According to the June 2005 blue-chip consensus forecast, the yield on ten-year U.S. treasuries is expected to average just under 5 percent (4.9 percent) in 2006.[98] On top of this expected increase in U.S. interest rates, we have speculated that if there were a disorderly adjustment to the large U.S. current account deficit (say, in the middle of 2006), then there could well be a further rise in U.S. interest rates (less at the short than the long end of the yield curve). Longer-term interest rates in other G-7 economies would also be expected to reflect a risk premium associated with tensions over global adjustment.[99] The issue at hand is how higher U.S. interest rates would affect the cost and availability of finance to emerging economies and which emerging economies would likely be the most affected.

Over the past dozen years, there has been quite a lot of empirical work analyzing the impact of financial conditions in industrial countries (or in global markets) on capital flows and on financing costs in emerging economies.[100] Much of that work has divided the factors affecting private capital flows to

97. Real GDP forecasts for 2005 changed less; for example, the blue-chip consensus forecast for 2005 real GDP growth was 3.6 percent in February 2005 versus 3.5 percent in June 2005.

98. In February 2005, the forecast for the ten-year yield was 5.3 percent.

99. Short-term interest rates in other G-7 countries could be the same or lower after such a shock, depending on whether countries with appreciating currencies vis-à-vis the dollar took monetary policy actions to offset the demand-shifting effects of more appreciated exchange rates. As suggested earlier, since February 2002 there has been little inclination to lower interest rates in Europe in the face of a depreciating dollar and a strongly appreciating euro.

100. See Calvo, Leiderman, and Reinhart (1993); Eichengreen and Mody (1998); Reinhart and Reinhart (2001); Arora and Cerisola (2001); Ferrucci and others (2004); IMF (2004a); Goldman Sachs (2005b).

emerging economies into either "push" factors, reflecting conditions in creditor countries, or "pull" factors, reflecting conditions in debtor countries. More recently, a complementary literature has also developed on the effects of "sudden stops" in private capital flows to emerging economies and on what features of these economies make such sudden stops more costly in some countries than in others.[101]

The recent empirical study by Ferrucci and others provides a good example of the push-pull framework.[102] They seek to explain, first, the lending flows of industrial-country banks to seventeen emerging economies over the 1986–2003 period and, second, the interest rate spread on J. P. Morgan's index of emerging-market bonds from 1991 to 2003. The borrower-specific "pull" factors are intended to capture factors affecting either the demand for credit by an emerging economy or the risks involved in lending to it; these factors are proxied by variables such as real GDP growth, the ratio of external debt to GDP, an index of local-currency equity returns, and bilateral exchange rate volatility.[103] The "push" factors are meant to reflect the opportunity costs of lending to the creditor, the risk appetite of the creditor, and the financial position of the creditor. Ferrucci and his co-authors attempt to capture those influences by including the global equity return, the yield spread between high- and low-rated U.S. corporate bonds, and real GDP growth in creditor countries. A few other variables are added as controls for other influences.

Ferrucci and his co-authors also find that this combination of push and pull factors does a decent job of explaining bank lending flows, with all the estimated coefficients (except for creditor-country GDP growth) being statistically significant with the expected signs. They find that push factors were, on average, just as important as pull factors in motivating bank flows over this period. Risk attitudes in creditor countries and returns on alternative investments (here, global equity returns) turn out to have a large influence on the results.

Turning to emerging-market bond spreads, they employ a similar framework. Here, pull factors are intended to capture the debtor's financial position and creditworthiness (represented by the ratio of external debt to GDP and the ratio of fiscal surplus to GDP), along with its ability to service its

---

101. See Calvo and Talvi (2005) and the earlier literature reviewed therein.
102. Ferrucci and others (2004).
103. Some authors also include the liberalization of financial markets and large-scale privatizations as among the "pull" factors.

foreign debt (proxied by trade openness, ratio of amortization to reserves, and ratio of current account to GDP). The push variables are supposed to reflect the opportunity cost of purchasing emerging-market bonds (yields on short- and long-term U.S. debt), investors' risk appetite (spread on BB and BBB bonds), and the macroeconomic environment in which the investment community operates (U.S. equity index). They argue that the expected sign on long-term creditor interest rates is ambiguous. Rising yields could be associated with increased borrowing costs to emerging markets and, hence, wider spreads. However, higher long-term interest rates could be linked to a steeper yield curve if short-term rates do not rise or rise by less than long-term yields; a steeper yield curve, in turn, could induce carry trades where investors borrow short in domestic markets and invest in higher-yielding, long-term debt in emerging markets, thereby compressing spreads.

A key finding is that external push factors are highly significant, especially short-term U.S. interest rates, which have a large, positive significant effect on emerging-market spreads; in contrast, long-term U.S. interest rates have a strong negative impact on spreads.[104] The main policy lesson is that since both banking flows and bond spreads are significantly influenced by push factors, emerging markets should not borrow heavily during times of a benign external environment, as a reversal in credit conditions is more often than not beyond the control of the borrower.

The IMF and Goldman Sachs have recently estimated models for emerging-market interest spreads that share some of the same conceptual foundations as those in Ferrucci and others.[105] Writing in the early fall of 2004, the IMF model generates the conclusion that if the U.S. federal funds rate would rise 275 basis points by mid-2005, the EMBIG spread would rise another 100 basis points or so. The Goldman Sachs study reports four noteworthy conclusions:[106]

—Of the 675-basis-point narrowing of emerging-market spreads between September 2002 and February 2005, about 40 percent is explained by domestic fundamentals in emerging markets, 17 percent by stronger export prices and global growth, 20 percent by greater availability of global liquidity, and 23 percent by greater risk appetite.

104. This contradicts the empirical results obtained by Arora and Cerisola (2001) but supports those of Eichengreen and Mody (1998).

105. Ferrucci and others (2004); Goldman Sachs (2005b); IMF (2004a).

106. Goldman Sachs (2005b).

—Domestic fundamentals played a much bigger role in the compression of Turkey's spread over this period than in that of Brazil's spread.

—If commodity prices and risk aversion remain at current levels and if global liquidity conditions return to a more normal level, defined as a 5.5 percent yield on ten-year U.S. treasuries, emerging-market spreads would widen by 120 basis points.

—The April 2004 bond market experience, where yields on ten-year U.S. treasuries increased by almost 100 basis points in six weeks and where Russian, Turkish, and Brazilian spreads rose by 108, 171, and 202 basis points, respectively, leads to the view that a 100-basis-point increase in yields on ten-year treasuries would probably push up spreads on riskier emerging-market credits by a further 200 basis points.

Although they do not test it, the Goldman Sachs team also conjectures that a very sudden increase in U.S. treasury yields would have a greater impact on emerging-market spreads than an increase spread out over a year. In the end, they do not believe that emerging-market spreads will blow out in the dramatic way seen in some earlier cycles of Fed tightening.

Since measures of risk appetite frequently appear in models explaining private capital flows to emerging economies and the spreads charged on those flows, it is worth mentioning another regularity in the empirical literature, namely, that such risk appetite variables—sometimes simply referred to as investor sentiment—tend to be quite volatile over time and typically show large falls in periods surrounding emerging-market financial crises (for example, the Asian financial crisis, the Russian crisis).[107]

A central thesis of the sudden-stop literature is that a collapse of capital flows to emerging markets is the dominant common characteristic of emerging-market financial crises. A related proposition is that domestic financial vulnerabilities in capital-importing countries largely determine how these countries fare after being hit with a sudden stop. Calvo and Talvi provide a revealing account of how the sudden stop triggered by the Russian crisis in

---

107. See, for example, Kumar and Persaud (2002). Gai and Vause (2004) review a number of measures of risk appetite. They emphasize that risk appetite and risk aversion should be kept distinct. They define risk appetite as the willingness of investors to bear risk and argue that it depends on both the degree to which investors dislike uncertainty (about their future consumption) and the level of that uncertainty (which, in turn, depends on the macroeconomic environment). Risk aversion is only about investors' dislike of uncertainty. Since risk aversion is about the intrinsic makeup of the investor, it should not change markedly or frequently over time; not so for risk appetite, which should change when the macroeconomic environment deteriorates. Gai and Vause (2004) report that, according to several measures, risk appetite was high in 2003 and 2004.

1998 affected Latin American emerging economies.[108] They make the following points:

—Beginning in 1989–90, there was a huge increase in capital flows going to emerging economies, including to Latin America, where these flows rose from an annual rate of minus 1 percent of GDP in 1989 to plus 5.5 percent of GDP in the year ending in the second quarter of 1998.

—The Russian default in August 1998 imposed losses on financial intermediaries investing in emerging markets, some of whom were highly leveraged, and this led to a liquidity crunch, forcing a sell-off of emerging-market bonds across-the-board at fire sale prices to meet margin calls.

—This, in turn, precipitated a sudden, synchronized, and large increase in interest rates in emerging markets, with spreads for Latin American countries rising from 450 basis points just before the crisis to 1,600 basis points in September 1998; it took five years for spreads to return to the levels prevailing before the Russian default.

—Capital inflows in Latin America came to a sudden stop, falling from 5.5 percent of GDP just before the crisis to less than 2 percent of GDP one year later.

—Every major country in Latin America was subject to the sudden stop, including Chile, which, despite its record of high growth and good policies, experienced the largest falloff in flows.

—The severe monetary tightening resulted in a severe drop in both asset prices and flows of domestic bank credit to the private sector.

—As a counterpart to the sudden stop in capital flows, there was both a sharp current account adjustment and a huge real currency depreciation.

—There were also a severe and sustained reduction in investment levels and a large decline in economic growth.

—Despite all this, Chile did not experience a crisis, whereas Argentina did.

—A comparison of the Chilean and Argentine experiences suggests that the two key domestic factors conditioning the impact of a sudden stop are the openness of the economy and the degree of liability dollarization: the more closed the economy, the larger the change in the real exchange rate needed to accommodate a sudden stop in capital flows. The higher the degree of liability dollarization, the more adverse the balance sheet effects induced by a depreciation of the domestic currency relative to the dollar.

---

108. Calvo and Talvi (2005).

The September 2004 issue of the IMF's *Global Financial Stability Report* also looks at sudden-stop case histories, focusing on four former Asian crisis economies, along with Russia, Argentina, Brazil, and Turkey.[109] One of the questions posed is what factors determine the length of the deleveraging process—that is, how long does the postcrisis reduction of external liabilities continue? The authors find that a very weak banking system (resulting in a crisis), a relatively underdeveloped domestic bond market, and a low share of securitized external debt relative to bank debt all are associated with a relatively long deleveraging process.

To sum up, we take a set of observations away from these studies on the cost and availability of private capital flows to emerging economies and links to U.S. monetary policy.

There is ample precedent for rapid and sizable shifts in risk appetite or market sentiment that can be reflected both in long-term bond yields in the major creditor countries and in the interest rate spread that emerging economies pay in excess of the yield on U.S. treasuries. Sometimes those shifts in market sentiment are initiated by unexpected changes in U.S. monetary policy and sometimes by unexpected developments in emerging markets themselves. Within the span of a few months, changes of several hundred basis points can occur and have occurred on the EMBIG and in the spread on an individual country's bonds. The amount of private capital that flows to and from emerging economies can also change quickly and markedly within a relatively short period.

As the U.S. Federal Reserve raises the federal funds rate toward a more neutral stance (say, 4–4.5 percent) and as long-term yields on U.S. treasuries also increase (say, to 5 percent or so on ten-year securities), the opportunity cost of investing in emerging markets will rise. Many empirical studies have confirmed that when U.S. short-term interest rates go up, private capital flows to emerging economies typically go down and the interest rate spread on emerging-market bonds rises. The move away from the very accommodating U.S. monetary conditions of the past few years—and away from such ample global liquidity more generally—should result in an increase of emerging-market spreads (say, in the neighborhood of 100–150 basis points). Since the U.S. yield curve will likely become flatter, not steeper, over the next eighteen months, it is unlikely that the rise in long-term U.S. rates will give rise to an upsurge in carry trades that will, in turn, lower the spread on emerging-market bonds. If the Federal Reserve gets behind the curve on inflationary

---

109. IMF (2004a).

developments and has to raise U.S. interest rates faster than now anticipated, the rise in emerging-market spreads will be larger.

If there is, on top of the expected tightening of U.S. monetary policy, a disorderly adjustment of the large and rising U.S. current account deficit, there will be a further rise in long-term interest rates, probably most pronounced in the United States but also likely evident in other G-7 countries. This increase in uncertainty could also produce a pronounced shift in sentiment away from high-risk investments, including emerging-market debt and equities. A sudden stop in private capital flows to many emerging economies and a further rise in the EMBIG spread (say, of another 100–200 basis points) might then occur, affecting a wide array of emerging economies, with the highest-yield credits probably being most affected initially.[110] A further round of selling pressure could follow if initial losses on some emerging-market bonds for cross investors are sufficient to trigger risk management strategies that call for further pullbacks in exposure to emerging economies in an effort to meet value-at-risk guidelines.

With their export prospects weaker and the costs of external finance higher, the creditworthiness of many emerging economies would decline some, notwithstanding improved fundamentals over the past two years or so. The higher cost and lower availability of external finance would probably spill over to domestic credit and equity markets, with negative consequences for investment and economic growth. Depending on the magnitude of the sudden stop and the amount of induced capital outflows, exchange rates of emerging economies could also depreciate, and their current accounts could go further into surplus.

The extent to which individual emerging economies would be adversely affected by such a global interest rate shock would depend not only on whether they were simultaneously subject to country-specific bad or good news but also on their structural characteristics. Emerging economies with high external financing needs, high ratios of both short-term external debt relative to reserves and of domestic debt service to GDP, low access to emergency sources of liquidity, floating interest rates, short remaining maturity on debt, a large share of foreign currency–denominated or foreign currency–indexed

---

110. Private capital flows to "many"—rather than all—emerging economies may stop suddenly. In a scenario in which *both* the United States and many emerging economies are regarded as less attractive destinations for investment, a large amount of capital flows would presumably want to go somewhere else. This "somewhere else" might include Europe, Japan, other OECD countries, *and* some emerging economies that are regarded as less vulnerable in the new risk environment. In this sense, the "flight to quality" need not involve exclusively the G-7 or G-10 countries.

debt, small domestic bond markets, low export openness, and weak domestic banking systems would be disadvantaged relative to others.

There could also be "contagion" of financial difficulties from one or more emerging economies to others.[111] One of the vulnerabilities now widespread among emerging economies is a level of public debt (relative to GDP) that is considerably higher than seems prudent. Thus, if one or more highly indebted emerging economies get into debt-servicing difficulties as a result of higher interest rates and a sudden stop in capital flows, other emerging economies with high debt might be adversely affected by contagion.

The next eleven tables bring together twenty-seven indicators that are often associated with vulnerability to higher interest rate spreads or a decline in private capital flows to emerging economies and ranks almost twenty emerging economies on each of those indicators.[112] Much of the data for the debt and debt-servicing variables come from the January 2005 issue of J. P. Morgan's *Emerging Debt and Fiscal Indicators*.[113] A notable advantage of this data set is that figures are provided not only for 2004 but also for 2005 and 2006 (based on projections made by their individual-country specialists, using a common set of assumptions about the global macroeconomic environment); a disadvantage is that the data on sovereign debt cover only the debt of the central government and appear to be on a gross rather than a net basis. Two other caveats worth mentioning are that the debt service data for Argentina are on an accrual basis through 2004 and then on a cash basis for 2005 and 2006 and that some countries with high sovereign domestic debt amortization payments (as a share of GDP), such

---

111. Both the Asian financial crisis of 1997–98 (which began in Thailand) and the Russian crisis of 1998 showed that the origin of such contagion need not be in an economy with a large weight in international financial markets. In addition, contagion need not operate exclusively, or even mainly, via bilateral trade and capital flow links from the country first affected to others. Two examples illustrate the point. Although financial sector weaknesses in Asian economies were evident for many years prior to 1997, it took the crisis in Thailand to remind and "wake up" investors of this fact. But once investors did awaken, they looked around the region and proceeded to write down economies with vulnerabilities similar to those in Thailand, particularly financial sector weaknesses; see Goldstein (1998). The losses suffered by Japanese banks in Thailand, coming on top of those suffered domestically in the bursting of the equity and land price bubble, induced them to pull back their exposure not only in Thailand but across the region more broadly. Those Asian economies that shared the same dominant external bank lender (Japanese banks) as Thailand suffered from this pullback, but the Philippines, which relied more heavily than others on U.S. banks, was much less affected; see Goldstein, Kaminsky, and Reinhart (2000).

112. Because the indicators use data obtained from different sources, the sample of emerging economies ranked under each indicator is not always the same (although the overlap across indicators is pretty high).

113. J. P. Morgan (2005).

Table 5-7. *External Sovereign Debt Service as a Share of Exports, 2004–06*

Country[a]	2004	Country[a]	2005[b]	Country[a]	2006[b]
Argentina	**55**[c]	**Argentina**	**23**[d]	**Colombia**	**23**
Brazil	**23**	**Colombia**	**23**	**Argentina**	**21**[d]
Turkey	**19**	**Brazil**	**21**	**Brazil**	**20**
Colombia	**17**	**Turkey**	**20**	**Turkey**	**17**
Indonesia	**13**	**Indonesia**	**13**	**Venezuela**	**13**
India	12	Venezuela	12	**Indonesia**	**13**
Venezuela	10	India	12	India	11
Mexico	8	Russia	8	Russia	6
Thailand	8	Mexico	7	Philippines	6
Russia	7	Philippines	7	Mexico	5
Philippines	7	Thailand	7	Poland	5
Chile	5	Poland	5	Thailand	5
South Africa	4	South Africa	4	South Africa	4
Poland	4	Hungary	4	China	3
China	4	Chile	3	Chile	2
Hungary	3	China	3	Hungary	2
Korea	2	Korea	1	Korea	1
Malaysia	0	Malaysia	0	Malaysia	0
Czech Republic	. . .	Czech Republic	. . .	Czech Republic	. . .

Source: J. P. Morgan (2005).
. . . Not covered.
a. From top to bottom, ranked from most to least vulnerable.
b. Forecast.
c. Accrual basis.
d. Cash basis.

as Turkey and Mexico, refinance their short-term maturities with short-term issuance.[114]

Table 5-7 looks at external sovereign debt service as a percent of exports for 2004, 2005, and 2006. Here, sovereign debt service includes interest payments and amortization. Exports are a good denominator to use because these external debt-service payments are made overwhelmingly in foreign exchange (predominantly in U.S. dollars). Argentina, Colombia, Brazil, and Turkey have the heaviest external debt service among this group of

114. A special problem with assessments of Argentina's vulnerability is that its cross-country ranking can be highly sensitive to whether the particular vulnerability indicator relies on data before versus after its recent debt restructuring.

Table 5-8. *Sovereign Domestic Debt Service as a Share of GDP, 2004–06*
Percent

Country[a]	2004	Country[a]	2005[b]	Country[a]	2006[b]
Turkey	**41**	**Turkey**	**35**	**Turkey**	**32**
Hungary	**29**	**Brazil**	**25**	**Brazil**	**23**
Brazil	**27**	**Hungary**	**17**	**Mexico**	**13**
Mexico	**14**	**Mexico**	**14**	**Hungary**	**9**
Chile	**13**	**Poland**	**11**	**Philippines**	**8**
Poland	12	Chile	10	**Poland**	**8**
Philippines	8	Philippines	9	Colombia	7
Malaysia	7	Colombia	7	Malaysia	7
Colombia	6	Malaysia	7	Venezuela	5
Venezuela	6	Venezuela	5	Chile	4
Argentina	4[c]	Argentina	4[d]	South Africa	4
South Africa	3	South Africa	3	Argentina[d]	3
Indonesia	3	Indonesia	3	Indonesia	3
China	2	Thailand	2	Thailand	3
Thailand	2	China	2	China	2
Russia	1	Russia	1	Russia	0
India	. . .	India	. . .	India	. . .
Korea	. . .	Korea	. . .	Korea	. . .
Czech Republic	. . .	Czech Republic	. . .	Czech Republic	. . .

Sources: J. P. Morgan (2005).
. . . Not covered.
a. From top to bottom, ranked from most to least vulnerable.
b. Forecast.
c. Accrual basis.
d. Cash basis.

emerging economies.[115] Argentina's external debt-service payments declined sharply after its recent debt restructuring in 2004, but it still ranks near the top of the pack even in 2006. Venezuela and Indonesia also sit rather high on the external debt-service ladder. In contrast, most Asian emerging economies and Eastern European economies have relatively low external debt-servicing burdens. Because an overlapping China–U.S. slowdown would both reduce emerging-market export earnings and increase their interest costs, it would produce a "double whammy" for emerging economies, especially those high up on the list.

115. Again, the figures for 2004 indicate what Argentina owed in external debt service in 2004, not what it actually paid.

Table 5-9. *Total Sovereign Debt Service as a Share of GDP, 2004–06*
Percent

Country[a]	2004	Country[a]	2005[b]	Country[a]	2006[b]
Turkey	**47**	**Turkey**	**41**	**Turkey**	**37**
Brazil	**31**	**Brazil**	**29**	**Brazil**	**27**
Hungary	**31**	**Hungary**	**19**	**Mexico**	**15**
Argentina	**20[c]**	**Mexico**	**16**	**Philippines**	**12**
Mexico	**17**	**Philippines**	**13**	**Hungary**	**11**
Chile	14	Poland	12	**Colombia**	**11**
Poland	14	Chile	11	Poland	10
Philippines	12	Colombia	10	Venezuela	9
Colombia	9	Argentina	10[d]	Argentina	9[d]
Venezuela	9	Venezuela	9	Malaysia	7
Indonesia	7	Malaysia	7	Indonesia	6
Malaysia	7	Thailand	7	Thailand	6
Thailand	7	Indonesia	6	Chile	5
South Africa	4	South Africa	4	South Africa	4
Russia	4	Russia	3	China	3
China	4	China	3	Russia	2
India	2	India	2	India	2
Korea	1	Korea	1	Korea	1
Czech Republic	. . .	Czech Republic	. . .	Czech Republic	. . .

Sources: J. P. Morgan (2005).
. . . Not covered.
a. From top to bottom, ranked from most to least vulnerable.
b. Forecast.
c. Accrual basis.
d. Cash basis.

Table 5-8 looks at sovereign domestic debt-service payments expressed as a share of GDP. Since there is arbitrage between international and domestic financial markets and since international investors are increasingly active in local bond markets, domestic interest rates may also be affected by a rise in global interest rates. Here, the country rankings change somewhat. Turkey now heads the list, followed by Brazil and Hungary.[116]

Table 5-9 brings together external and domestic debt-servicing obligations to get a picture of total sovereign debt service as a share of GDP. Turkey's ratio exceeds everyone else's by a significant margin in all three years, with

116. Again, large short-term debt issuance is associated with high amortization payments.

Table 5-10. *Private Sector Debt Service as a Share of GDP, 2006*

Country[a]	Percent of GDP
Argentina	**6**
Indonesia	**4**
Chile	**4**
Turkey	**3**
Brazil	**3**
Poland	3
Philippines	3
Colombia	3
Mexico	2
Malaysia	2
Thailand	2
Hungary	2
Korea	2
Venezuela	1
China	1
Russia	1
South Africa	. . .
India	. . .
Czech Republic	. . .

Source: J. P. Morgan (2005).
. . . Not covered.
a. From top to bottom, ranked from most to least vulnerable.

Brazil, Hungary, Mexico, and the Philippines next in order. Of the seven economies with the heaviest total sovereign debt service in 2006, three come from Europe, three from Latin America, and one from Asia.

Debt-servicing difficulties that begin in the private sector of the economy can generate a crisis for the economy as a whole, as we saw in the Asian financial crisis. The private sector, like the public sector, would find its financing costs increased by a rise in global interest rates. Table 5-10 looks at the private sector's debt service relative to GDP in 2006. Argentina, Chile, and Indonesia have the heaviest (projected) burdens. The next tier encompasses Brazil, Colombia, Poland, Turkey, and the Philippines.

Other things being equal, the higher the share of government debt with floating interest rates and, within the floating-rate component, the higher the share indexed to domestic interest rates, the greater the country's vulnerability to suddenly higher global interest rates. Table 5-11 uses data obtained from Borensztein and others on the structure of domestically issued

Table 5-11. *Structure of Domestically Issued Government Bonds, End 2001*
Percent of total

Country[a]	Fixed-interest-rate debt	Country[a]	Floating domestic government debt tied to domestic interest rate
Brazil	10	**Venezuela**	90
Venezuela	10	**Malaysia**	80
Turkey	15	**Mexico**	60
Malaysia	20	**Brazil**	53
Chile	21	**Turkey**	50
Indonesia	25	**Indonesia**	31
Mexico	36	Hungary	21
Hungary	79	Poland	11
Poland	89	Chile	0
South Africa	98	Czech Republic	0
Czech Republic	100	India	0
India	100	Philippines	0
Philippines	100	South Africa	0
Thailand	100	Thailand	0
Argentina	. . .	Argentina	. . .
China	. . .	China	. . .
Colombia	. . .	Colombia	. . .
Korea	. . .	Korea	. . .
Russia	. . .	Russia	. . .

Source: Borensztein and others (2004).
. . . Not covered.
a. From top to bottom, ranked from most to least vulnerable.

government bonds (at end-2001).[117] Here, the economies with the lowest share of fixed-interest-rate debt in the total are Brazil, Venezuela, Turkey, Malaysia, and Chile. This reflects the broader tendency for Latin American emerging economies to have a much lower share of fixed-rate debt than either Asian or European emerging economies. The table also compares economies with respect to the share of floating-rate, domestic government debt that is tied to the domestic interest rate. On this yardstick, the economies most vulnerable to a rise in domestic interest rates are Venezuela, Malaysia, Mexico, Brazil, Turkey, and Indonesia.

117. Borensztein and others (2004).

Table 5-12. *Three Measures of External Financing Needs*
Percent of reserves

Country[a]	Current account plus external debt amortization, 2004	Country[a]	Current account plus external debt amortization, 2005	Country[a]	Current account plus external debt amortization minus foreign direct investment, 2004
Turkey	**113**	**Turkey**	**115**	**Turkey**	**118**
Hungary	**100**	**Hungary**	**110**	**Hungary**	**117**
Argentina	**96**	**Indonesia**	**54**	**Argentina**	**101**
Mexico	**49**	**Colombia**	**54**	**Chile**	**81**
Indonesia	**45**	**Poland**	**49**	**Mexico**	**75**
Chile	40	Mexico	45	Colombia	48
Poland	35	Argentina	38	Poland	46
Colombia	31	Chile	25	Indonesia	42
Czech Republic	20	Czech Republic	21	Czech Republic	34
India	7	India	9	India	11
Thailand	6	Thailand	2	Thailand	9
China	−6	China	−2	China	3
Korea	−8	Korea	−3	Korea	−6
Philippines	−9	Philippines	−9	Philippines	−8
Malaysia	−20	Malaysia	−13	Brazil	−11
Brazil	−30	Brazil	−18	Malaysia	−17
Russia	−40	Russia	−26	Russia	−38
Venezuela	−47	Venezuela	−39	Venezuela	−43
South Africa	. . .	South Africa	. . .	South Africa	. . .

Source: J. P. Morgan (2005).
. . . Not covered.
a. From top to bottom, ranked from most to least vulnerable.

In the rest of this section, we look at vulnerability indicators that are tied primarily to a sudden decline in private capital flows.

Table 5-12 examines three measures of external financing needs in 2004–05. The first measure is the sum of the current account plus external debt amortization (public and private), expressed as a share of the country's international reserves. Turkey, Hungary, Argentina, Mexico, and Indonesia show the greatest need for external financing in 2004, and the top five rankings are similar in 2005, except that Argentina drops out (again, reflecting the effect of Argentina's recent restructuring of its external debt), while Colombia and Poland move up in the vulnerability rank-

Table 5-13. *Current Account as a Share of GDP, 2004*

Country[a]	Percent of GDP
Hungary	−9
Czech Republic	−6
Turkey	−4
South Africa	−2
Poland	−2
Mexico	−1
Colombia	−1
Chile	1
India	1
Argentina	1
Brazil	1
China	2
Philippines	3
Indonesia	3
Korea	3
Thailand	4
Russia	10
Malaysia	12
Venezuela	14

Source: Deutsche Bank (2005).
a. From top to bottom, ranked from most to least vulnerable.

ing.[118] There are quite a few Asian emerging economies (along with Russia and Venezuela) where the current account surplus exceeded external debt amortization in 2004. The table also subtracts from (the numerator of) external financing needs (in 2004) the flow of inward foreign direct investment; the rankings are broadly similar. Table 5-13 gives just the current account position as a share of GDP. What we see here is that whereas in Hungary, the Czech Republic, Turkey, and South Africa current account deficits add substantially to external financing requirements, the opposite prevails in most other emerging economies, especially in Russia, Malaysia, and Venezuela, which are currently running large external surpluses.

In table 5-14, we show three indicators that bear some relationship to rollover risk in external and domestic debt. The first indicator is the ratio of

118. The rankings for 2006 are identical to those for 2005, at least as regards to the eight most vulnerable economies. In Turkey, Hungary, Colombia, Indonesia, and Poland, estimated external financing needs are larger in 2006—in some cases, substantially so—than in 2004; the opposite is true for Argentina, Mexico, and Chile.

Table 5-14. *Three Indicators of Rollover Risk in External and Domestic Debt*

	Short-term external debt				Average
Country[a]	*Percent of total external debt, 2004*	*Country[a]*	*Percent of domestically issued government bonds, 2001*	*Country[a]*	*original maturity of new issuance (number of years), 2004*
China	**43**	**Czech Republic**	**59**	**Thailand**	**5**
Czech Republic	**33**	**Philippines**	**36**	**Russia**	**5**
Korea	**31**	**Poland**	**27**	**India**	**5**
Thailand	**23**	**Mexico**	**24**	**Poland**	**7**
Mexico	**21**	**Hungary**	**23**	**South Africa**	**8**
Turkey	19	Chile	21	**Hungary**	**8**
Chile	19	Malaysia	20	**Chile**	**8**
Poland	18	India	18	**Malaysia**	**8**
Venezuela	16	Turkey	15	South Korea	9
Malaysia	15	Venezuela	10	China	9
Hungary	15	Thailand	9	Argentina	9
Argentina	15	South Africa	5	Czech Republic	10
Colombia	10	Brazil	0	Indonesia	10
Brazil	10	Indonesia	0	Philippines	10
Philippines	10	Argentina	. . .	Colombia	12
India	3	China	. . .	Brazil	12
South Africa	. . .	Colombia	. . .	Turkey	13
Russia	. . .	Korea	. . .	Mexico	16
Indonesia	. . .	Russia	. . .	Venezuela	16

Source: Bank for International Settlements (2005).
. . . Not covered.
a. From top to bottom, ranked from most to least vulnerable.

short-term to total external debt, the second is the share of short-term debt in domestically issued government bonds, and the third is the average original maturity of new bond issues.[119] Topping the economies with high ratios of short-term to total external debt are China, the Czech Republic, Korea, and Thailand, countries that have not heretofore been high up on our indicators of external financing vulnerability; they are followed by Mexico, Turkey, Chile, and Poland. With regard to the share of short-term debt in domestic public debt, the Czech Republic, the Philippines, Poland, Mexico, and Hungary seem to be the most disadvantaged. As ranked by the original

119. Short-term debt is defined as an initial maturity of less than one year.

Table 5-15. *Measures of Liquidity Risk*

	Short-term external debt				Available
Country[a]	Percent of reserves, September 2004	Country[a]	Percent of net foreign reserves, 2003	Country[a]	amount of emergency IMF assistance, 2003[b]
Argentina	101	Turkey	152	Korea	934
Hungary	100	Brazil	132	Turkey	722
South Africa	85	South Africa	125	Mexico	413
Turkey	76	Indonesia	88	Brazil	371
Brazil	74	Hungary	61	Philippines	369
Chile	70	Philippines	49	Chile	360
Philippines	67	Czech Republic	38	Hungary	325
Mexico	45	Korea	30	Argentina	293
Indonesia	39	Colombia	27	Thailand	288
Russia	32	Russia	25	Poland	273
Colombia	30	Poland	24	Malaysia	215
Korea	29	Thailand	24	Indonesia	203
Poland	28	Chile	22	China	170
Venezuela	25	Malaysia	20	South Africa	152
Malaysia	22	Mexico	18	Colombia	138
Thailand	20	Venezuela	18	Russia	123
Czech Republic	20	China	13	India	118
India	18	India	7	Venezuela	35
China	8	Argentina	−706	Czech Republic	. . .

Sources: For shorter-term external debt as a percent of reserves and of net reserves, International Institute of Finance; for the available amount of emergency IMF assistance, International Monetary Fund.

. . . Not covered.

a. From top to bottom, ranked from most to least vulnerable.

b. Short-term external debt as a percentage of 250 percent of the country's quota in the International Monetary Fund.

maturity of new bond issues, Thailand, Russia, India, and Poland have the shortest maturities.

Liquidity risk also merits attention. The ratio of short-term external debt to reserves—a measure that combines elements of liquidity and currency mismatch—is shown in table 5-15. Several empirical studies have found that countries with a high ratio of short-term external debt to reserves (unity and higher) were far more likely to have had a currency crisis in the 1990s than countries with relatively low ratios.[120] Using the data for Sep-

120. See Frankel and Rose (1996).

Table 5-16. *Vulnerability to Sudden Stops, 2004*

Country[a]	Currency mismatch measure, 2004[b]	Country[a]	Ratio of sovereign external debt to sovereign domestic debt, 2004	Country[a]	Current nominal interest rate (overnight policy rate), March 2005
Argentina	**−115**	**Russia**	**4.1**	**Brazil**	**19**
Philippines	**−18**	**Venezuela**	**1.6**	**Venezuela**	**16**
Turkey	**−11**	**Argentina**	**1.5**	**Turkey**	**16**
Brazil	**−11**	**Indonesia**	**1.2**	**Russia**	**13**
Chile	**−5**	**Philippines**	**1.2**	**Mexico**	**9**
Hungary	−5	Colombia	0.9	**Philippines**	**9**
Mexico	−4	Mexico	0.8	Hungary	8
Colombia	2	Turkey	0.6	South Africa	8
Indonesia	2	Malaysia	0.6	Indonesia	7
South Africa	2	Chile	0.5	Colombia	7
Poland	2	Poland	0.4	Poland	7
China	3	Brazil	0.4	India	5
Thailand	4	Hungary	0.3	Korea	3
Malaysia	4	Thailand	0.3	Argentina	3
Korea	4	India	0.2	Chile	3
Czech Republic	5	China	0.2	Malaysia	3
India	5	Korea	0.2	China	2
Russia	16	South Africa	0.2	Czech Republic	2
Venezuela	57	Czech Republic	. . .	Thailand	2

Sources: For the currency mismatch measure, Goldstein and Turner (2004); otherwise, J. P. Morgan (2005).
. . . Not covered.
a. From top to bottom, ranked from most to least vulnerable.
b. Combines data on net foreign currency liabilities, the foreign currency share of total debt, and export openness of the economy.

tember 2004, the countries that have the weakest liquidity position are Argentina, Hungary, South Africa, Turkey, and Brazil; China and India are at the bottom of the list. The table also looks at a related liquidity concept, namely, the ratio of short-term external debt to net foreign reserves, where net reserves are gross reserves less total credit and loans outstanding to the IMF. As of 2003, the rankings are broadly similar, except that Turkey and Brazil appear to be more liquidity constrained under the net reserves indicator, reflecting their large loans from the IMF. To bring in a crude proxy for the available amount of emergency official assistance from the IMF, the table also compares countries' short-term external debt to 250 percent of their quota in the IMF. The implicit assumptions here are that a country in dire straits might get an IMF loan equal to, say, 500 percent of quota but that probably only half that amount would be available early in the IMF program. South Korea appears most vulnerable on this measure, reflecting its relatively small quota in the IMF. Turkey, Mexico, Brazil, and the Philippines also face small credit lines from the IMF relative to their short-term external debt.[121]

Table 5-16 picks up our earlier discussion about what structural characteristics make sudden stops more costly in some emerging economies than in others. Three such structural characteristics are considered: the foreign currency share of debt, the export openness of the economy, and the size of the sovereign domestic bond market relative to reliance on international bonds. The first indicator shows the Goldstein-Turner measure of aggregate effective currency mismatch, which combines data on net foreign currency liabilities, the foreign currency share of total debt, and the export openness of the economy.[122] The larger the negative number, the more currency mismatched is the economy and, ceteris paribus, the more vulnerable to adverse balance sheet effects from a large currency depreciation.[123] According to this currency mismatch indicator, the most vulnerable emerging economies (in 2004) are Argentina, the Philippines, Turkey, Brazil, Chile, and Hungary. The second indicator is the ratio of sovereign external debt to sovereign domestic debt. The basic idea here is that countries with a large domestic bond market are less vulnerable to a sudden stop in external finance than those with a smaller domestic bond

---

121. We also analyze how various liquidity measures have changed over the 1997–2003 period by examining the ratio of liquidity in 2003 to that in 1997; a figure greater (less) than 1 implies an improvement (deterioration) in liquidity. One measure uses the ratio of gross international reserves to short-term external debt, while two others use, respectively, the ratio of net international reserves to short-term external debt and the ratio of gross international reserves to total external debt. The three main conclusions from these comparisons are (a) the degree of improvement in liquidity positions is more widespread among emerging economies when one looks at the ratio of gross reserves to short-term debt than when one looks at the ratio of gross reserves to total external debt or the ratio of net reserves to short-term external debt; (b) there is considerable variation across emerging economies in these liquidity ratios, with some economies showing a worsening of liquidity ratios since 1997; and (c) several of the emerging economies in Europe—namely, Poland and Hungary—show up as having relatively low liquidity in terms of reserves.

122. Goldstein and Turner (2004). The foreign currency share of total debt is an estimate of the foreign currency shares of domestic bonds, domestic bank loans, and international bonds.

123. This conclusion follows only for economies that have a net liability position in foreign exchange; a positive number means a net foreign asset position in foreign exchange; see the discussion later in this section.

market.[124] Russia, Venezuela, Argentina, Indonesia, and the Philippines are the countries most vulnerable under this metric.

Last but not least, one might ask which economies would be most susceptible to a pullback in private capital flows if there were either a sharp decline in risk appetite or contagion from debt problems elsewhere. The IMF reports that when there was a rapid increase in U.S. long-term interest rates between early April and May 2004, there was a tendency for investors to pull back markedly from local currency, emerging-market bonds in those economies with relatively high nominal interest rates—that is, from the most risky credits.[125] The table therefore orders emerging economies according to the nominal interest rate on overnight loans (as of March 2005). Brazil, Venezuela, Turkey, Russia, and Mexico head the list.

In table 5-17, we present two summary statistics that ought to be indicative of relatively high indebtedness, namely, the ratio of total external debt to exports and the ratio of total sovereign debt to GDP, both for 2004. On external debt, Argentina tops the list, followed by Colombia, Brazil, Indonesia, and Turkey; the rankings are almost identical if one redoes the exercise for 2005 and 2006 (although Argentina's ratio falls significantly). On the public debt front, the top five are Argentina, the Philippines, Turkey, India, and Brazil.

For what it is worth, the economies in tables 5-7 to 5-17 that appear most often in the top five vulnerability spots—spanning the whole set of indicators—are Turkey, Brazil, Argentina, Hungary, and Mexico.[126] Comparing the ranking for vulnerability to global financial conditions with the ranking for vulnerability to a slowdown in China–United States import growth, it is interesting to note that Mexico is the only economy to make the top five on both criteria and that Turkey, which heads the vulnerability list on global financial conditions, is far down the vulnerability list for slower China–U.S. import growth, presumably because it does most of its trade with other regions (Europe). The same result, albeit to a lesser degree, applies to Argentina, Brazil, and Hungary. All this reinforces the point made earlier—namely, that the type of transmission mechanism by which a China–U.S. slowdown spills over to emerging markets will have a lot to say about which individual emerging economies are most vulnerable.

124. Ideally, this measure should also include private debt.
125. IMF (2004c).
126. In addition to the twenty-seven indicators listed in tables 5-7 through 5-17, we also draw on the change in liquidity ratios summarized in note 121.

Table 5-17. *Summary Statistics of Relatively High Indebtedness, 2004*

Country[a]	Total external debt as a percent of exports	Country[a]	Total sovereign debt as a percent of GDP
Argentina	**396**	**Argentina**	**121**
Colombia	**221**	**Philippines**	**89**
Brazil	**187**	**Turkey**	**88**
Indonesia	**183**	**India**	**76**
Turkey	**174**	**Brazil**	**73**
Chile	122	Malaysia	62
India	119	Hungary	60
Philippines	117	Indonesia	58
Poland	108	Colombia	54
Russia	101	Poland	51
Hungary	87	Thailand	50
Venezuela	86	South Africa	41
South Africa	81	Venezuela	39
Mexico	66	Chile	34
Korea	56	Mexico	27
Thailand	43	Russia	24
Malaysia	36	China	21
China	33	Korea	19
Czech Republic	. . .	Czech Republic	. . .

Source: J. P. Morgan (2005).
. . . Not covered.
a. Ranked from most to least vulnerable.

Exchange Rate Changes for the U.S. Dollar and for Emerging-Market Currencies

In the China–U.S. slowdown scenario outlined above, at least two kinds of changes are likely to occur in the exchange rate: a large, disorderly decline in the dollar (say, on the order of 20 percent from its current level) and a sharp decline in some emerging-market currencies in response to the assumed sharp decline in private capital flows to them. As noted earlier, a marked depreciation of emerging-market currencies has been a prominent feature of previous sudden-stop episodes (for example, Mexico, the Asian financial crisis, the aftermath of the Russian crisis, and so forth); indeed, the size of the change in the nominal exchange rate (along with the size of the change in international reserves) is the metric that is commonly used to judge whether a currency "crisis" has taken place.

It turns out, however, that it is not easy a priori to make sweeping generalizations about the likely effects of exchange rate changes on the vulnerability to crisis in individual emerging economies because the outcome depends on a number of key factors, including:

—Whether the country's currency is "pegged" (de jure) or not to the dollar,

—If not pegged to the dollar, whether the country's currency depreciates or appreciates relative the falling dollar,

—Whether the country has a net asset versus a net liability position in foreign exchange,

—How the currency composition of the country's liabilities and foreign exchange payments compares with that of its assets and foreign exchange receipts,

—Whether the country's currency is significantly overvalued or significantly undervalued,

—Whether the domestic economy is overheated or operating well below capacity, and

—Whether the country suffers a country-specific shock in addition to any generalized reduction in the risk appetite for high-yield bonds.[127]

It is clearly not possible with the aid of only a few variables to capture all of the factors conditioning the effect of exchange rate changes on vulnerability to crisis. Nevertheless, in tables 5-18 to 5-22, we bring together seventeen indicators that are relevant for assessing potential exchange rate–related problems.

Empirical research on currency crises in emerging economies often finds that overvaluation of the real exchange rate is one of the best-performing indicators of a crisis.[128] Undervaluation of the real exchange rate also carries risks, but they typically are less pressing than those associated with overvaluation. In table 5-18, we present three measures of the misalignment of the real, trade-weighted exchange rate. The first measure provides Goldman Sachs's recent estimates of misalignment of the (dynamic) real equilibrium exchange rate (DEER),[129] covering overvaluation and undervaluation. It models the real equilibrium exchange rate as a function of productivity differentials, measures of long-term capital inflows, the degree of trade openness, and the terms of trade. The currencies of Venezuela, Hungary, Indonesia, Turkey, and

---

127. To convey the flavor of why these distinctions matter for crisis vulnerability, Goldstein (2005a) considers three hypothetical cases that combine these characteristics in various ways.

128. See Goldstein, Kaminsky, and Reinhart (2000); Berg, Borensztein, and Pattillo (2004).

129. Goldman Sachs (2005b).

Table 5-18. *Measures of Misalignment of the Real Trade-Weighted Exchange Rate*

Goldman Sachs dynamic real equilibrium exchange rate (DEER)				Deviation from ten-year moving average				Real effective exchange rate (REER)[b]			
Country[a]	Over-valuation	Country[a]	Under-valuation	Country[a]	Over-valuation	Country[a]	Under-valuation	Country[a]	Appreciation	Country[a]	Depreciation
Venezuela	29	Hong Kong	−17	Czech Republic	26	Argentina	−26	Russia	61	Argentina	−41
Hungary	23	Taiwan	−14	Russia	22	Malaysia	−16	Czech Republic	28	Malaysia	−6
Indonesia	17	Philippines	−14	Turkey	22	Philippines	−7	Turkey	17	Philippines	−4
Turkey	17	China	−8	Brazil	20	Indonesia	−6	Poland	21	China	−4
Korea	12	Argentina	−5	Hungary	17	Colombia	−3	Brazil	21	Indonesia	−2
Poland	9	Malaysia	−2	South Africa	17	China	−3	Hungary	20	Colombia	−2
Czech Republic	8	Brazil	−2	Poland	16			Poland	15		
Chile	8	Colombia	−2	Venezuela	14			Venezuela	2		
Mexico	7			Mexico	9			Mexico	3		
Thailand	4			Korea	8			Korea	3		
Russia	2			Chile	2			Chile	4		
South Africa	1			India	2			India	2		
				Thailand	2			Thailand	0		

Sources: For DEER, Goldman Sachs (2005a); for deviation from ten-year moving average, authors' calculations; for real movement of the exchange rate, J. P. Morgan (2005).
. . . Not covered.
a. Ranked from most to least vulnerable.
b. Percent changes, 2000–04.

Korea top the overvaluation estimates, with the currencies of Poland and the Czech Republic not far behind. On the undervaluation side, Goldman Sachs estimates that the currencies of Hong Kong, the Philippines, Taiwan, China, and Argentina have the largest misalignments.

The results of two more mechanical approaches to estimating real exchange rate misalignment are also shown. The second measure in table 5-18 presents positive (overvaluation) and negative (undervaluation) deviations from a ten-year moving average of the real trade-weighted exchange rate, while the third measure displays the positive (overvaluation) and negative (undervaluation) percentage change in the real trade-weighted exchange rate over the 2000–04 period. Using deviations from the ten-year moving average, we find that the most overvalued real exchange rates are in the Czech Republic, Russia, Turkey, Brazil, Hungary, South Africa, and Poland, while the most undervalued ones are in Argentina, Malaysia, the Philippines, Indonesia, Colombia, and China. Using the percentage change in the real exchange rate over the 2000–04 period yields a similar identification of the most overvalued and undervalued emerging-market currencies.

As regards the size of real exchange rate misalignments, one ought to take the estimates in table 5-18 with a large grain of salt. There are, of course, many alternative approaches to estimating real exchange rate misalignments, and no single approach is without drawbacks. There is, for example, no consensus in the literature on the role of productivity differentials and trade openness in determining the real exchange rate. For oil producers (for example, Venezuela), the volatility of oil prices is apt to dominate the exchange rate calculations. Deviations from a ten-year average may not give enough weight to large changes in the balance of payments that occur over just a few years, while four-year percentage changes can be misleading when the country has had an exchange rate crisis, and hence a very low exchange rate, near the early part of the four-year period (for example, Argentina in 2001; Brazil in 2002). Still, warts and all, the estimated large overvaluation in much of Eastern Europe and undervaluation in much of emerging Asia seem to agree with recent exchange rate studies for individual countries and for regional groups. For example, Bulir and Smidkova use a model of equilibrium real exchange rates to estimate misalignments in several new EU accession countries and find that, at end-2003, the Czech koruna was overvalued by about 15 percent, the Hungarian forint by about 40 percent, and the Polish zloty by about 20 percent.[130] Similarly, Anderson estimates misalignment (using a basic-balance

---

130. Bulir and Smidkova (2005).

framework) for a group of Asian emerging economies and finds undervaluations ranging from 5 to 25 percent.[131] Goldstein estimates the equilibrium real exchange rate for the Chinese renminbi (using both underlying balance-of-payments and global adjustment approaches) and finds that the renminbi is undervalued by 15–25 percent.[132] And given Turkey's large external deficit and its appreciating real exchange rate, it seems difficult to argue that the Turkish lira is anything but overvalued.

Since the distinction between a net liability and a net asset position in foreign exchange is crucial for assessing the balance sheet effects of exchange rate changes, table 5-19 signifies which emerging economies fall in which camp (using the Goldstein-Turner measure of currency mismatch to differentiate net liability from net asset positions).[133] Other things being equal, those with net liability positions in foreign exchange (Argentina, Brazil, Chile, Colombia, Hungary, Mexico, the Philippines, and Turkey) are more vulnerable to a depreciation of the local currency vis-à-vis reserve currencies than are the other emerging economies listed in table 5-19.

In table 5-20, we present several indicators that are often referred to in discussions of currency mismatch.[134] As outlined earlier, the presumption is that a large currency mismatch makes it more costly if the country undergoes a large currency depreciation. When a large currency mismatch is paired with a large overvaluation of the domestic currency, the risk is particularly high, as Argentina sadly discovered during its 2001–02 crisis. The first indicator is the Goldstein-Turner measure of aggregate effective currency mismatch (in 2004).[135] On this indicator, the most currency-mismatched economies are Argentina, the Philippines, Turkey, Brazil, Chile, and Hungary. The second indicator is the share of total public debt that is either denominated in, or indexed to, foreign currency (for 2003). On this liability measure, the more vulnerable economies are Chile, Russia, Argentina, Indonesia, and Venezuela. The third indicator is the currency composition of long-term debt among the euro, the Japanese yen, and the dollar. These indicators are relevant to cases where the local emerging-market currency might depreciate much more (in a period of financial strain) relative to the euro and the yen than with respect

---

131. Anderson (2004b).
132. Goldstein (2004).
133. Goldstein and Turner (2004).
134. See Goldstein and Turner (2004) for a discussion of what attributes a good measure of aggregate currency mismatch should possess and why measures that look at just the liability side of the balance sheet can be misleading.
135. Goldstein and Turner (2004).

Table 5-19. *Net Asset or Net Liability Position in Foreign Exchange, 2003*

Country[a]	Net position
Argentina	**Net liability**
Turkey	**Net liability**
Brazil	**Net liability**
Philippines	**Net liability**
Chile	**Net liability**
Hungary	**Net liability**
Colombia	**Net liability**
Mexico	**Net liability**
South Africa	Net asset
Malaysia	Net asset
Poland	Net asset
Korea	Net asset
India	Net asset
China	Net asset
Czech Republic	Net asset
Thailand	Net asset
Russia	Net asset
Indonesia	Net asset
Venezuela	Net asset

Source: Goldstein and Turner (2004).
a. Ranked from most to least vulnerable.

to the dollar. Three of the new EU accession countries (Hungary, Poland, and the Czech Republic) are, ceteris paribus, the most vulnerable to an appreciation of the euro vis-à-vis their currencies; Argentina and Turkey are next in line on euro appreciation. Turning to the yen-denominated liabilities, it is apparent—and not surprising—that the Asian emerging economies, led by Thailand, the Philippines, Indonesia, and Malaysia, have the highest shares of yen debt; Hungary and China also have relatively high percentages of yen-denominated liabilities. Continuing the same kind of regional focus, with the notable exception of South Africa, the emerging economies with the largest share of dollar-denominated long-term debt are U.S. neighbors in Latin America (namely, Mexico, Chile, Colombia, Venezuela, and Brazil). Without having parallel information on the currency composition of reserve holdings, one cannot go further in assessing vulnerabilities to different potential patterns of exchange rate movements among the three major reserve currencies.

If banking sector fragility constrains an interest rate defense of a rapidly falling domestic currency, which economies would be most constrained

Table 5-20. *Indicators of Currency Mismatch*

Country[a]	Aggregate effective currency mismatch, 2004	Country[a]	Foreign currency or foreign currency-linked debt, 2003	Country[a]	Euro debt as a percent of long-term debt, 2002	Country[a]	Yen debt as a percent of long-term debt, 2002	Country[a]	Dollar debt as a percent of long-term debt, 2002
Argentina	**−115**	**Chile**	**88**	**Hungary**	**63**	**Thailand**	**57**	**South Africa**	**92**
Philippines	**−18**	**Russia**	**82**	**Poland**	**46**	**Philippines**	**41**	**Mexico**	**90**
Turkey	**−11**	**Argentina**	**73**	**Czech Republic**	**35**	**Indonesia**	**28**	**Chile**	**89**
Brazil	**−11**	**Indonesia**	**69**	**Argentina**	**35**	**Malaysia**	**21**	**Colombia**	**78**
Chile	**−5**	**Venezuela**	**63**	**Turkey**	**25**	**Hungary**	**19**	**Venezuela**	**77**
Hungary	−5	Colombia	52	Russia	24	China	15	Brazil	74
Mexico	−4	Turkey	50	Venezuela	13	India	12	India	74
Colombia	2	Philippines	49	Brazil	12	Brazil	9	China	73
Indonesia	2	Mexico	45	Colombia	11	Turkey	8	Malaysia	71
South Africa	2	Poland	38	Indonesia	9	Argentina	5	Russia	70
Poland	2	Hungary	28	India	6	Mexico	5	Turkey	65
China	3	Brazil	26	Chile	6	Poland	5	Argentina	56
Thailand	4	Thailand	22	China	6	Colombia	4	Indonesia	56
Malaysia	4	Malaysia	20	Philippines	5	South Africa	4	Czech Republic	54
Korea	4	China	16	Malaysia	3	Chile	3	Philippines	39

(*continued*)

Table 5-20. *Indicators of Currency Mismatch (continued)*

Country[a]	Aggregate effective currency mismatch, 2004	Country[a]	Foreign currency or foreign currency–linked debt, 2003	Country[a]	Euro debt as a percent of long-term debt, 2002	Country[a]	Yen debt as a percent of long-term debt, 2002	Country[a]	Dollar debt as a percent of long-term debt, 2002
Czech Republic	5	South Africa	14	South Africa	3	Czech Republic	2	Thailand	38
India	5	India	8	Thailand	2	Venezuela	1	Poland	36
Russia	16	Czech Republic	7	Mexico	1	Russia	0	Hungary	16
Venezuela	57	Korea	. . .	Korea	. . .	Korea	. . .	Korea	. . .

Sources: For effective currency mismatch, Goldstein and Turner (2004); for foreign currency or foreign currency–linked debt as a share of total public debt, Bank for International Settlements (2004); for the currency composition of long-term debt, World Bank (2004).

. . . Not covered.

a. From top to bottom, ranked from most to least vulnerable.

Table 5-21. *Indicator of Banking Sector Soundness*

Country[a]	Moody's weighted average bank financial strength index, May 2004
Argentina	**0**
Indonesia	**7**
Venezuela	**8**
China	**10**
Russia	**11**
Thailand	17
Turkey	19
Philippines	19
Korea	20
Colombia	24
Brazil	24
India	28
Poland	30
Malaysia	37
Mexico	37
Czech Republic	38
Hungary	43
South Africa	50
Chile	57

Source: International Monetary Fund.
a. From top to bottom, ranked from most to least vulnerable.

under that criterion? In table 5-21, we present one indicator of banking-system soundness, namely, Moody's financial strength index. One advantage of this measure (unlike some other ratings) is that it does not incorporate the probability of a government bailout of the banking system but rather concentrates on the underlying strength and viability of the banking system. The tale told is that, among the countries identified in table 5-18 as having overvalued real exchange rates, Argentina, Indonesia, Venezuela, and Turkey have the most to worry about when it comes to banking-sector fragility.

What about the emerging economies with undervalued exchange rates? As argued earlier, the main risks they face from a large decline in the dollar are either that the reserve accumulation associated with "managing" the exchange rate conflicts with efforts to maintain domestic financial stability or that letting the local currency appreciate induces large balance sheet losses on the international reserve position. Table 5-22 presents several indicators loosely related to those risks. The consumer price index (CPI)

Table 5-22. *Indicators of Risk from an Undervalued Exchange Rate*

Country[a]	CPI inflation rate for undervaluation cases, 2004	Country[a]	Domestic to foreign interest rate spread, January 2005	Country[a]	Exchange rate–adjusted spread, January 2005	Country[a]	International reserves as a percent of GDP, 2004
Colombia	**6**	**Turkey**	**16.8**	**Russia**	**8.0**	**Malaysia**	**57**
Philippines	**5**	**Russia**	**9.8**	**China**	**7.6**	**China**	**38**
Argentina	**5**	**Indonesia**	**6.0**	**Indonesia**	**3.4**	**Thailand**	**31**
China	**4**	**Mexico**	**5.6**	**India**	**1.8**	**Korea**	**29**
Malaysia	**2**	**Poland**	**3.3**	**Mexico**	**1.3**	**Venezuela**	**23**
		Philippines	3.2	Thailand	1.0	Russia	21
		China	2.4	Poland	0.2	India	18
		India	2.3	Czech Republic	−0.2	Poland	16
		Malaysia	−0.5	Turkey	−0.6	Indonesia	14
		Brazil	−0.6	Philippines	−0.9	Czech Republic	. . .
		Czech Republic	−0.7	Brazil	−14.9	South Africa	. . .
		Thailand	−1.2	Malaysia	. . .		
		Argentina	. . .	Argentina	. . .		
		Chile	. . .	Chile	. . .		
		Hong Kong	. . .	Hong Kong	. . .		
		Hungary	. . .	Hungary	. . .		
		Korea	. . .	Korea	. . .		
		Singapore	. . .	Singapore	. . .		
		Venezuela	. . .	Venezuela	. . .		

Sources: For CPI inflation rate, International Monetary Fund; for spread, World Bank (2005a); for international reserves, Deutsche Bank.

. . . Not covered.

a. From top to bottom, ranked from most to least vulnerable.

inflation rate is given for 2004, albeit only for the economies identified as having an undervalued real exchange rate. The assumption is that the higher the inflation rate, the higher the risk that capital inflows complicate the task of monetary policy. Topping the (inflation) list are Colombia and the Philippines, followed in turn by Argentina, China, and Malaysia. The table also provides two measures of the costs of sterilizing reserve inflows put together by the World Bank in a recent *Global Development Finance* report.[136] The first measure is the difference between the interest rate on domestic bonds and that on two-year U.S. government bonds (as a proxy for the nominal return on dollar reserves); there are substantial differences in the interest rate costs across emerging economies that have large reserve holdings, with the estimated costs highest in Turkey, Russia, Indonesia, and Mexico and lowest (indeed, negative) in Thailand, the Czech Republic, Brazil, and Malaysia. In the table, these interest costs of sterilization are then supplemented by estimates of the expected change in the exchange rate between the local currency and the U.S. dollar.[137] This changes quite markedly the ordinal rankings of sterilization costs, with higher (lower) costs now evident in those countries where the World Bank estimates that the local currency will appreciate (depreciate) nontrivially relative to the dollar; for example, expected appreciation of the renminbi increases significantly China's sterilization costs, while expected depreciation of the lira decreases markedly Turkey's sterilization costs. Russia then emerges as the economy with the largest sterilization costs, followed by China, Indonesia, and India.

Some other researchers have obtained quite different results on sterilization costs, at least among Asian emerging economies. Anderson, for example, considers only the interest rate differential between domestic and foreign assets in his estimates but concludes that all Asian central banks have positive net balance sheet earnings from sterilization operations, while Singapore, Taiwan, and China have the largest gains.[138] He also notes that, in the year ending February 2005, only China and Malaysia were sterilizing more than they did during the previous twelve months. Finally, the table shows the ratio of international reserves to GDP in 2004. The presumption is that the higher this ratio, the larger the balance sheet effects linked to an appreciation of the local currency vis-à-vis the dollar. The rank-

---

136. World Bank (2005a).

137. Unfortunately, World Bank (2005a) does not indicate where or how the expected changes in emerging-market exchange rates were derived.

138. Anderson (2005a).

ing is done only for the economies identified as having a net asset position in foreign exchange. Heading the list is Malaysia, followed by China, Thailand, South Korea, and Venezuela.

To sum up, looking broadly at potential exchange rate problems shows that the emerging economies in Europe as a group (especially Turkey, Russia, Hungary, and the Czech Republic) are prominent on the list of countries vulnerable to overvaluation, while the list of countries vulnerable to undervaluation is made up mainly of Asian emerging economies (especially the Philippines, Malaysia, and China). There is some overlap with the high-vulnerability positions for other transmission mechanisms (for example, Turkey and Hungary are high up on the list of vulnerability to global financial conditions, Malaysia is in the top five on the list of vulnerability to a slowdown in China–U.S. imports, and Russia has a relatively high share of primary commodities in its total exports), but it is not striking.

Fiscal and Monetary Policies in Emerging Economies

Thus far, we have concentrated on external shocks to emerging economies: slower import growth in China and the United States, lower prices of primary commodities, higher global interest rates, reduced private capital flows to emerging economies, and, probably, downward pressure on emerging-market exchange rates. But one can argue that fiscal and monetary policies in emerging economies also need to be brought into the picture for at least three reasons.

First, if there is a diminished risk appetite for emerging-market securities, the behavior of fiscal and monetary policies in individual emerging economies might be one of the criteria by which investors decide how to apportion their pullback from that asset class. Second, if a debt crisis in one emerging economy does occur as a result of global plus country-specific shocks, contagion might take the form of penalizing other emerging economies with high debt levels and with large actual or prospective fiscal deficits. And third, the conduct of fiscal and monetary policy after the onset of more difficult global financial conditions could be either part of the solution to stabilizing growth in emerging economies or part of the problem in turning financial difficulties into a crisis. For those economies with relatively good reputations on fiscal and monetary policies, it is apt to be easier to conduct countercyclical policies than for those with poor track records.

In a recent paper, Goldstein makes a comprehensive effort to determine which emerging economies would face the greatest challenges in conducting fiscal and monetary policy during a period of deteriorating global financial conditions.[139] In ranking economies according to their vulnerabilities, the general presumption is that those economies with relatively low debt ratios and more favorable debt dynamics, more disciplined fiscal and monetary policies, a history of lower procyclicality for fiscal and monetary policy, lower volatility in growth and foreign trade, better inflation histories, less pressure to sterilize large capital inflows, an inflation-targeting framework in place, a larger cushion of international reserves, and a relatively sound domestic banking system face less adverse external pressures and have more room for maneuver in conducting fiscal and monetary policy.

Goldstein uses a set of thirty-five indicators to capture these influences on monetary and fiscal policies in emerging economies. The indicators include:

—Four measures of public and external debt,

—Three indicators of "debt intolerance,"[140]

—Ten indicators that relate to the sustainability of public and external debt, encompassing the recent trend in public debt ratios, measures of the primary balance in the budget, the ratio of the trade balance to GDP, various measures of real interest rates on public and external debt, ratios of interest payments to GDP and to government revenues, the recent rate of real economic growth, and an index of political stability,

—Measures of the variability of both real economic growth and the real exchange rate,

—An index of the procyclicality of fiscal policy,[141]

—Eight indicators relating to monetary policy, encompassing measures of recent inflation performance, the scale of recent capital inflows, the size of sterilization operations directed at capital inflows, the recent pace of domestic credit expansion, two measures of "excess" holdings of international reserves, and the presence or not of an inflation-targeting regime in the country,

—Seven indicators of banking system fragility, encompassing the change in real GDP growth between 2003–04 and projected for 2005–06, Moody's financial strength index, the ratio of nonperforming loans to total bank loans, the ratio of bank regulatory capital to risk-weighted assets, the ratio

139. Goldstein (2005b).

140. Reinhart, Rogoff, and Savastano (2003) define "debt intolerance" to mean the extreme duress that many emerging economies experience at debt levels that seem quite manageable by the standards of industrial countries.

141. As constructed by Kaminsky, Reinhart, and Vegh (2004).

Table 5-23. *Vulnerability to Different Transition Mechanisms*[a]

Bilateral trade	Primary commodity prices	Interest rates and capital flows	Exchange rate overvaluation	Fiscal and monetary policies
Hong Kong	Venezuela	Turkey	Czech Republic	Turkey
Singapore	Russia	Brazil	Hungary, Turkey	Argentina
Malaysia	Philippines	Argentina	Russia	Brazil
Venezuela	Chile	Hungary	Venezuela	Venezuela
Mexico	Singapore	Mexico	Poland	Hungary

a. Countries are ranked from top to bottom from most to least vulnerable.

of government debt to deposits in the banking system, and two measures constructed by Barth, Caprio, and Levine of regulatory limits on banking activities and of private sector monitoring of banks.[142]

Goldstein looks across this set of thirty-five fiscal and monetary policy indicators to see which economies appear most frequently in the top five vulnerability spots.[143] The answer is Turkey, Argentina, Brazil, Venezuela, Hungary, and Mexico. With the exception of Venezuela, these are the same economies that also head up the high-vulnerability list when we look at vulnerability to adverse global financial conditions, a factor that presumably reflects the importance of public and external debt positions in both sets of indicators as well as links between high inflation and high interest rates.

Summarizing the Vulnerability Rankings

Table 5-23 brings together the vulnerability rankings presented previously under the five transmission channels. The five (most vulnerable) economies are listed under each channel.

For exchange rates, only the overvaluation cases are presented (under the assumption that overvaluation problems are more pressing than undervaluation ones).[144] In terms of frequency of appearance in the table, Venezuela heads the hit parade, appearing in four of the five vulnerability channels;

---

142. Barth, Caprio, and Levine (2005). Goldstein (2005a) offers a more thorough description and analysis of these thirty-five indicators of pressures operating on fiscal and monetary policies in emerging economies.

143. Goldstein (2005b).

144. To determine the ordinal ranking for overvaluations, the three overvaluation measures listed in table 5-18 are averaged.

next in line are Turkey and Hungary, which each appear in three of the five channels. And the next tier of vulnerability is represented by Argentina, Brazil, Mexico, and Russia, which each appear in two of the five transmission channels. If the criterion is instead the number of appearances in the top-three vulnerability positions, then Turkey tops the list (appearing in that spot under three channels), followed by Argentina and Brazil (each with top-three vulnerability rankings under two channels).[145] Given the focus of this chapter on cross-country differences in vulnerability across various transmission channels, we do not think it is useful to push the conclusions about average vulnerability beyond that.

Concluding Remarks

In this chapter we have outlined a story in which an overlapping growth slowdown in China and the United States, along with a deterioration in global financial conditions linked to a disorderly correction of global payments imbalances, could put emerging markets on the threshold of a new financial crisis. We have emphasized that it makes a great deal of difference to emerging-market prospects if the U.S.–China slowdown is or is not accompanied both by a large increase in emerging-market interest rate spreads and by a large decline in private capital flows to them. A recent issue of the World Bank's *Global Development Finance* comes to a similar qualitative conclusion: it finds that a rise by 200 basis points in short- and long-term U.S. interest rates (relative to the baseline scenario) slows developing-country growth (again relative to the baseline) by 1 percentage point in each of 2005 and 2006.[146] But if that same rise in U.S. interest rates is accompanied by a return of emerging-market interest rate spreads to "normal" levels, then the decline in developing-country growth is much larger: more than 2 percentage points in 2005 and roughly 4.5 percent points in 2006 (relative to the baseline).

We have also tried to highlight the point that identifying those emerging economies most vulnerable to a crisis is not invariant either to the way in which the crisis unfolds or to the different characteristics of individual emerging economies themselves. Some emerging economies have strong

---

145. If the cutoff were instead the top seven economies under each transmission channel, then Venezuela and the Philippines lead the pack, appearing in four of the five channels.

146. World Bank (2005a).

bilateral export links with China, the United States, or both, while others do not. Some have a relatively high concentration of exports in those primary commodities where China or the United States could affect the world price, and others do not. Some have financing requirements and debt positions that make them quite sensitive to large increases in global interest rates and to large declines in private capital flows, while others are much less sensitive. Some have net foreign asset positions in foreign exchange, while others have net liability positions. Some have significant debt in foreign currencies other than the dollar; others do not. Some still have relatively serious currency mismatches or large real exchange rate misalignments to contend with, while others do not. Some have good monetary policy frameworks in place, have turned in very good inflation performance of late, and might well be able to take some countercyclical policy action if hit with a serious external shock; others do not, have not, and could not. Some have to carry the baggage of fragile banking systems, while others are much further along on banking reform. The various indicators included here represent a first pass at dealing with some of those cross-country differences.

But if the threat of a new emerging-market crisis is not something to be dismissed lightly, it is natural to ask what might be done to reduce the risk and to strengthen the forces of crisis prevention going forward.

Since our crisis story is linked to a disorderly correction of global payments imbalances, a good place to start on crisis prevention would be to make the payments-adjustment process more orderly and more effective. That entails at least three complementary sets of policy actions. In the United States, there needs to be a credible plan to reduce the structural budget deficit to less than 1 percent of GDP by 2010; there is no such plan on the table right now. Also, the U.S. Federal Reserve needs to continue with its ongoing tightening of monetary conditions so that growth in U.S. domestic demand is brought beneath the growth of output and stays there until the U.S. current account deficit is roughly half its present size. In Europe, the European Central Bank should be cautious in raising interest rates so that domestic demand in the EU can grow faster than output. In Asia, the imperative is to get more appreciation of key Asian currencies, especially the Chinese renminbi, so that the needed second wave of dollar depreciation can be both broadly distributed among currencies other than the dollar and large enough to perform its expenditure-switching function.

The emerging markets too still have plenty to do so that they are both better equipped to withstand a shift toward less benign global financing conditions and less likely to throw fat on the fire with their own country-specific difficulties. This means continuing to work toward reducing high public debt ratios and currency mismatches, taking action to remove large overvaluations and undervaluations of their real exchange rates (before the markets force such a change on them), persuading more emerging economies to adopt transparent frameworks for the conduct and evaluation of monetary policy, building deeper local bond markets, and increasing efforts to reduce the fragility of domestic banking systems.

The fact that (almost) everybody has heard this diagnosis and prescription before does not make it any less relevant.

References

Anderson, Jonathan. 2004a. "China Exposure Chartbook." Hong Kong: UBS Investment Research, October.

———. 2004b. "The New RMB Handbook." Hong Kong: UBS Investment Research, September.

———. 2005a. "The First Cracks in the Dam." Hong Kong: UBS Investment Research, March 21.

———. 2005b. "The One Number to Watch This Year." Hong Kong: UBS Investment Research, March 10.

Arora, Vivek, and Martin Cerisola. 2001. "How Does U.S. Monetary Policy Influence Sovereign Spreads in Emerging Markets?" *IMF Staff Papers* 48, no. 3: 3.

Asian Development Bank. 2004. "Economic Scenarios for Asia." In *Asian Development Outlook.* Manila.

Baily, Martin. 2003. "Persistent Dollar Swings and the U.S. Economy." In *Dollar Overvaluation and the World Economy,* edited by C. Fred Bergsten and John Williamson. Washington: Institute for International Economics.

Bank for International Settlements. 2004. *74th Annual Report.* Basel, June.

———. 2005. "Foreign Exchange Market Intervention in Emerging Markets: Motivation, Techniques, and Implications." BIS Paper 24. Basel, May.

Bank of England. 2004. *Financial Stability Review.* London, December.

Barth, James, Gerard Caprio, and Ross Levine. 2005 forthcoming. *Rethinking Bank Regulation and Supervision: Till Angels Govern.* Cambridge University Press.

Berg, Andrew, Eduardo Borensztein, and Catherine Pattillo. 2004. "Assessing Early Warning Systems: How Have They Worked in Practice?" IMF Working Paper 04/52. Washington: International Monetary Fund.

Bernanke, Ben. 2005. "The Global Saving Glut and the U.S. Current Account Deficit." Sandridge Lecture, Virginia Association of Economics, Richmond, Va., March 10.

Borensztein, Eduardo, Marcos Chamon, Olivier Jeanne, Paulo Mauro, and Jeromin Zettelmeyer. 2004. "Sovereign Debt Structure and Crisis Prevention." Washington: International Monetary Fund, July.

Bulir, Ales, and Katerina Smidkova. 2005. "Exchange Rates in the New EU Accession Countries: What Have We Learned from the Forerunners?" IMF Working Paper 05/27. Washington: International Monetary Fund, February.

Bureau of Economic Analysis. 2005. National Income and Product Accounts Tables. Washington: U.S. Department of Commerce, March.

Calvo, Guillermo, Leo Leiderman, and Carmen Reinhart. 1993. "Capital Inflows and Real Exchange Rate Appreciation in Latin America: The Role of External Factors." *IMF Staff Papers* 40, no. 1: 108–51.

Calvo, Guillermo, and Ernesto Talvi. 2005. "Sudden Stop, Financial Factors, and Economic Collapse in Latin America: Learning from Argentina and Chile." NBER Working Paper 11153. Cambridge, Mass.: National Bureau of Economic Research, February.

Caprio, Gerard, and Daniela Klingebiel. 1996. "Bank Insolvency: Cross-Country Experience." Washington: World Bank.

Cline, William. 2005 forthcoming. *The United States as a Debtor Nation: Prospects, Policies.* Washington: Institute for International Economics.

Committee on the Global Financial System. 2005. "Stress Testing at Major Financial Institutions: Survey Results and Practice." Bank for International Settlements, Basel.

Croke, Hilary, Steven Kamin, and Sylvain Leduc. 2005. "Financial Market Developments and Economic Activity during Current Account Adjustments in Industrial Countries." International Finance Discussion Paper 827. Washington: Board of Governors of the Federal Reserve System, February.

De Rato, Rodrigo. 2005. "Correcting Global Imbalances: Avoiding the Blame Game." Remarks before the Foreign Policy Association, New York, February 23.

Deutsche Bank. 2005. "Emerging Markets Monthly." London, March 10.

Dooley, Michael, David Folkerts-Landau, and Peter Garber. 2003. "An Essay on the Revived Bretton Woods System," NBER Working Paper 9971. Cambridge, Mass.: National Bureau of Economic Research, September.

———. 2004a. "Direct Investment, Rising Real Wages, and the Absorption of Excess Labor in the Periphery." NBER Working Paper 10626. Cambridge, Mass.: National Bureau of Economic Research, July.

———. 2004b. "The Revived Bretton Woods System: The Effects of Periphery Intervention and Reserve Management on Interest Rates and Exchange Rates in the Center Countries." NBER Working Paper 10332. Cambridge, Mass.: National Bureau of Economic Research, March.

———. 2004c. "The U.S. Current Account Deficit and Economic Development: Collateral for a Total Return Swap." NBER Working Paper 10727. Cambridge, Mass.: National Bureau of Economic Research, August.

Eichengreen, Barry. 2004. "Global Imbalances and the Lessons of Bretton Woods." NBER Working Paper 10497. Cambridge, Mass.: National Bureau of Economic Research, May.

Eichengreen, Barry, and Ashoka Mody. 1998. "What Explains Changing Spreads on EM Debt: Fundamentals or Market Sentiment?" NBER Working Paper 6408. Cambridge, Mass.: National Bureau of Economic Research.

Erceg, Christopher, Luca Guerrieri, and Christopher Gust. 2005. "Expansionary Fiscal Shocks and the Trade Deficit." International Finance Discussion Paper 05/825. Washington: Board of Governors of the Federal Reserve System, January.

Ferrucci, Gianluigi, Valerie Herzberg, Farouk Soussa, and Ashley Taylor. 2004. "Understanding Capital Flows to Emerging Market Economies." *Bank of England Financial Stability Review* 16 (June): 89–97.

Frankel, Jeffrey, and Andy Rose. 1996. "Exchange Rate Crises in Emerging Markets." *Journal of International Economics* 41, no. 3: 341–68.

Frankel, Jeffrey, and Nouriel Roubini. 2000. "Industrial Country Policies." In *Economic and Financial Crises in Emerging Market Economies,* edited by Martin Feldstein. National Bureau of Economic Research and University of Chicago Press.

Gai, Prasanna, and Nicholas Vause. 2004. "Risk Appetite: Concept and Measurement." *Bank of England Financial Stability Review* 17 (December): 127–36.

Geithner, Timothy. 2005. "Key Challenges in Risk Management." Speech before RMA/Risk Business KRI's Global Operational Risk Forum, January 13.

Goldman Sachs. 2005a. *Global FX Monthly Analyst.* New York, March.

———. 2005b. "Global Risks from Liquidity-Fueled Emerging Markets?" *Goldman Sachs Global Economics Weekly* 05/09 (March 9).

Goldstein, Morris. 1998. *The Asian Financial Crisis: Causes, Crises, and Systemic Implications.* Washington: Institute for International Economics, June.

———. 2004. "Adjusting China's Exchange Rate Policies." IIE Working Paper 04/1. Washington: Institute for International Economics, June.

———. 2005a. "The International Financial Architecture." In *The United States and the World Economy,* edited by C. Fred Bergsten. Washington: Institute for International Economics.

———. 2005b. "What Might the Next Emerging Market Financial Crisis Look Like?" IIE Working Paper 05-7. Washington: Institute for International Economics, July.

Goldstein, Morris, Graciela Kaminsky, and Carmen Reinhart. 2000. *Assessing Financial Vulnerability: An Early Warning System for Emerging Markets.* Washington: Institute for International Economics, June.

Goldstein, Morris, and Nicholas Lardy. 2004a. "Don't Hail China's Soft Landing Too Soon." *Financial Times,* October 6.

———. 2004b. "What Kind of Landing for the Chinese Economy?" IIE Economics Policy Brief 04/7. Washington: Institute for International Economics, November.

———. 2005. "China's Role in the Revived Bretton Woods System: A Case of Mistaken Identity." IIE Working Paper 05/2. Washington: Institute for International Economics, March.

Goldstein, Morris, and Philip Turner. 2004. *Controlling Currency Mismatches in Emerging Markets.* Washington: Institute for International Economics.

IMF (International Monetary Fund). 1994. *International Capital Markets Report,* led by Morris Goldstein and David Folkerts-Landau. Washington, September.

———. 2003. *World Economic Outlook.* Washington, September.

———. 2004a. *Global Financial Stability Report.* Washington, September.

———. 2004b. *World Economic Outlook.* Washington, April.

———. 2004c. *World Economic Outlook.* Washington, September.

———. 2005. *World Economic Outlook.* Washington, April.

———. Various years. *International Financial Statistics.* Washington.

Institute for International Finance. 2005. "Capital Flows to Emerging Market Economies." Washington, January.

J. P. Morgan. 2005. *Emerging Markets Debt and Fiscal Indicators.* New York, January.

Kaminsky, Graciela, Saul Lizondo, and Carmen Reinhart. 1998. "Leading Indicators of Currency Crises." *IMF Staff Papers* 45, no. 1: 1–48.

Kaminsky, Graciela, and Carmen Reinhart. 1999. "The Twin Crises: Causes of Banking and Balance-of-Payments Problems." *American Economic Review* 51, no. 1: 473–500.

Kaminsky, Graciela, Carmen Reinhart, and Carlos Vegh. 2004. "When It Rains, It Pours: Procyclical Capital Flows and Macroeconomic Policies." NBER Working Paper 10780. Cambridge, Mass.: National Bureau of Economic Research, September.

Kumar, Manmohan, and Avinash Persaud. 2002. "Pure Contagion and Investors' Shifting Risk Appetite: Analytical Issues and Empirical Evidence." *International Finance* 5, no. 3: 401–36.

Lachman, Desmond. 2005. "Not in Tango." *Financial Times,* March 28, 2005.

Lardy, Nicholas. 2005. "China: The Great New Economic Challenge?" In *The United States and the World Economy,* edited by C. Fred Bergsten. Washington: Institute for International Economics.

Lindgren, Carl, Gillian Garcia, and Matthew Saal. 1996. *Bank Soundness and Macroeconomic Policy.* Washington: International Monetary Fund.

Makin, John. 2004. "China: The Unplannable Planned Economy." AEI Economic Outlook. Washington: American Enterprise Institute, June.

Manasse, Paolo, Nouriel Roubini, and Axel Schimmelpfennig. 2003. "Predicting Sovereign Debt Crises." IMF Working Paper 03/221. Washington: International Monetary Fund, November.

Mann, Catherine. 2004. "Managing Exchange Rates: Achievement of Global Re-balancing or Evidence of Global Co-dependency?" *Business Economics* (July): 20–29.

Mussa, Michael. 2005. "Sustaining Global Growth while Reducing External Imbalances." In *The United States and the World Economy,* edited by C. Fred Bergsten. Washington: Institute for International Economics.

National Bureau of Statistics of China. 2004. *China Statistical Yearbook 2004.* China Statistics Press.

Reinhart, Carmen, and Vincent Reinhart. 2001. "What Hurts Most? G-3 Exchange Rate or Interest Rate Volatility?" NBER Working Paper 8535. Cambridge, Mass.: National Bureau of Economic Research, October.

Reinhart, Carmen, Kenneth Rogoff, and Miguel Savastano. 2003. "Debt Intolerance." NBER Working Paper 2003. Cambridge, Mass.: National Bureau of Economic Research, August.

Roubini, Nouriel, and Brad Setser. 2005. "Will the Bretton Woods 2 Regime Unravel Soon? The Risk of a Hard Landing in 2005–2006." Paper written for the symposium "The Revived Bretton Woods System: A New Paradigm for Asian Development?" Federal Reserve Bank of San Francisco, San Francisco, February 4.

Setser, Brad. 2005. "Bernanke's Global Savings Glut." Brad Setser's web log (www.roubiniglobal.com/setser/archives/2005/05/index.html [May 21, 2005]).

Simpfendorfer, Ben. 2004. "China and the World Economy." New York: J. P. Morgan, April.

Stracke, Christian. 2005. "Brazil: Pre-History of a Currency Crisis." *Credit Insights,* May 8.

Summers, Lawrence. 2004. "The United States and the Global Adjustment Process." Stavos Niarchos Lecture, Institute for International Economics, Washington, March 23.

Truman, Edwin. 2005a. "The Euro and Prospects for Policy Coordination." In *The Euro at Five: Ready for a Global Role?* edited by Adam Posen. Washington: Institute for International Economics.

———. 2005b. "A Revived Bretton Woods System: Implications for Europe and the United States." Paper presented at the symposium "The Revived Bretton Woods System: A Paradigm for Asian Development?" Federal Reserve Bank of San Francisco, San Francisco, February 4.

U.S. Office of the Comptroller of the Currency. 2004. *Bank Derivatives Report* (Fourth Quarter).

U.S. Treasury. 2005. "Report to Congress on International Economic and Exchange Rate Policies." Washington (www.treas.gov/press/releases/reports/js2448report.pdf [May 17, 2005]).

Verleger, Philip. 2005. "The Oil Price Increase: Permanent Structural Change or Transitory Bubble?" *Petroleum Economics Monthly* 12, no. 2 (February).

World Bank. 2004. *World Development Report 2004.* Oxford University Press.

———. 2005a. *Global Development Finance: Mobilizing Finance and Managing Vulnerability.* Washington, April.

———. 2005b. *Global Economic Prospects.* Washington, March.

Xie, Andy. 2005. "China: Searching for a Soft Landing." Morgan Stanley (www.morganstanley.com/GEFdata/digest/20050201-tue.html [February 1, 2005]).

Financial Risks Ahead

Views from the Private Sector

O ne of the unique characteristics of the annual World Bank–Brookings conference is that it brings together academic scholars and practition- ers from the "real world" to discuss developments in emerging-markets finance. This year's conference featured a panel of three practitioners with expertise in the field: David Wyss, chief economist of Standard & Poor's; Don Hanna, managing director and global head of emerging markets eco- nomic and market analysis of Citigroup; and Khalid Sheikh, senior vice pres- ident of ABN Amro Bank. A summary of their views and their responses to some questions from the participants follows.

David Wyss led off the panel by noting that the general ratings environ- ment is currently very favorable. Country ratings are at their historical best. Of the 107 countries being rated, more countries are rated investment grade than ever before; a record number of countries received upgrades in 2004; and few country governments have defaulted on their debt. Rating emerging economies is a relatively new phenomenon. But with ratings, more countries have access to the international bond market. More than half of the rated countries now issue investment-grade debt.

Wyss acknowledged that ratings are not perfect, but he contended that they still are fairly reliable. For example, over the long run, CCC bonds have a 45 percent default rate, whereas A bonds default less than 2 percent of the time. The default rate rises sharply as ratings decline. Investors currently tend to view lending money very favorably, because the economic environment is generally healthy, they have short memories, and they are searching for higher yields in a world of low interest rates. All the major industrial countries (with the exception of Japan) have bond yields of around 2 to 3 percent, which is a very benign environment. Growth rates have not displayed the same degree of convergence, with a noticeable split between high-growth "Anglosphere" countries and low-growth continental European countries. With respect to Europe in particular, concerns remain over the extent and number of the long-term unemployed. Wyss believes that many of them will be difficult to reintegrate into the work force.

The benign interest rate environment may be coming to an end, with the Federal Reserve's steady lifting of short-term interest rates. However, Wyss expected the "Fed funds" rate to be between 4 and 4.5 percent by the end of 2005. Wyss also believed that the record-low yields on speculative-grade bonds were not sustainable. Normal default rates on such bonds are 3.5 percent, which Wyss argued is inconsistent with the 3 percent yield spread on those bonds (relative to safe government bonds) prevalent at the time of the conference.

Wyss pointed to another anomaly: sovereign debt is being priced at interest rates that are similar to those on speculative corporate bonds. Sovereigns used to have a small advantage, the disappearance of which could indicate decreased awareness of default risk.

Wyss suggested that, despite media stories to the contrary, the U.S. budget deficit is not out of line with the deficits of other industrial countries, taking account of growing social security obligations. Indeed, Japan is already beginning to run into pension financing problems.

He was much more concerned about the U.S. current account deficit, both because it is larger than the fiscal deficit and because he does not see what mechanism will lead to a substantial reduction of the trade gap. Normally, trade deficits are reflected in exchange rate declines, which already has happened, with the dollar falling against the euro. But in other countries that are growing slowly and where much of that growth is from exports, governments have intervened in foreign exchange markets to keep their currencies cheap relative to the dollar. This exchange rate policy began when the United States had a fiscal surplus and has continued now that the United States has a budget deficit. The essential problem is that every other country agrees that the U.S. deficit is too large, but no country seems to want to allow its currency to appreciate and thereby curtail its exports.

The U.S. trade deficit may, in fact, continue longer than most people expect. The U.S. state of New York, for example, has had a trade deficit with the rest of the United States for 200 years, with no signs of stopping. Furthermore, countries can keep their currencies undervalued, with nothing external forcing them to stop. Wyss noted that if countries are trying to support the dollar, they are doing so by selling their own currencies into the market to buy dollars and accumulating U.S. liabilities, public and private. When are the central banks in these countries going to stop this accumulation? Moreover, there are some other anomalies. Wyss pointed to the Japanese purchase of dollars, in particular, which normally would be inflationary. But Japan has seen deflation for the past decade. So, from the Japanese standpoint, buying dollars with yen has been a win-win proposition.

The other way that trade imbalances usually stop is that the country with the trade deficit complains. Although the United States is complaining about trade issues, the counterpart to the United States' current account deficit is that it is investing more than it saves, and Japan is financing much of this. So it is in the interest of the United States to let this process continue. In effect, another country's central bank is monetizing the U.S. trade deficit. Meanwhile, the level of investment in the United States is contributing to the fact that productivity has been rising more rapidly in the United States than in either Europe or Japan.

Of course, the United States and the rest of world still run the risk that this process will come to an abrupt halt: other countries at some point no longer will be so willing to sell their own currencies to prop up the dollar. At that point, the United States will be forced to save more and invest less. The result will be higher U.S. bond yields (perhaps much higher), a weaker dollar, and perhaps a recession in the United States and elsewhere.

Don Hanna also addressed global financial vulnerabilities, beginning with the sustainability of the U.S. current account deficit and its financing, but from a somewhat different viewpoint. He felt that non-U.S. central banks that were buying dollars were doing so out of their own free will and presumably making rational decisions. Indeed, there is a good argument for these dollar purchases in countries like Malaysia, where exports are more than 100 percent of GDP, and in China, where exports are around 37 percent of GDP.

Only a change in their domestic economies would make them change their behavior, and inflation is the only likely phenomenon that could put enough pressure on them to stop deflating their currencies. However, inflation is low in most of those countries. Indeed, by various measures, inflation in Asia over the last four years has barely moved, despite higher prices for oil and other commodities.

Hanna also noted the contention that foreign central banks eventually may stop their dollar purchases in order to avoid a large capital loss due to a sudden and sharp decline in the value of the dollar. In the short term, however, countries like China, where domestic interest rates are low, are making money by purchasing higher-yielding U.S. treasury bonds. Still, China's international reserves represent almost a third of its GDP, so a revaluation could cause capital losses in the future.

Hanna felt that, overall, Asia has better regulatory supervision, better current account status, and lower inflation than it did before the 1997–98 crisis, which supports the higher credit ratings assigned to debt issued in Asian economies. He questioned, however, whether information transparency and the legal framework have improved. For example, the Doing Business database of the World Bank shows that East Asia has below-average levels of disclosure, despite high-disclosure areas in a few countries in the region— Hong Kong and Singapore. East Asia also has weak mechanisms for collecting collateral and creditor information for the financial intermediaries.

Korea has been aggressive and successful at improving its supervisory environment and improving property rights. In China, however, enforcing a contract costs 25 percent of its value on average. It costs 125 percent of the value in Indonesia. In contrast, the corresponding figure in Korea and Taiwan is just 5 percent.

Hanna noted that some work has already been done on analyzing which financially related issues are easiest to tackle. It is very difficult to get well-functioning courts in place. It can be easier to create a culture of disclosure and compliance if the correct incentives are set up. Creating rules is easy, although they may be difficult to implement. Even China has some rules about property rights. It is easy to import accountants and lawyers, but difficult to establish true information transparency. Change is possible, but it is unlikely to occur quickly.

Finally, Hanna observed that the marginal efficiency of investment in China is decreasing. Money is still cheap, and investment is forecast to rise to 50 percent of GDP, but much of that is being wasted. This will be a serious problem that undoubtedly will cause a slowdown at some point, but that Hanna believed was some ways off in the future.

Khalid Sheikh expressed concern that some unforeseen trigger could "turn the tide" on rising ratings and economic growth in emerging markets. Indeed, he saw evidence of some nervousness in the market, which, combined with some bad news and the typical herd-like behavior of investors, could lead to the much feared downturn.

Sheikh noted that many Asian countries already have become very dependent on China, which could prove dangerous if China's growth slows significantly. By the same token, the excessive dependence of many Eastern European economies on Germany has hurt those economies as German growth has slowed.

Meanwhile, the countries that have been attracting large inflows of foreign capital have had difficulty sterilizing those inflows (which is necessary to avoid undue expansion of the domestic money supply). Many countries still have excessive public debt, much of which is concentrated among banks. Thus any untoward event that triggers a downturn could easily be magnified by a downturn among banks.

Discussion. Morris Goldstein argued that Hanna did not take into account the effect of lower exports from China should the United States put import restrictions on Chinese goods. This would cost China much more than currency appreciation would. Goldstein added that China's low inflation was attributable in part to administrative controls, which can be costly and lead to inefficiencies.

Hanna responded that, in his view, there was nothing inherently wrong or illegal with having a fixed exchange rate and that a nominal exchange rate is not equivalent to a real exchange rate. He agreed that Chinese administrative controls of inflation have costs, and, as a result, he sees further inflationary pressure in China in the future. In fact, Chinese officials want to lower investment, and, to do that, they need a higher interest rate—much higher than rates in the United States. This will probably happen slowly, however, because Chinese government policy usually moves slowly.

David Wyss agreed with Hanna on the economics, but not the politics, of the United States–China trade situation. The U.S. trade deficit with China may look larger than it really is, but it remains an attractive target for protectionist U.S. politicians, especially because China does not have fully open markets. Khalid Sheikh commented that U.S. protectionism would both slow growth in that country and inspire retaliatory Chinese action.

In response to a question, Hanna did not agree with the argument that a country cannot control both its interest and exchange rates. Right now, Chinese reserves are only a fifth of the money supply. China's size makes its reserve situation more manageable. More speculative money may arrive, but speculation on revaluation has existed for a long time without forcing a major revaluation of the yuan. The current account surplus may continue to rise, but that may have more effect on the rest of Asia than on the United States. Hanna also noted that, according to one study by Federal Reserve economists, only about 20 percent of exchange rate movements get passed through to final product prices. As a result, even revaluation of the yuan may have relatively little impact on consumer behavior.

Hanna observed, however, that a real exchange rate revaluation already could be under way. Coastal China is seeing labor shortages, which are driving up wages. As this process continues there and eventually in the rest of the country, the government will feel greater pressure to revalue its exchange rate in an effort to rein in inflation.

Wyss noted that the reserve accumulation in China will continue if China is able to keep sterilizing the inflows. He added that many commentators underestimate American saving because net worth has been rising faster than national income account saving, which is the same thing as saving from the perspective of individual Americans (although it does not appear in the national accounts).

Sheikh said that although revaluation of the yuan probably would not make a large economic impact, it would be an important political gesture that would reinforce market stability. In response to a question, he said that ABN Amro does take into account World Bank and International Monetary Fund actions in making lending decisions, because the actions of these institutions lend credence to governance issues and political commitment to reform.

Scott Bugie, managing director of financial services, Standard and Poor's, asked the panelists how banks are diversifying their portfolios against the different crisis scenarios presented at the conference. Hanna responded that the sorts of possible downturns already discussed are not the baseline forecast for Citigroup, but that they still are limiting Citigroup's exposure to currencies where imbalances present strong risk. Hanna added that Citigroup also tries to limit excessive exposure to particular sectors and countries as a general part of risk management. Sheikh said that ABN Amro has similar internal risk limits and conducts extensive stress testing of its portfolio.

In response to a question from the floor on ratings, Wyss said that the ratings agencies share a certain sense of myopia because their ratings are based on present financial conditions. He suggested that Argentina might see its ratings rise right after defaulting on some of its loans (as it has since the conference), because it is in a better position to service its remaining debt. Any true myopia might be due to the fact that many defaults have political causes as much as economic causes and that the politics do not change as fast as the economics do.

GERARD CAPRIO
PATRICK HONOHAN

7

Starting over Safely

Rebuilding Banking Systems

When the financial crisis breaks, the first priority of policymakers is containment. In that acute phase, the urgent may displace the important in the scramble for survival. Already, however, the decisions taken can determine much of the loss allocation and have a long-lasting and hard-to-unwind influence on moral hazard through the expectations and perceptions of market participants. Once the acute phase is over and the resolution phase has begun, policymakers tend to be more aware of the longer-term implications of their actions, even if they see themselves as cleaning up a mess rather than setting the financial system on a more secure and effective foundation.

In many cases a lasting recovery should also include a fundamental reshaping of the financial system, in particular when financial sector distortions have played a major role in causing or contributing to the cost of the crisis. This chapter addresses the stage of recovery that follows the acute phase of the crisis. In other words, it asks what the key priorities for financial regulatory authorities should be when the panic has subsided and the future design of the system is the focus, rather than merely its survival. How can the system be best protected from future vulnerability to crisis, while at the same time ensuring that it delivers the services needed for growth (and is there a poten-

The authors would like to thank Liliana Rojas-Suárez, James Hanson, and participants at the conference for their comments.

tial conflict between these two goals)? Many of the messages of this chapter are valid even for policymakers who are not actively managing a "morning-after" situation but are simply concerned with making their financial system more robust and better able to serve the needs of the economy.

The first section describes the experience of postcrisis countries in the past decade or so, highlighting distinctive features of the resolution process and examining some objective, quantitative indicators of overall postcrisis economic performance and changes in assets, liabilities, capital, and owner-ship of the banking system. Postcontainment policy calls for both resolu-tion and infrastructure-building work; these are dealt with in the second and third sections, respectively.

Over the past few years a degree of technical consensus has emerged over many elements of what constitutes good policy in the resolution phase, and this has been reflected in resolution practice, with deviations often attribut-able to implementation shortcomings or political interference. But there are several open questions and disagreements, or at least differences of empha-sis, as to what choice of resolution policy will place the banking system in the best possible position going forward. The second section highlights two of the most important of these, relating to capital and ownership, the treat-ment of delinquent assets, and their replacement in the banks' balance sheet.

Bearing in mind the policy challenges emerging from recent postcrisis experience, the third section suggests several general lessons for placing the postcrisis financial system on a more secure medium-term basis. These fall under three main headings:

—The need to create an active but carefully balanced engagement with global finance, exploiting the benefits of opening up to reputable foreign banks and foreign equity listings as well as avoiding a buildup of excessive exchange risk in the economy (for nonfinancial corporates as well as for banks). Of course, this is especially important for smaller economies.

—The need to create the conditions for market discipline to work well. This is important given the limitations of official supervision (and, in partic-ular, the danger of overstretching local capacity by introducing the complex-ities of the Basel II capital regime, which for many countries could increase rather than decrease the risks of a future crisis).

—The need to promote a broader range of financial services with greater reach (small and microenterprises, start-up finance, households, and so forth). This agenda, in particular, requires not only a coherent policy on such matters as macro stability, privatization, taxation, and the building of information and legal infrastructures, but also efforts to avoid crowding out and to remove the distortions that hamper the deepening of equity-based finance.

A warning is in order: anyone who claims to be able to establish a system that is immune to financial crises either is wrong or will do so by eliminating intermediation. But the measures discussed in this chapter can reasonably be expected to reduce the risk of crisis and, should one occur, its fiscal and real economic cost.

How Has the Recovery Phase Panned Out in Practice?

Contrary to a common view, not all banking crises are the same, but neither are they all different. Episodes of systemic banking distress can be traced to one of three distinct syndromes. First, some of the banking crises reflected unstable macroeconomic conditions and were triggered mainly by a collapse of confidence in the fiscal stance and exchange rate regime. The resulting collapse of the banking system typically amplified the macroeconomic crisis, with a positive feedback loop onto banking conditions themselves. But even before the collapse in confidence, the banking system was in a weak position, often reflecting the same widespread overconfidence that had supported an unsustainable macroeconomic stance for too long. Indeed, although devaluations worsened the situation because banks or their borrowers were unhedged, much of the weakness of the banking portfolio and much of the loss predated the economic downturn and were revealed only when the macroeconomic situation deteriorated to the point where the losses could no longer be hidden. To different degrees, the cases of Mexico (1994), East Asia (1997),[1] Russia (1998), and Argentina (2001) can be placed in this category. In most of these cases (and more than in earlier episodes), banks left themselves in speculative or unhedged foreign exchange positions, often linked with exposure to national government debt; this accelerated and amplified the collapse.

A second group of crises reflects the unraveling of prior government policies that effectively imposed unviable lending obligations on the banking sys-

---

1. These countries did not start out with particularly weak macroeconomic and fiscal conditions, but they were reliant on sustaining the confidence of external investors. The failure of finance companies in Thailand triggered an outflow of funds from that country, and when this resulted in depreciation of the Thai baht, a contagion effect swept through the region. The currencies of Indonesia and Korea, in particular, collapsed, worsening and revealing the weak position of banks and corporate borrowers in those countries.

tem. The largest case by far is China, where government arranged from the early 1990s for the four large state-owned commercial banks to provide cash-flow support for numerous public enterprises. The resulting balance sheet deficiencies gave rise, beginning in 1998, to extensive bank recapitalization efforts by the Chinese authorities that, so far, account for 25 percent of China's GDP. Of course, there was no open crisis in China: the large state-owned banks receive the full backing of the government. However, the size of the recapitalizations required means that this too must be regarded as a systemic banking failure. State-controlled banks in Vietnam (where there have been sizable recent recapitalizations of the large state-owned banks) and Zambia (whose main bank has, like those of many African countries, recently been recapitalized and privatized to foreign owners) also exemplify this pattern.

A third group is associated chiefly with management failures, including corruption, that no doubt are attributable, in part, to the prevailing incentive and discipline structures. Outright fraud was at the center of a number of systemic crises, notably in Venezuela (1994) and the Dominican Republic (2003), and was present in several other poorly regulated and opaque banking systems as well.[2] Several such cases involved the use of "diverted deposits" fraud, where most of the deposits placed by customers were simply not registered on the bank's official books. The very high loss-given-default ratios noted in banking failures in many other countries also raise questions about the degree to which these loans were originally made in good faith and with an intention to repay.

The resolution strategy needs to be adapted to the type of crisis being experienced. This can be a subtle task. For instance, several transition economies in Eastern Europe and Central Asia have experienced a complex mixture of inherited quasi-fiscal losses at state-owned banks and the results of fraud or imprudent lending in the volatile early years of transition by private or privatized banks.

Four Distinctive Features of the Resolution Phase

Turning from the pattern of causes to the pattern of cleanups, it is worth highlighting four not-so-obvious features of recent experience that need to be kept in mind when considering policy choices for the postcrisis era.

---

2. Barth, Caprio, and Levine (2006) show that complaints of banking corruption are highest in countries that adopt overly prescriptive and autocratic regulatory style without sufficient use of transparency and market discipline.

First, the distribution of loan losses and other sources of capital deficiency was not uniform from bank to bank. Although the entire system was under water in a few cases—mostly in very poor countries—not all banks failed. Indeed, in most crises only a moderate fraction of the banks were found to be insolvent. This suggests that crises should not normally be seen as the result of overwhelming forces that would have destroyed any bank no matter how well managed; as such, it points to the continued importance of private sector incentives and market discipline in strengthening the future resilience of the system.

Second, resolution efforts had to address both privately owned and state-owned banks. While the pattern of large capital deficiencies at state-owned banks was already familiar from the experience of transition countries in the early 1990s, as well as from the widespread (but unspectacular)[3] distress in many African countries, several of the more recent high-velocity crises displayed particularly heavy losses at government-owned banks. State-owned banks accounted for about half or more of the total costs of fiscal resolution in Indonesia (1997–98), at least as large as their share in the total assets of the system;[4] in Turkey by 2002, the share of state-owned banks in total resolution costs was just over half (well above their one-third share in the system's assets), mostly attributable to "duty losses" (see box 7-1). In addition, the capital deficiencies created by the asymmetric "pesification" in Argentina in 2002 can be attributed to a form of directed credit subsidy.

Third, information about the extent and incidence of losses among banks often evolved slowly. Rarely do we observe a one-shot resolution and recapitalization.[5] More often there are several waves, each separated by some months. (The different waves are often dealt with using different resolution techniques. This may reflect a learning process by the authorities or differences in the successive waves of banks that come to the point of resolution.) This shows how difficult it is for regulators to determine with precision a bank's capital (often negative) and calls into question the practical realism of some policy recommendations, especially those calling for speed and pre-

3. The African systemic failures were not as conspicuous because the banks were not relying on mobile wholesale funds. As a result, the typical symptoms were bank illiquidity, limited lending capacity, and repeated recapitalizations by the fiscal authorities.

4. Batunanggar (2002).

5. De Luna Martínez (2000) contrasts the gradualist approach of Mexico with what he characterizes as a big-bang approach in Korea. Even Korea has taken its time completing the resolution (see also Scott 2002). The interaction between delayed recognition and resolution in Bulgaria and the slide into hyperinflation are described in Enoch, Gulde, and Hardy (2002).

Box 7-1. *The Complexity of Modern Banking Crises: Turkey, 2000–01*
The Turkish crisis illustrates several distinctive features of the recent crises. Already
in late 2000 liquidity and profitability were severely strained. For one thing, the large
state-owned banks, accounting for about one-third of the system, were quite illiquid,
reflecting an inherited and accumulating condition of "duty losses" (old claims on
the government that resulted from loans that had been made by the banks at the
behest of government, had not been repaid, and on which unpaid interest was accru-
ing at very high rates). Second, lengthy delays in implementing legislation for an
independent regulatory agency meant that, when it was finally implemented in 1999,
five failing banks were quickly intervened by SDIF, the deposit guarantee agency,
adding to three already on its books. These had an estimated capital deficiency of
$6 billion but continued to operate without recapitalization, resulting in much
higher ultimate costs. Third, a lengthy period of high nominal interest rates had generated an uncompetitive banking environment in which large spreads encouraged an
accretion of excessive operating costs.

The macroeconomic disinflation program initiated in late 1999, entailing a
crawling-peg exchange rate regime, resulted in a sharp fall in nominal interest rates that
had the effect of tightening competitive conditions and interest margins in banking; as
a result, banks sought to cover their operating expenses by speculative plays, such as
increasing their uncovered foreign exchange position, borrowing in foreign exchange,
and on-lending in local currency at a nominal spread that was insufficient to compensate for the depreciation that followed abandonment of the crawling peg. One medium-
size bank (Demir, the ninth largest), having established a highly speculative position in
government securities, failed to meet its obligations in the interbank market in November 2000, triggering a jump in interest rates to 1,900 percent before it was intervened
by SDIF and a blanket deposit guarantee was announced. Subsequently, political
uncertainty placed pressure on the exchange rate peg, and interbank interest rates
jumped to 6,200 percent in February 2001, before resulting in a currency collapse. The
associated fall of almost 20 percent of GNP in 2001 further worsened loan performance. By March 2001, SDIF had intervened in a total of thirteen banks.

There was also "a high incidence of fraud and criminal activity on the part of
shareholders and managers" (World Bank 2001). In mid-2003, well into the resolution phase, a further major setback was experienced when Imar Bank failed, revealing understated deposits on the order of $5 billion, almost ten times the reported
level (World Bank 2004). Imar had long been on the banking watch list and had even
had a regulator appointed as a board member with veto power during part of the crisis period (Fort and Hayward 2004).

Total fiscal costs of the crisis (including the accumulated "duty losses" of about
$19 billion) were $50 billion, or 34 percent of GDP (Pazarbasioglu 2003; Steinherr,
Tukel, and Ucer 2004).

cision either in precrisis actions (so-called prompt corrective actions) or in postcontainment resolution policy. Such uncertainty about the value and recoverability of loan portfolios also highlights the difficulty of reestablishing lending confidence.

Fourth, a sharp currency depreciation was often in the background, influencing the timing, nature, and scale of the recapitalization. Although its role as a trigger of bank failure is discussed more often, whether because of direct or indirect exposure of banks to foreign exchange risk, deep exchange rate collapses, with their partial knock-on effects on local prices, also reduced the real value of *local* currency liabilities. This served to offset the decline in economic activity, making it easier than it otherwise would have been for borrowers to repay. Devaluation in these circumstances tended to improve the country's international economic competitiveness, speeding the recovery of output and employment. And where government stepped in to compensate the depositors of failed banks, the real value of this compensation was lower because of the currency devaluation, thereby lowering the overall real fiscal costs of the crisis. Devaluation also helped recovery in more complex ways.[6] Compulsory conversion of foreign currency deposits at off-market rates following a devaluation was a feature in several countries, including Mexico (1982), Russia (1998), and the well-known case of Argentina (2002).[7]

Postcrisis Systemic Performance

Postcrisis macroeconomic and financial sector performance was astonishingly varied in the past decade, reflecting the varied causes and severity of the forty-two crises documented even in that limited period. Figures 7-1 to 7-6 compare conditions before and after these banking crises in the countries for which data are available.[8] Some general trends can be detected, but they only apply as averages, around which there is much variation.

---

6. An interesting example is the case of Russia, where exchange rate depreciation during the September 1998 moratorium allowed banks to settle frozen ruble liabilities arising from earlier forward foreign exchange transactions at favorable rates (Steinherr 2004).

7. Gelpern (2004).

8. Each country for which a systemic crisis is documented in the World Bank's database (Caprio and others 2005) as having started since 1994 is included. This gives forty-two crises in thirty-eight countries and includes cases of systemwide insolvency of state-owned banks that did not result in open distress. The comparison is made between conditions just before the onset of the crisis and the latest available data. Specifically, except where stated, for each country the data are for the last full year before the onset of the crisis as recorded in the database and compared with 2003 or the most recent date for which the data were available in *International Financial Statistics* at the time of writing (IMF various years).

GDP growth often slowed following crisis, especially if we ignore the transition economies, as seen in figure 7-1 (which shows a simple comparison of mean GDP growth in the three years before the crisis broke with the mean growth rate in the years beginning one year after the crisis broke). Some cases—Argentina, Ecuador, and Venezuela, particularly—experienced very sharp falls in growth rates from between 5 and 10 percent before the crisis to 1 percent or less after. These collapses in growth were not all caused by the banking crisis (for example, in Argentina the main cause was the exchange rate collapse triggered by sovereign default risk, and this, along with the associated policies, created an insolvent and dysfunctional banking system for months after the shock). Furthermore, where precrisis growth rates were unsustainably high (perhaps fueled by an overly rapid expansion of credit), a fall was inevitable and need not reflect poor crisis resolution policies.

Most countries had lower *inflation* after crisis than before, with five very high-inflation countries managing to vanquish inflation in the postcrisis era (figure 7-2). Only Zimbabwe showed an increase, reflecting its wider economic and political crisis, which was still unresolved at the time of writing. In such cases, the banking crisis probably did not cause the disinflation but instead came toward the end of a wider process that also brought inflation to an end.

Perhaps surprising, almost all countries experienced increased *financial depth* after the crisis (figure 7-3). China is outstanding in this respect; although undercapitalization of the major banks and the problem of nonperforming loans have been widely canvassed, including in official statements, and although there have been numerous failures of small institutions, depositor confidence has not faltered in China in recent years. Other crisis countries with deep financial systems—Korea, Malaysia, and Thailand—also experienced striking postcrisis financial deepening, suggesting that depositor confidence in these countries has been fully restored. In general, transition economies tended to show fairly rapid financial deepening from a low point reached after the initial inflationary surge. However, dollarization of deposits also increased in most cases.

In contrast, *bank credit* to the private (nongovernment) sector as a share of GDP displayed a mixed outcome in different crisis countries (figure 7-4). Once again China experienced the greatest increase (although for China the only available data series includes a substantial fraction of bank credit going to government-owned enterprises).

Wholesale *interest rates* tended to fall, and (although the data are not reliably comparable across countries) quoted intermediation spreads declined

Figure 7-1. *GDP Growth before and after Crisis in Select Countries*

After (percent)

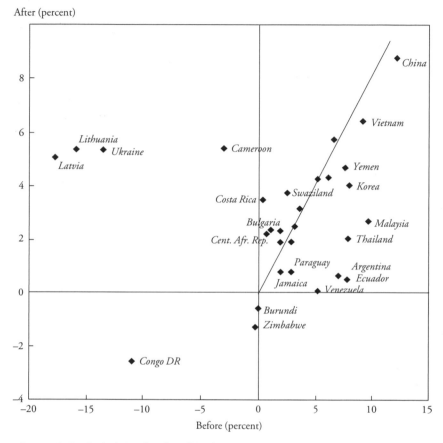

Sources: Authors' calculations based on GDP data in IMF (various years) and crisis dates from the World Bank's Banking Crisis Database (Caprio and others 2005).

(figure 7-5). An independent source of information (based on aggregation of bank accounts) is available only for a shorter list of countries, but it confirms a tendency toward narrower margins as well as a fall in overhead costs, especially in countries where bank concentration was declining.

As for *bank ownership,* a sizable fraction of most postcrisis systems for which we have data is now controlled by private and foreign-owned banks. In three out of four of these postcrisis countries, less than one-third of the system is controlled by government. This shows that, even if temporary nationalization had been a feature of many containment and resolution

Figure 7-2. *Inflation before and after Crisis in Select Countries*

After (percent)

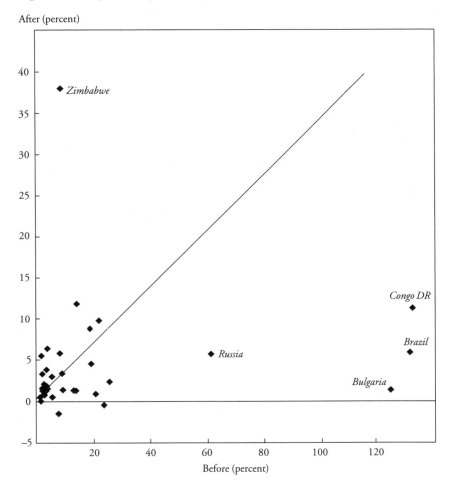

Before (percent)

Sources: Authors' calculations based on consumer price inflation data in IMF (various years) and crisis dates from the World Bank's Banking Crisis Database (Caprio and others 2005).

strategies, privatization or reprivatization was adopted relatively quickly (figure 7-6).

As shown by the outliers, positive and negative, in the figures, countries lacking a consistent policy direction experienced the worst performance. This includes a number of countries gripped by political instability—for example, Venezuela and Zimbabwe as well as Indonesia and the Philippines. Results were also disappointing for Argentina, whose apparently coherent

Figure 7-3. *Aggregate Liquidity as a Percentage of GDP before and after Crisis in Select Countries*

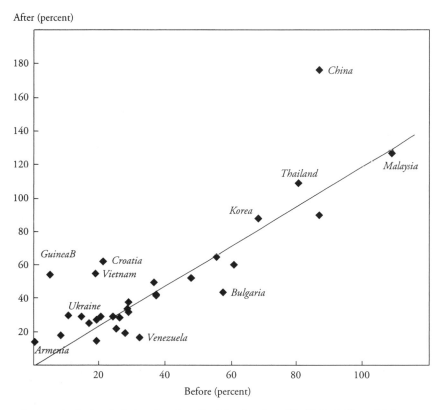

After (percent)

Before (percent)

Sources: Author's calculations based on liquidity data from World Bank Financial Structure Database (March 2005 version) and crisis dates from the World Bank's Banking Crisis Database (Caprio and others 2005).

financial sector policies of the 1990s were badly derailed by the external collapse attributed to a fiscal crisis and whose subsequent financial sector policy strategy remained unclear through most of 2002–03. Lack of clarity and certainty in Mexico's postcrisis resolution policies may also have contributed to its disappointing score.

Summary

The wide variety of country experiences, both in the run-up to the crisis and since, provides a rich laboratory for policy analysis. The next section

Figure 7-4. *Bank Credit to the Private Sector as a Percentage of GDP before and after Crisis in Select Countries*

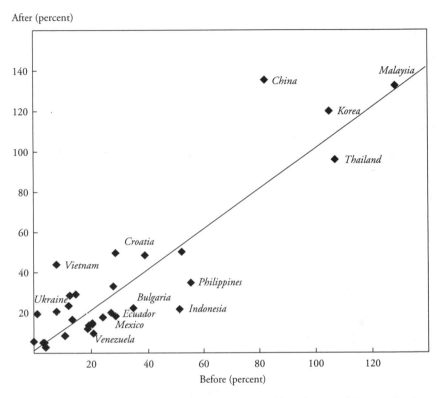

After (percent)

Sources: Author's calculations based on credit data from World Bank Financial Structure Database (March 2005 version) and crisis dates from the World Bank's Banking Crisis Database (Caprio and others 2005).

distills some policy lessons, distinguishing between areas in which a general consensus has emerged and those where differences of opinion remain.

Policy Issues Arising during Postcontainment Resolution

Resolution addresses the debris of the crisis: ensuring that the financial, ownership, and management structures of the banks are reestablished on a solid and incentive-compatible basis.

Figure 7-5. *Spreads before and after Crisis in Select Countries*

After (percent)

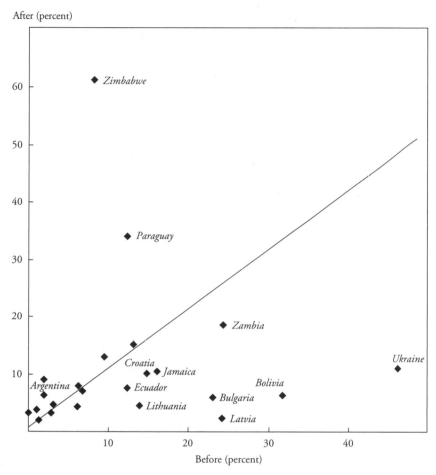

Before (percent)

Sources: Author's calculations based on interest rate data in IMF (various years) and crisis dates from the World Bank's Banking Crisis Database (Caprio and others 2005).

As crises arose with increasing frequency during the 1980s and 1990s, accumulated experience consolidated around a set of good resolution practices. Although it would be going too far to say that financial regulators had a resolution toolbox ready for the next crisis, let alone the capacity and political independence to implement that toolbox, they certainly were better prepared.

Figure 7-6. *Share of the Banking System Controlled by Foreign and Domestic Private Sector*

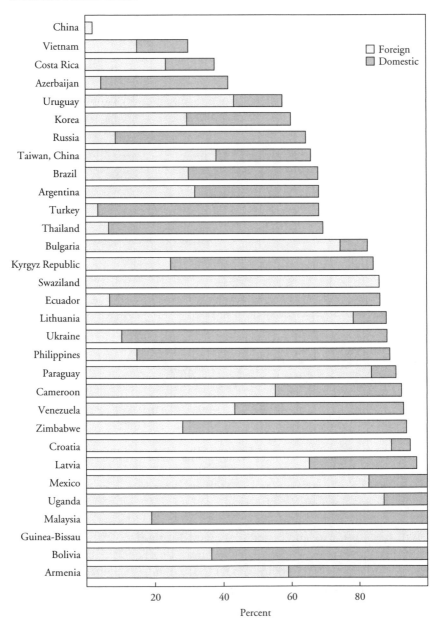

Source: Barth, Caprio, and Levine (2006).

Indeed, the degree of consensus among expert commentators about the best way to approach both containment and resolution issues seems to be quite high. The handbook-like tone of recent contributions epitomizes this.[9] And, in broad terms, the conduct of crisis resolution in recent cases around the world reflects this consensus.

Thus good-practice handbooks stress the value of having a clear and transparent resolution policy in place and of working with speed, noting that uncertainty over the amounts needed and opacity of the cleanup process can greatly increase the transfer of resources to the incumbent private sector. They also insist on the importance of parallel work to deal with corporate distress, because even a banking system that is fixed cannot safely lend to a distressed nonfinancial corporate sector. Handbooks also point out the merits of an all-private resolution and, failing that, of avoiding a full socialization of losses, instead imposing these first onto shareholders, then onto subordinated claimholders (if any), and finally onto uninsured depositors.

Thus all recent crises saw interventions into failing banks by the regulatory authorities (sometimes the deposit insurer, sometimes the banking supervisor, sometimes the central bank) where at least some of the powers of the incumbent management and shareholders were suspended while the scale of the losses was assessed. Sometimes this involved freezing the banks' operations (perhaps with the deposits being transferred to another bank). But more often an open-bank approach was pursued, whether supported by liquidity lending from the central bank or by a merger.[10]

Of course, all of this is a counsel of perfection, hard to achieve in developing-country environments, not only because of technical and administrative shortcomings[11] but also because of the political interests that come into play. Politicians are reluctant to see even uninsured depositors lose. Bankers often have powerful political connections that can protect even the unscrupulous in the process of looting or gambling with the remaining assets of an insolvent bank.

The correspondence between best and actual practice is, therefore, imperfect. In some cases, regulators provided no more than lip service to the prin-

---

9. See, for example, Hoggarth, Reidhill, and Sinclair (2004); Honohan and Laeven (2005).

10. Some of the banks are kept open for political more than technical reasons, as described by an Indonesian official: "Some politically well-connected banks known to be insolvent were kept open. Based on BI's supervisors and recommendations from the IMF staff, there were at least 34 more politically linked insolvent banks that should have also been closed down at the time" (Batunanggar 2002: 11).

11. Enoch, Gulde, and Hardy (2002) provide an interesting and detailed account of how the Mongolian authorities at first failed, and then worked with speed, to close two large insolvent banks in 1996.

ciple that an insolvent bank must be intervened in such a way that insiders cannot loot the bank's remaining assets. In their haste to privatize or reprivatize, several countries transferred ownership rights to unsuitable shareholders, whose investments were financed in a shady manner and who were tempted to loot.

Reflecting, as mentioned, how slowly full information about the extent of the insolvencies emerged, numerous countries took too optimistic a view of the recoverability of assets. As a result, they either permitted banks to reopen in a de facto insolvent position or committed to large contingent liabilities for the state (for example, by granting put-back options to the new owners of the banks or assistance to borrowers). In particular, government commitments to recapitalize insolvent banks remain, all too often, in the form of unenforceable policy indications rather than bonds, or, if they are bonds, they are not marketable or are valued well above what the promised stream of payments would be priced on the market.[12] These transactions are often quite opaque—indeed, the reluctance to provide marketable bonds is typically driven by a desire on the part of politicians to conceal the true fiscal impact of the recapitalization—making it difficult for participants and outsiders to assess the true value of the commitments made.[13]

Many such deficiencies in the implementation of resolution policy can be attributed to political pressures, including the limited independence of financial regulators from the self-serving pressure of political elites. Limited administrative or technical capacity of the regulators has often been a contributing factor.

---

12. Honohan (2005). This is mentioned as an implementation deficiency rather than an open question, although it occurs so often that it raises some doubts as to whether the principle that resolution bonds should be bankable has been fully accepted. Among the numerous instances, the following cases are illustrative. In China, the asset management companies that bought nonperforming loans at par from the four big commercial banks were not in a position to service the resulting debt to the banks from their own resources. That the asset management company promissory notes were fully guaranteed by the government of China remained vague for several years. In Mexico, banks received government guarantees for the value of injected assets, but at first these were on an annually renewable basis so there was some risk (after a vigorous political debate the guarantees have been put on a permanent basis). Furthermore, the long-term, nonmarketable bonds that were injected at below-market rates meant that the banks remained truly undercapitalized, although this was not reflected in accounting practice. In Vietnam, bonds with ten-year maturity were injected into the banks but were not tradable for the first five years; they also carried a 3.3 percent fixed coupon as against market rates in the vicinity of 8–10 percent, implying a marked-to-market net present value discount of 50 percent or more on face value.

13. Brazil provides some interesting examples in which a weak bank was merged into a stronger bank with some quite opaque financing assistance through below-market interest rates on loans from the central bank and from two large state-owned banks as well as through special tax concessions (Baer and Nazmi 2000).

Yet there are some substantial points on which disagreements or at least differences of emphasis arise.[14] We discuss two of these. First is the approach to recapitalization and the degree of emphasis given to finding new capital and new owners, including foreign owners. A subordinate question here relates to the appropriate timing of recapitalization for troubled state-owned banks. Second is the question of asset quality and, in particular, the extent of a role that should be given to asset management companies.

Capital and Ownership: Where to Cast the Net

There are clear differences of emphasis in the way different countries approached the question of securing capital injections for a bank whose business was to be kept as a going concern. There are five main ways of doing this: (a) rely as much as possible on existing shareholders, assisted as necessary by public funds; (b) seek a domestic merger partner; (c) sell to other domestic entities; (d) take the bank into state ownership (usually envisaged as a temporary step); and (d) seek new foreign partners to have a strategic stake in or take over the failed bank(s). Most countries have employed more than one of these techniques in resolving a systemic crisis, and all have their advocates. (It would, in particular, be difficult to quantify the relative importance attached by a particular country to each, especially as strategies have shifted over time.)[15] Political considerations are central to the choices made.

Yet each technique is problematic in different ways:

—Relying on the existing shareholders is highly risky in terms of the danger of self-dealing or looting, even if the regulator has installed a conservator or otherwise is constraining the activities of the insiders.[16] The recent experience with Imar Bank in Turkey is cautionary in this regard

14. There are more acute differences of opinion among experts regarding containment-phase policy. These center around the questions of regulatory forbearance, liquidity support, closure policy, blanket deposit guarantees, and the allocation of losses to depositors and other claimants. While many continue to recommend accommodating policies along these dimensions in the containment phase, there is evidence that such an approach tends, on average, to add to the fiscal costs of crises without improving economic growth (Honohan and Klingebiel 2003).

15. The three largest Central European countries collectively display the shifting diversity of strategies in a transition environment. Thus, for example, Poland encouraged new bank entry almost from the start; the Czech Republic did not. Hungary opened early to foreign banks; the Czech Republic did not; Poland proceeded gradually. Hungary had a sweeping bankruptcy law for corporates; Poland instead encouraged negotiated solutions to insolvency.

16. This is typically considered only where there is no political backlash against retaining owners seen as responsible for the crisis.

(box 7-1). Furthermore, giving existing shareholders preferred status in the recapitalization clearly risks ending with a bad financial bargain for the state in deciding how to divide the costs of recapitalization.

—Seeking a domestic merger partner is a widely used approach, especially for small banks, but it clearly carries the risk of weakening the acquiring bank, especially if, as is frequent, the transaction is done under official pressure. If things go wrong with the merged entity, the regulators are put on the defensive and find it difficult not to forbear.

—Finding other new local owners is difficult. The wealth of local groups that would normally be candidates for bank ownership has often been eroded by the crisis, and they are frequently unable to put up the funds needed for a controlling stake.[17] In principle, an initial public offering could attract the necessary capital, but if broad equity ownership is not well developed and the capital market lacks a track record of ensuring transparent operations and governance of public firms, this may leave the door open in practice to weak governance by self-interested managerial insiders.[18]

—Nationalization can also seem a step backward, given what we know about the problematic performance of systems dominated by state-owned banks, especially if the new managers have limited relevant commercial experience.[19]

—A foreign buyer can bring new capital and expertise into the system. Some observers remain concerned that there may be hidden risks in relying heavily on foreign-owned banks, despite much recent evidence that acquisition by foreign banks does not diminish the systemic availability of credit.[20] All in all, allowing (and even encouraging) the entry of reputable

17. Indeed, in such circumstances, they could be tempted to use various stratagems to leverage their resources in order to come up with the needed funds. In Portugal, one former bank owner tried to use loans from an insurance company he controlled as the basis for the capital required to acquire his family's old bank when it was slated for denationalization. Some of the new owners of Mexico's privatized banks in 1991 employed complex cross-lending arrangements in much the same way; in aggregate they placed little of their own funds at stake (see, for example, Haber and Kantor 2004).

18. In Eastern Europe, former owners sought control of their own banks by participating in initial public offerings of restructured entities.

19. Several Central Asian transition economies sold to the general public minority stakes in banks that remained state controlled; to the extent that retail holders consider these equity stakes to be little more than long-term deposits likely to be protected by government, these banks are not really fully capitalized. However, if the shareholders truly are at risk, then the fact that many of these banks often have a weak underlying financial position (known to the government but not to the small shareholders) amounts to fraud.

20. For concerns about the hidden risks, see, for example, Barros and others (2005); for recent evidence that those concerns are unfounded, see Clarke and others (2003).

foreign-owned banking groups seems to offer the ideal solution. It has been adopted widely, but not universally, postcrisis, not only in Latin America and Eastern Europe (by now ten Central and Eastern European countries have at least 65 percent of their banking system in foreign hands, several with more than 95 percent) but increasingly also in Africa. Nevertheless, the enthusiasm of the major banking groups has waxed and waned over the years. The Argentine experience was a considerable setback—even though only one large foreign bank withdrew from that country—and indications are that many of the larger banking groups are much less interested than they used to be.[21]

But foreign does not always imply good or long-lasting. Certainly the interesting phenomenon of non-banking private equity investors acquiring privatized banks with a view to resale shows how foreign investors may have a short-term horizon. (In the most famous of these cases, Newbridge Capital eventually sold its stake in Korea First Bank to another foreign entity, Standard Chartered, for which control of banks throughout Africa and Asia is the core of its business model; Carlyle also sold its stake in Korean banking to Citigroup.) Yet large international banks have considerable cost advantages, and they tend to globalize their operations so that exit would involve abandoning most of the investment (as the local operation is not fully functional as a bank). However, even if their horizon is not always as long as some suppose, these major players can be valuable providers of capital and confidence in the early postcrisis days.

Much less satisfactory is the risk that, in the desire to find new owners, the door is opened to unprofessional or unfit international bankers, typically those active on a regional scale. For one thing, it is hard for host regulators to assemble sufficient information about the shareholders to determine whether they are, in the jargon, fit and proper to be controlling a major local bank. The notorious case of Meridien-BIAO, where a failing ex-colonial bank in francophone West Africa was taken over by an over-aggressive Zambian-based regional concern, only to collapse in a costly manner within a few years, is the most striking cautionary tale along these lines. But there are others. In Uganda, pressure on the part of international financial institutions to privatize a badly performing state-owned bank that had been dominant in the

---

21. Foreign bank setbacks in Latin America were not confined to Argentina and cooled the previous enthusiasm for foreign entry in that region. Even where exogenous factors did not intervene, a process of consolidation resulted in some net exit of foreign banks in much of the Caribbean. And foreign entry remains surprisingly low in East Asia, despite some liberalization of host-country attitudes.

country resulted in its acquisition by a foreign concern that proved to be only a front for unfit local investors; the deal had to be unwound.

Circumstances differ from country to country, and not all of the five techniques may be equally available. The choice needs to be made with explicit consciousness of the risks of each. Certainly it is not the highest bidder who should necessarily be accepted: capacity, reputation, and willingness to place capital at risk are also key requirements for a suitable new owner.

But an additional dimension deserves consideration, especially where the preexisting regime was a closed and clubby system designed to preserve the power of—and effectively funnel credit to—an incumbent elite.[22] This is the opportunity created by the demise of a dysfunctional banking system to create a new and more open ownership structure that does not confine itself to financing the former incumbents. Of course, the new elite may be no better than the old, as has been observed during the transition experience in some countries of the former Soviet Union. If this is the situation, there is even more to be said (from the point of view of broad social welfare) for eschewing the routes that privilege the existing shareholders, and other wealthy groups in society, in favor of energetically seeking foreign owners. Self-serving politicians do not always perceive matters in the same light: while some postcrisis countries have welcomed foreign owners as part of the solution, others have not.

A Special Issue in Recapitalization of Troubled State-Owned Banks

Should recapitalization of technically insolvent state-owned banks be done early or late in the process of governance reform? We are so accustomed to assuming that an undercapitalized bank presents risks for the system and that it is natural to include recapitalization of any bank as an early requirement for permission to operate. But does this apply to a state-owned bank? Many commentators believe that it does,[23] but an alternative view is that fully capitalizing a state-owned entity risks reintroducing the soft-budget constraint that was an essential ingredient of previous losses. While the underlying governance, management, systems, and policy environment that resulted in the insolvency of such state-owned banks are being fixed, might it not be more

---

22. See, for example, Rajan and Zingales (2003).

23. As suggested, for example, for China by OECD (2002). The huge recapitalization of China's big-four banks has been spread over seven years and four main waves, yet it was not until June 2005 that the first sale of a stake to private investors was agreed.

prudent to hold off on the recapitalization?[24] These issues are of central importance in the many countries that still retain large and often troubled state-owned banks. Allowing an undercapitalized state-owned bank to operate cannot be a long-term solution, but the sequencing of the needed restructuring is important: the recapitalization should come late.

Cleaning Up the Assets: Asset Management Companies Not the Only Solution

While several systemic failures in recent years have been associated with either massive deposit fraud or failed financial market speculation, almost always there has been a legacy of nonperforming loans. What is to be done about them? The problems relate both to what is on the books and the reluctance of the banks to accumulate new credit risks in a situation where so much information capital has been destroyed either by a changed macro environment or by the losses incurred by existing customers.

Should doubtful and irrecoverable loans be separated from the restructured bank, for example, by transfer to an asset management company? The dominant view is that old banking relationships that have resulted in loan losses should be separated, and numerous crises featured the establishment of an asset management company or at least the segregation of the new bank from the old bank. The argument is that such a separation would allow the bank to move forward without contamination from the past and also that specialized recovery agencies would do as good a job—or better—at recovering as much as possible from the nonperforming assets.

Transferring assets to an asset management company does not necessarily recapitalize the bank; it all depends on the agreed price. In China in 1998, the transfers of nonperforming loans were priced at full original book value, whereas in Japan the transfers were deeply discounted, corresponding on average to just 7 percent of face value.[25]

---

24. The experience of Tanzania in restructuring its insolvent National Bank of Commerce is instructive. Following recapitalization, this bank was split in two: the larger portion, comprising most of the business banking and the larger branches, was privatized to a reputable foreign bank. The remainder, a cash-rich entity constituted as the National Microfinance Bank and incorporating most of the smaller branches, was until 2005 fully retained in public ownership with contract management that operated under a memorandum of understanding that restrained it from using most of the liquid assets for lending, effectively creating, for the time being, a "narrow" bank. Here, then, the recapitalization, though early, was qualified by the memorandum of understanding, limiting the risk that the bank's resources would be dissipated.

25. Fung and others (2004).

The most famous case is that of Sweden, where the delinquent assets were backed with real estate and where a highly professional and well-incentivized set of management companies succeeded in disposing of the carved-out assets so profitably (into a rising market) as to recover all of the government's initial outlay. More often, however, the loan portfolio is backed by assets that are less easily valued or disposed of (sometimes embedded in industrial-commercial groups related to the controlling shareholders of the failed bank or the state) or is a broad portfolio of business interests in the economy at large. Recovery rates are often low, and disposal is slow, especially where the asset management companies are tasked with corporate restructuring as distinct from simple rapid disposal or liquidation of assets.[26]

The use of asset management companies can have adverse implications for development if they destroy banking information capital unnecessarily or if they prove to be simply a form of soft-budget constraint for politically favored borrowers. To be sure, where the information capital is based mainly on corrupt or dysfunctional banking relationships, its destruction may be no great loss. However, in most cases the baby may be thrown out with the bathwater. Instead, with new owners and managers, clearly untarnished by previous relationships, the loan book and documentation, even if severely impaired, contain much information capital that can be exploited to the mutual advantage of bank and borrower. This has certainly been the experience of some of the foreign entrants acquiring privatized commercial banks in African countries. Very often regional and sectoral patterns of specialization mean that the book is of greatest value to the bank being restructured. This is a consideration to be set against the traditional advocacy of a clear separation.

The soft-budget problem can be illustrated by the financial restructuring of a borrowing enterprise whose nonperforming loans have been purchased by an asset management company. If the enterprise receives a debt-equity swap from the asset management company while remaining fundamentally unprofitable, this injection of equity will strengthen the creditworthiness of the firm, which can continue to borrow to cover losses for a considerable interval as it eats its way through the new equity capital. If they are careful, the banks may make such loans without exposing themselves to undue risk,

---

26. As noted by Klingebiel (2000) and Fung and others (2004). Even in the rapidly growing Chinese economy, by late 2004, asset management companies had disposed of about half of the original loans purchased in 2000–01 from the banks, reporting an average recovery rate of 26 percent on the original face value.

but social welfare declines as value-reducing firms are allowed to remain in business. Case studies from China purport to illustrate this pattern.[27] The policy lesson is that commercial goals must guide the resolution decisions of asset management companies, which then adopt a least-cost solution and liquidate firms whose continued functioning would be value reducing. Politically driven asset management companies will not escape from this trap.

Therefore, two strong reasons exist for reassessing the almost universal enthusiasm for asset management companies. They may have their role in the cleanup, but not all nonperforming loans should be transferred to them. Many cases have been resolved successfully without the use of asset management companies.[28]

Moving On: Reshaping the Financial Sector in the Medium Term

Many financial systems are less vulnerable to subsequent crises because policy actions were taken during the last crisis, market participants made adjustments (for example, increased risk aversion), or, less happily, the financial system, particularly private credit, shrank so dramatically that risk-taking was sharply curtailed. This is good news for crisis prevention, perhaps—assuming that the state does not go bankrupt—but disastrous for development! Policymakers should seek to support a financial system that both is reasonably protected from the risk of financial crisis and does a good job of delivering services to the economy. In particular, they need to consider both the extent to which the "shape" of the financial system contributed to the crisis or to its cost as well as how the sector might be vulnerable to another crisis.

Countries need to pay particular attention to the role of incentives in their financial system, as many of the most expensive, developing-country crises have been characterized by looting, which can be thought of in its broadest sense not just as literal stealing or fraud but as any lending that is not at arm's-length, including Ponzi finance (here, lending that only pays off when additional loans are granted). Looting may be facilitated—and enlarged—when a pegged exchange rate is prolonged, as this can allow insiders to convert their funds into another currency at an artificially high exchange rate.

---

27. Steinfeld (2001).
28. Norway and (the second round in) Poland are examples (see, for example, Moe, Solheim, and Vale 2004; Huibers 2004).

Thus an early question following a crisis must be how this looting was permitted, and taking a hard look at the regulatory environment should be the first task on the agenda.

We begin this section with a discussion of approaches to bank regulation and supervision and the general issue of the role of financial sector standards in countries that want not only to avoid crises but also to enjoy a healthy pace of economic growth. In fact, a financial system that underwrites sustainable growth is critical to avoiding or minimizing crises. We then move on to discuss a series of medium-term issues that need to be considered as the system is rebuilt: links with the global financial system and, in particular, the issue of small financial systems; the dependence of the financial system on debt and banking; and improvements in debt finance.

Bank Regulation and Supervision

Notwithstanding differences in approach, even among industrial countries, a remarkable consensus has been achieved regarding the supervision of bank regulation. The new Basel Capital Accord, or Basel II as it is called, promotes three pillars as the foundation for a safe and sound banking system: risk-adjusted capital, supervisory oversight, and market discipline. This new accord is far broader than its predecessor, which focused exclusively on capital and had a quite simple method of constructing risk weights. Basel II contains four variants, with the more advanced approaches relying partly on banks' internal models.[29] Thus, in the most advanced approach, pillar one allows bank supervisors to set capital requirements for individual banks based on their particular risk profile, in a mostly formulaic approach. Pillar two allows supervisors to have discretion in further modifying individual bank capital requirements. Market discipline, the third pillar, gets relatively little attention, perhaps because this pillar is thought to be relatively well developed in the financial systems of the advanced economies that form the Basel committee. In addition to timely disclosure of accurate information, though, market discipline requires an effective incentive system: where governments bail out most creditors, markets will not bother to discipline banks, no matter how good the supply of information.

Is this a model for developing countries, and will it allow them to achieve the goal of having a banking sector that is both pro-development and also stable? First, it is important to note that there is significant opposition to Basel

29. Powell (2004).

II even for industrial economies. The shadow financial regulatory committees of Europe, Japan, Latin America, and the United States have criticized the plan for its excessive emphasis on supervision, lack of attention to market discipline, and enormous complexity, which results from its attempt to replicate market forces.[30] Moreover, Basel II's approach to risk modeling is, arguably, seriously deficient and, if taken literally as the basis for risk management, could exacerbate the likelihood of crisis as well as the procyclicality of regulation.[31]

Second, a number of observers, and many developing-country officials, think that the advanced features of Basel II are far beyond their means to implement. Moreover, the accord is not based on a systematic empirical study of what works but instead represents a synthesis of practitioner judgment, drawing on the experience of regulatory and supervisory officials from rich countries, in consultation with a few developing-country officials.[32] According to Barth, Caprio, and Levine, based on their investigation of a large cross-country database on bank regulation and supervision, countries that want to prevent crises need to ensure that their banks diversify, both internally, to the extent that the country is sufficiently large, and externally, especially for the many small countries.[33] Reducing the restrictions on bank activity also helps with diversification and is empirically linked with greater bank stability. As mentioned, generous deposit insurance schemes increase the likelihood of crises, and therefore curtailing these schemes where they exist and raising their price, which is set below an actuarially fair value in most developing countries, are important.

Unfortunately, the core Basel recommendations do not enjoy empirical support for crisis prevention: the links between capital regulation and stability are not robust, and supervision essentially is found to bear little relationship to bank stability. According to Barth, Caprio, and Levine, supervision only works well in countries that are in the "top ten" in the strength of their democratic institutions, such as checks and balances in government and independence of the media.[34] Moreover, measures of supervisory power are neg-

---

30. Links to the websites of these regional committees can be found at http://www.aei.org/research/projectID.15/project.asp.

31. Shin and others (2001). Some characterize these criticisms as "academic," notwithstanding the fact that a number of the shadow financial regulatory committees and Shin and his coauthors are well-known policy advisers or former policy officials.

32. Sophisticated risk management systems are so recent—indeed, more accurately are barely developed even in advanced countries—that they cannot be evaluated.

33. Barth, Caprio, and Levine (2005).

34. Barth, Caprio, and Levine (2005).

atively linked with lending integrity, except in the institutionally most advanced countries.[35] This points to a potentially serious hidden risk in mechanically applying to weak institutional environments what may be considered good regulatory practice in advanced economies. Supervisors in rich countries, who apparently want to have this discretion (essentially they are the ones who agreed in the Basel committee on this approach), must believe that democracy and supervisory independence with accountability are sufficiently strong in their countries that abuses would be rare. Unfortunately, this cannot be taken for granted in many countries, and indeed, abuses were seen in the U.S. savings and loan crisis.

Aside from stability, Barth, Caprio, and Levine show that private monitoring seems to have beneficial effects on the development and efficiency of the banking sector, on the governance of banks, and on the integrity of the lending process. Capital regulation has no positive effect on any of these variables. As the authors note, the use of cross-country survey data suffers from some drawbacks. Most notably, they are unable to measure supervision directly, and supervisory effectiveness on the ground is very difficult to evaluate. Instead they have measures of supervisory powers and budgets and of the institutional environment supporting supervision (independence and the strength of different democratic institutions). Similarly, they have a number of proxies or components of market monitoring, but again they do not measure the actual monitoring in practice. Still, the fact that they consistently find that an approach emphasizing private monitoring has desirable effects on most of the banking system characteristics of concern is important. They conclude that governments should stress improving the information environment to facilitate the ability of markets to monitor and should strengthen the incentives that markets have to do so, such as by limiting deposit insurance and possibly by encouraging subordinated debt.[36]

At a minimum, this approach suggests that bank supervision should attempt to ensure the accuracy of the data disclosed by banks; at a maximum, it suggests that, in sharp contrast to its role in the Basel approach, supervision should not be charged with second-guessing bank management as to how to model risk. Returning to our earlier theme of financial sector development, we are unaware of any other sector whose development has been led by supervisors, so a more ancillary role seems entirely appropriate.

---

35. This finding is based on survey data that ask borrowers about the degree of corruption in the lending process.

36. See also World Bank (2001).

And as Barth, Caprio, and Levine point out, the dramatic widening of pay differentials in favor of those with deep skills in risk management make it unlikely that supervisory agencies will be able to attract and retain the best risk managers in what is sure to be a fast-changing field.

More broadly, we fear that Basel II might lead to a convergence in the way banks model risk.[37] This might be an advantage if one assumes that there is just one correct way to do so, but also a disadvantage, not only because that assumption likely is false, but also because it could provoke banks to reallocate their portfolios simultaneously, with clear consequences for asset price volatility. Long-Term Capital Management might not have been such an urgent issue for policymakers if the commercial banks had not been imitating some of the asset allocations of that hedge fund. Although Basel committee members deny that their goal is to eliminate differences in risk modeling, it is uncommon for regulators to feel comfortable with a range of approaches. Some have focused on the impact of a "one-size-fits-all" approach for the volatility of capital flows to developing countries.[38] We are also concerned that, internally, domestic supervisors in developing countries might be particularly disposed either to impose a uniform approach to risk management on the banks within their borders or to make excessive, possibly corrupt, use of discretion. Getting the right balance is both difficult and unlikely without a substantial degree of oversight of the supervisory process.

These concerns are sufficiently legitimate as to advise great caution for the adoption of Basel II in developing countries. Moreover, the costs of adoption are now being borne by rich countries, and much undoubtedly will be learned in the process, so late adopters may well be spared some costs if they postpone the decision. And some Basel committee members already are discussing further revisions: a Basel II.1, II.2, and so forth. As with computer software, let the early adopters of Basel II.0 beware!

Perhaps most important, developing-country authorities know well that the crises they suffered were not caused by factors that the advances of Basel II are meant to address: simple currency mismatches, loan concentrations, connected lending, fraud, liberalization cum privatization, and absence of any real capital in the banking system, all of which were recognized without sophisticated models, were some of the main domestic factors behind many banking crises. Rather than a rush to Basel II, developing-country authorities should focus on the specific types of vulnerabilities they have experienced,

37. As do Shin and others (2001).
38. Griffith-Jones, Segoviano, and Spratt (2002).

long before becoming preoccupied with Basel II. Indeed, without first-rate information and data systems, many of the advanced features of Basel II *cannot* be adopted. The worst fear is that there will be a rush to models with no data—meaning that the data will be "estimated" or "imported" (for example, using U.S. numbers), no doubt to show a result that banks will like, yielding yet another reason why early adoption in developing countries could be destabilizing. Finally, given the limited political independence and technical capacity of most developing-country supervisory systems, it is all too easy to imagine the nightmare scenario of banks being permitted to calculate required capital on the basis of meaningless risk calculations, whether based on off-the-shelf models calibrated to some other economy or on external credit ratings prepared by inexperienced and conflicted rating agencies.

Financial Sector Standards, Growth, and Crisis Prevention

A broader concern that goes beyond Basel II is the explosion of best-practice standards in the financial sector and related areas—from accounting and auditing, bank supervision, and securities regulation to corporate governance, money laundering, and so forth—a total of a dozen well-established ones, each with numerous parts. Yet industrial countries saw massive governance failures in Enron, Parmalat, and WorldCom at the roughly same time as the experts from these countries were preparing standards for corporate governance! And even if the standards worked in the highest-income countries, which has not been demonstrated, it is a leap of faith to assume that they will work elsewhere. This approach to standards often is driven by the idea that certain features of the experts' home or favorite country are just what other countries either need or (occasionally) need to avoid rather than based on serious empirical research. As Dani Rodrik puts it,

> The Augmented Washington Consensus is problematic from a number of different perspectives. For one thing, there is an almost tautological relationship between the enlarged list (on the revised Washington Consensus list) and economic development. The new "consensus" reflects what a rich country *already* [emphasis in the original] looks like. If a developing country can acquire, say, Denmark's institutions, it is already rich and need not worry about development. The list of institutional reforms describes not what countries need to do in order to develop—*the list certainly does not correspond to what*

today's advanced countries did during their earlier development [our emphasis]—but where they are likely to end up once they develop.[39]

A question that rarely is addressed is the possibility that, having gotten rich, residents of high-income countries would like to protect their gains, in which case policies that reduce volatility, at the possible expense of growth, are quite understandable. However, it does not follow that those policies are optimal for developing countries, and in fact this quite likely is not the case.

Why would developing-country authorities go along with this logic? The paucity of empirical research in any of the areas affected by the standards make them ripe for experts, both instant and genuine, to claim the creation of a standard worthy of emulation. But the experts in narrow areas are rarely experts in the interaction between their own narrow area and the broader institutional environment—the set of institutions that they take for granted. And as Rodrik points out, the approach to recommending best-practice standards is essentially unfalsifiable, as it is always possible to find something wrong with government's implementation. We would add that it can distract from understanding better the institutional environment in the countries that are trying to implement policy reform and how these policies will interact in a world very different from the one in which the standards were designed. Barth, Caprio, and Levine's example of the relationship between supervisory powers and the development of democratic institutions stands out as an example here.

Standards may contain much that is good, but in developing-country contexts they should be treated as a checklist of issues to be considered rather than as a template to be mechanically applied. They clearly do not contain a blueprint for financial sector reform, not least because they convey no information about how different areas should be sequenced. But perhaps even more important, their critical drawback is that they focus attention on a principle that comes from outside a developing country, rather than on the institutional reality within the country that determines how that principle will operate once implemented. Instead of tinkering with their system solely to achieve compliance with the phrasing of some possibly irrelevant international standard, it is far more important for authorities to focus attention on building the basic infrastructure in the financial sector and on the incentives that will drive performance.

---

39. Rodrik (2004).

Stability through Development

It is plausible to argue that one of the sources of a future round of financial (or other) crises in developing countries will be the lack of access to financial services and the policy responses to this problem. Recall the role of development banks and directed credit schemes—and even public sector commercial banks—in the last round of crises. These came about in response to banking systems in the 1970s that did not appear to be doing much for domestic residents and that were accused of only helping foreign firms that were operating in the economy. Access to credit from the commercial banking system was also restricted by high reserve and liquidity requirements in many countries. At least the reserve and liquidity requirements were designed partly to keep the banking system safe, this being prior to the days in which there was much reliance on prudential supervision. Lending to the private sector was also restrained because the information and contracting environment was so poor and, it was thought, would take a long time to develop. As a result, commercial credit could not be provided, except in the very short term to a narrow range of well-known clients with exceptionally high collateral requirements. The joke that bankers only lend to those who do not need the money was not far off. Bankers also lend to themselves or their family members, the group for which their information is relatively good.

Early attempts to improve access to credit (except for deposit facilities, most other financial services were largely ignored) by and large failed, especially where subsidies were included.[40] In many countries, preferred credit schemes saw abysmal repayment rates, and in many cases these programs either weakened the incentives to repay or did not contribute to establishing a better "credit culture," by which we mean an incentive system that encourages timely repayment. Subsidies, of course, tended to be largest where there were interest rate ceilings and very high inflation.

---

40. See Calomiris and Himmelberg (1993) for an early exception, namely the Japan Development Bank during the 1950s and early 1960s. The directed credit programs in Malaysia also appear to have been successful, in part because, as in Japan, they left much discretion in choosing borrowers with the commercial banking system (for example, all native Malaysians—Bumiputras—were eligible), and banks were allowed to charge a markup of up to 400 basis points over their average cost of funds. In contrast, in many directed credit schemes in other parts of the world, banks were forced to make loans below their cost of funds, and the high inflation subsequently drove the real interest rates to significantly negative real rates. Thus directed credit became a way to allocate massive subsidies (in high-inflation settings), and it is not surprising that these programs not only bankrupted their providers but also directed large subsidies to groups that were not targeted. Much of the subsidized credit went to governments and to public enterprises by design, not to small borrowers (where large borrowers wormed their way in).

To be sure, a variety of other domestic and international factors, including macroeconomic developments, contributed to many crises, but the shocks were affecting financial systems whose foundations—information, contract enforcement, incentives—all were vastly underdeveloped, as they were not important when the discretion permitted to banks was far less. Indeed, in the worst of cases, resources were grotesquely misallocated, or there was widespread looting of the banking system, so that the foundation of the financial system was completely eroded. In effect, rather than being built to withstand significant economic shocks, the financial system was in distress and waiting to topple over. In Mexico, credit immediately prior to the crisis was being allocated mainly to a handful of sectors in which the interest spreads were the highest and were highly exposed to dollar devaluation. This portfolio allocation could only make sense for a banker if the probability of devaluation was zero, which is difficult to believe, or if the real net worth of the banking system was zero or negative.[41] In other words, the portfolio was allocated in a highly risky fashion, whereas Wilson, Saunders, and Caprio show that if banks had been diversifying their lending throughout the economy (behaving like a well-diversified mutual fund), they would have been able to weather the 1994 devaluation. In Indonesia by the mid-1990s and in Russia prior to the 1998 crisis, liberal entry had permitted the creation of "banks" that were closer to Ponzi finance than to safe and sound commercial banks. But even in less dramatic cases, the long-standing inability of the financial system to meet developmental needs was the hallmark of financial systems prior to crisis.

Countries that survived a financial crisis in the past decade still may be suffering from the legacy of these earlier problems to varying degrees. The (last) crisis may be over, and some facets of the regulatory system aimed at reducing vulnerability may be stronger, but the financial system's reach may still be as limited as it was in the 1970s. Certainly it is sensible for authorities to address egregious weaknesses that contributed to the earlier crisis and that are still a source of vulnerability (for example, foreign currency mismatches associated with dollarization). And no doubt some improvements designed to address crises might ultimately lead to a banking system that can more prudently take a variety of risks. Still, once headline problems in a crisis have been tackled, an important way to achieve financial stability is to make financial sector development the top priority. Thus building the foundations that will encourage better access to financial services should make the system more

41. Wilson, Saunders, and Caprio (2000).

robust. Otherwise, as pressure builds to improve access to financial services, policymakers once again might resort to solutions that undermine sound finance. For example, there is now talk of "smart subsidies," as if the previous generation of attempts to subsidize and target finance had been willfully designed as unintelligent, whereas, in fact, they failed because borrowers not in the target group were able to grab the built-in subsidies and even the target borrowers failed to repay. The answer, as shown in the Calomiris and Himmelberg study of Japan, is to limit significantly the subsidies, keep the scheme small relative to total credit, and force borrowers to repay and graduate to fully commercial financing.[42] These lessons are well understood, but the political pressure for subsidies and directed credit persists.

Rather than attempting to find some "quick fixes," there is a strong case in favor of focusing on infrastructure and incentives in the financial sector.[43] Admittedly this can seem a politically uninteresting recommendation. Improving accounting and auditing, reforming a judiciary biased in favor of debtors, improving the disclosure of information by financial intermediaries or the incentives of depositors and market participants to monitor, and educating the media so that they can perform a useful watchdog function on the financial sector all take a long time to show results, whereas most governments have a short time horizon. In a world in which "results orientation" and "best practice" are the new buzzwords, how does one elevate the need for judicial reform to a top priority, particularly when there is no checklist of best practices to convince judges that excessively favoring debtors actually reduces access to credit?

Since there is no evidence that a healthy financial system—one that contributes to economic growth—can be achieved without these building blocks, we emphasize continuing with this uphill battle in two ways. First, some large retail banks in the United States are able to make small-business loans at a marginal cost of virtually pennies by using credit-scoring models, relatively sophisticated electronic databases, and a loan approval process linked automatically with the risk management system. Developing-country authorities could ask why this is not possible in their countries, as the answers would point the way to a program for improving their own financial infrastructure. For example, this focus might lead them to encourage the growth of credit registries as an information base or to make improved incentives to repay a national priority. They might also become motivated to attract the entry of

42. Calomiris and Himmelberg (1993).
43. World Bank (2001).

foreign banks that could provide not only better banking skills but also better risk management and credit systems.

Second, developing countries no doubt will want to learn from relatively advanced emerging markets to see if this strategy has functioned in an environment outside of high-income countries. In this respect, Mexico's recent success is of interest. From the late nineteenth through the early twenty-first century, Mexico's financial system did not provide wide access to financial services. After nationalizing its banks in 1982, then recognizing the failure of this approach and privatizing them rapidly in 1992, only to experience a financial crisis two years later, the authorities finally allowed foreign banks to enter the system, improved the regulatory environment, and strengthened the enforcement of contracts. Only a decade later—in 2004—were there finally encouraging reports that credit to the private sector was beginning to grow rapidly (25 percent in real terms), with corporate, consumer, and mortgage lending all advancing rapidly.[44] This system is dominated by large foreign banks (about 85 percent of commercial bank assets are in foreign-owned banks). While this rapid increase is from an exceptionally low base, and it is far too early to impute a trend from developments over just one year, it is at least a hopeful sign that attention to financial sector infrastructure and a large foreign bank presence can improve the developmental impact of the banking sector.

In addition to stressing the developmental reach of the financial sector, what are some of the other key medium-term issues for developing-country financial systems? Priorities here will differ dramatically, depending on the initial conditions that confront the authorities. Here we treat some of the major issues for different groups of countries.

Global Finance and Small Financial Systems

Although there is impressive empirical evidence that finance contributes to growth and, more recently, to poverty alleviation, there is no evidence that countries must produce their own financial services.[45] Opening up to some trade in financial services need not require removing all barriers to capital flows. For years, some well-known industrial-country commercial banks have been established in countries with capital controls. Moreover,

---

44. According to the *Financial Times*, March 3, 2005, "Mexican banks ride a strong wave of lending: After years of stagnant growth the industry is seeing a dramatic upturn."
45. World Bank (2001).

advances in technology are making it increasingly difficult to close off one's borders to capital flows. Thus some opening is both optimal and inevitable. International banks, thanks to increasingly cheap technology, can provide developing-country markets with world-class depository services, insurance, and pension fund management, in addition to credit services.

Opening is an especially important issue in countries with small financial systems. A major problem facing most of the 125 developing countries is that their financial market is too small to operate well as a separate, independent entity.[46] Brazil, China, and India aside, most developing countries' financial systems are so small that integration with a larger financial system is a necessary ingredient of financial sector stability.[47] Domestic banks in small countries typically have highly concentrated portfolios; where one or two commodities are important in an economy, it is difficult to avoid exposure to these sectors, as savings and loans banks in Texas discovered.

There are a number of ways to achieve better diversification, such as by allowing the entry of more foreign banks, participating in a regional banking system, having domestic banks do business abroad, and achieving portfolio diversification for domestic financial intermediaries. The interest of international banks in diversifying in different countries has waxed and waned over the last hundred years or more, but banks seem to be retrenching, again in response partly to Basel II but also to the asymmetric way they were treated in the Argentine crisis (and the fear that other countries might follow this example). Thus providing a sufficiently attractive investment climate for foreign banks has become more difficult, and in the near term regional banking may be more promising, as seen in recent years in southern Africa. Perhaps a more radical solution—because it is hard for policymakers to acknowledge that capital might be better invested overseas—would be a policy to encourage banks in small countries to hold a fraction of their assets in diversified investments abroad, as some are already doing.[48] Another approach might be to create a global bond fund that could recycle capital to developing countries meeting certain criteria, so it need not entail a loss of investable resources. The rapidly growing credit default swap market in advanced mar-

46. Hanson, Honohan, and Majnoni (2003).

47. This does not imply that the very large developing countries can or should cut themselves off from foreign financial systems. Rather we suggest that, within these very large and more diversified countries, it is at least possible for banks and other financial intermediaries to diversify risk reasonably well within their borders. In contrast, in very small financial systems, this type of diversification just is not possible. There are also issues of costs, innovation, and the need to deal with crises.

48. The net holdings of foreign assets have become positive for a number of developing-country banking systems.

kets could also provide some useful instruments for diversifying or hedging small-economy credit risks.

Excessive Reliance on Debt and on Banks

Another concern for many developing countries is that their relatively riskier environment would be more conducive to equity-based finance, yet most countries are overwhelmingly characterized by debt-based finance through the commercial banking system. In part, this imbalance represents a natural step in the evolution of financial systems. Equity requires much finer and more detailed information than bank finance, which in its early stages is based more on relationships and only later more on arm's-length transactions. Underdeveloped financial infrastructures—poor accounting and auditing, an inefficient legal and judiciary system—bias financial development in favor of relationship-based banking and make it more difficult for small and new firms to obtain access to credit or even more to equity. This, in turn, can make the financial system more vulnerable to the extent that a higher debt-to-equity ratio leaves firms with a more fragile financing structure.[49] Consequently, to improve both the breadth and the resiliency of the financial sector, authorities should make the development of this infrastructure a top priority, rather than aim for a particular structure. In other words, the priority should be to remove distortions that bias the development of the financial system, with the understanding that, in most countries, the bias is in favor of banks.[50] Equity-based finance is also underdeveloped wherever information is weak and minority shareholders do not enjoy effective protection, creating another clear area in which government action would have a favorable effect. This does not mean that small countries need their own exchanges; larger firms in many countries already are listing offshore.

Governments need to consider removing other distortions that bias the development of the financial system in favor of banks. One important source of bias is the provision of underpriced deposit insurance. As Laeven shows, most developing countries with explicit deposit insurance significantly under-price it, having for the most part copied pricing from industrial countries, notwithstanding the considerably greater risks in lower-income countries.[51]

---

49. In other words, debt always has to be serviced, regardless of how a firm is doing, whereas with equity-based finance, risks are more diversified. The fragility associated with a high debt-equity ratio was seen most clearly in the Korean banking crisis.

50. This bias may reflect a number of factors, not least of which is the political power of bankers in many countries.

51. Laeven (2002).

Thus authorities in countries with explicit deposit insurance need to consider either raising its price or significantly reducing coverage, either of which would favor the development of non-bank finance. Countries might also encourage debt finance through their tax code, such as when interest payments are deductible, whereas dividends are fully, double-, or even triple-taxed. In sum, wherever the banking sector is effectively subsidized, removing or reducing the subsidies relative to non-bank finance should be given high priority.

Improving Debt Finance

In addition to reducing reliance on debt, addressing the quality and term structure of debt is important. Problems in both areas stem from the unfriendly contractual environment and weak information base of many low-income countries. Although some developing-country banks are already acquiring familiarity with or beginning to use credit-scoring models, which permit the efficient supply of small loans in most advanced countries, they lack the accurate, online information systems and the reliable judicial and legal framework to support a significant expansion of access to credit or even a modest lengthening of its term structure. Encouraging the rapid development of credit registries is one critical ingredient to improving debt finance. Retraining the judiciary, streamlining judicial processes, and developing extrajudicial processes to correct the bias against creditors are a related priority. These measures do not grab headline-winning attention, but they do contribute to what should be headline-winning stories about poverty alleviation and development.

Institutional investors, who provide both long-term and high-risk funding, are barely nascent in low- and middle-income countries. Developing the insurance industry and moving to at least a partially funded pension system would not only improve the risk position of the main clients of these two industries but also indirectly benefit the development of the debt and equity markets in a country. Again, these areas are not amenable to quick fixes, but they are critical ingredients to the development of a healthy financial system.

Finally, as long as governments maintain their own currencies, developing local debt markets will reduce currency risk and also, as maturity lengthens, interest rate risk, relative to the situation in which borrowing is mostly short term and in foreign exchange. Domestic government debt markets can also encourage the growth of domestic debt markets, in part by providing a benchmark for corporate securities. Still, in many countries, large fiscal deficits threaten to crowd out the private sector, so this macroeconomic imbalance can easily undermine the positive effects of debt market development (and other financial sector reform). A fitting reminder that, with all of the improvements recommended here in the financial sector, success in the macro policy area is a sine qua non for a safe and sound financial sector that contributes effectively to development.

References

Baer, Werner, and Nader Nazmi. 2000. "Privatization and Restructuring of Banks in Brazil." *Quarterly Review of Economics and Finance* 40, no. 1: 3–24.

Barros, Pedro Pita, Erik Berglöf, Paolo Fulghieri, Jordi Gual, Colin Mayer, and Xavier Vives. 2005. *Integration of European Banking: The Way Forward.* London: Centre for Economic Policy Research.

Barth, James, Gerard Caprio, and Ross Levine. 2005 (forthcoming). *Rethinking Bank Regulation: Till Angels Govern.* Cambridge University Press.

Batunanggar, Sukarela. 2002. "Indonesia's Banking Crisis Resolution: Lessons and the Way Forward." Bank Indonesia Working Paper (www.bi.go.id/NR/rdonlyres/FF08B4FB-08A8-4835-9B39-E35EB615545A/517/ibcr0212.pdf).

Calomiris, Charles, and Charles Himmelberg. 1993. "Directed Credit Programs for Agriculture and Industry: Arguments from Theory and Fact." In *Proceedings of the World Bank Annual Bank Conference on Development Economics,* pp. 113–54. Washington: World Bank.

Caprio, Gerard, Daniela Klingebiel, Luc Laeven, and Guillermo Noguera. 2005. "Banking Crisis Database." In *Systemic Financial Distress: Containment and Resolution,* edited by Patrick Honohan and Luc Laeven. Cambridge University Press.

Clarke, George R. G., Robert J. Cull, María Soledad Martínez Peria, and Susana M. Sánchez. 2003. "Foreign Bank Entry: Experience, Implications for Developing Countries, and Agenda for Further Research." *World Bank Research Observer* 18, no. 1: 25–59.

De Luna Martínez, José. 2000. "Management and Resolution of Banking Crises: Lessons from the Republic of Korea and Mexico." World Bank Discussion Paper 43. Washington: World Bank.

Enoch, Charles, Anne-Marie Gulde, and Daniel Hardy. 2002. "Banking Crises and Bank Resolution: Experiences in Some Developing Countries." IMF Working Paper WP 02/56. Washington: International Monetary Fund.

Fort, Jean-Louis, and Peter Hayward. 2004. "The Supervisory Implications of the Failure of Imar Bank." Mimeo. Ankara: Government of Turkey, Treasury Department (www.treasury.gov.tr/duyuru/basin2004/rapor_20040831.pdf).

Fung, Ben, Jason George, Stefan Hohl, and Guonan Ma. 2004. "Public Asset Management Companies in East Asia." FSI Paper 3. Basel: Financial Stability Institute (www.bis.org/fsi/fsipapers03.pdf).

Gelpern, Anna. 2004. "Systemic Bank and Corporate Distress from Asia to Argentina: What Have We Learned?" *International Finance* 7, no. 1: 151–68.

Griffith-Jones, Stephany, Miguel Segoviano, and Stephen Spratt. 2002. "Basel II and Developing Countries: Diversification and Portfolio Effects." Mimeo. Basel: Institute for Development Studies (www.stephanygj.com/_documents/Basel_II_and_Developing_CountriesDiversification_and_Portfolio_Effects.pdf).

Haber, Stephen, and Shawn Kantor. 2004. "Getting Privatization Wrong: The Mexican Banking System, 1991–2003." Paper presented at the World Bank conference Bank

Privatization in Low- and Middle-Income Countries, Washington, November 23. Forthcoming in *Journal of Banking and Finance.*

Hanson, James A., Patrick Honohan, and Giovanni Majnoni, eds. 2003. *Globalization and National Financial Systems.* Oxford University Press.

Hoggarth, Glen, Jack Reidhill, and Peter Sinclair. 2004. "On the Resolution of Banking Crises: Theory and Evidence." Working Paper 229. London: Bank of England.

Honohan, Patrick. 2005. "Bank Recapitalization: Fiscal, Monetary and Incentive Implications." In *Systemic Financial Distress: Containment and Resolution,* edited by Patrick Honohan and Luc Laeven. Cambridge University Press.

Honohan, Patrick, and Daniela Klingebiel. 2003. "The Fiscal Cost Implications of an Accommodating Approach to Banking Crises." *Journal of Banking and Finance* 27, no. 8: 1539–60.

Honohan, Patrick, and Luc Laeven, eds. 2005. *Systemic Financial Distress: Containment and Resolution.* Cambridge University Press.

Huibers, Fred E. 2004. "Initial Public Offerings." In *The Future of State-Owned Financial Institutions,* edited by Gerard Caprio, Jonathan Fiechter, Robert Litan, and Michael Pomerleano. Brookings.

IMF (International Monetary Fund). Various years. *International Financial Statistics.* Washington.

Klingebiel, Daniela. 2000. "The Use of Asset Management Companies in the Resolution of Banking Crises: Cross-Country Experiences." Policy Research Working Paper 2284. Washington: World Bank.

Laeven, Luc. 2002. "Pricing of Deposit Insurance." Policy Research Working Paper 2871. Washington: World Bank.

Moe, Thorvald G., Jon A. Solheim, and Bent Vale, eds. 2004. *The Norwegian Banking Crisis.* Occasional Paper 33. Oslo: Norges Bank.

OECD (Organization for Economic Cooperation and Development). 2002. *China in the World Economy: The Domestic Policy Challenges.* Paris.

Pazarbasioglu, Ceyla. 2003. "Costs of European Union Accession: The Potential Impact on the Turkish Banking Sector." Mimeo. Ankara: Banking Regulatory and Supervisory Agency.

Powell, Andrew. 2004. "Basel II and Developing Countries: Sailing through the Sea of Standards." Policy Research Working Paper 3387. Washington: World Bank.

Rajan, Raghuram G., and Luigi Zingales. 2003. *Saving Capitalism from the Capitalists.* New York: Crown Business.

Rodrik, Dani. 2004. "Rethinking Growth Policies in the Developing World." Mimeo. Harvard University, October.

Scott, David. 2002. "A Practical Guide to Managing Systemic Financial Crises: A Review of Approaches Taken in Indonesia, the Republic of Korea, and Thailand." Policy Research Paper 2843. Washington: World Bank.

Shin, Hyun Song, Felix Muennich, Charles Goodhart, Paul Embrechts, Jon Danielsson, and Con Keating. 2001. "An Academic Response to Basel II." FMG Special Paper sp130. London School of Economics, Financial Markets Group.

Steinfeld, Edward S. 2001. "China's Program of Debt-Equity Swaps: Government Failure or Market Failure?" Paper presented to a Harvard University conference and forthcoming in

Financial Sector Reform in China, edited by Yasheng Huang, Anthony Saich, and Edward S. Steinfeld. Harvard University.

Steinherr, Alfred. 2004. "Russian Banking since the Crisis of 1998." CEPS Working Document 209. London: Centre for Economic Policy Studies, October.

Steinherr, Alfred, Ali Tukel, and Murat Ucer. 2004. "The Turkish Banking Sector: Challenges and Outlook in Transition to EU Membership." EU-Turkey Working Paper 4. London: Centre for Economic Policy Studies, August.

Wilson, Berry, Anthony Saunders, and Gerard Caprio. 2000. "Mexico's Financial Sector Crisis: Propagative Links to Devaluation." *Economic Journal* 110, no. 460 (January): 391–408.

World Bank. 2001. "Turkey: Programmatic Financial and Public Sector Adjustment Loan Project, President's Report." P7463-TU. Washington.

———. 2004. "Turkey: Third Programmatic Financial and Public Sector Adjustment Loan Project, President's Report." P27595-TU. Washington.

ROBERT HOLZMANN 8

Old-Age Income Support in the Twenty-first Century

Conceptual Framework and Select Issues of Implementation

The past decade has brought increased recognition of the importance of pension systems for the economic stability of nations and the security of their aging populations. In developing countries, the traditional systems of support for the elderly are being eroded by migration, urbanization, and other factors that break down extended families. At the same time, pension systems, where they exist, are proving limited and increasingly costly in fiscal terms.

For the past ten years, the World Bank has taken a leading role in addressing these challenges through its support for pension reform around the world. The World Bank has been involved in pension reform in more than eighty countries and provided financial support for reform to more than sixty countries. The demand for such support continues to grow.

What has emerged from interactions with policymakers, pension experts, and representatives from civil society in client and donor countries is the continued relevance of the main objectives of pension systems—poverty alleviation and consumption smoothing—and of the broader goal of social protection. The World Bank continues to perceive advantages in multipillar

This paper draws heavily on the recently published World Bank report on pension reform (Holzmann, Hinz, and Bank Team 2005). It was written to clarify and update the World Bank's perspective on pension reform, incorporating the lessons learned from recent experience and research that has advanced the understanding of how best to proceed in the future. It does not announce a new approach.

designs that contain some funded element when conditions are appropriate but increasingly recognizes that a range of choices can help policymakers to achieve effective old-age protection in a fiscally responsible manner.

The suggested pension system is composed of some combination of five elements or pillars: (a) a basic, noncontributory or "zero pillar" (in the form of a demogrant or social pension) that provides a minimal level of protection; (b) a "first-pillar" contributory system that is linked to varying degrees to earnings and seeks to replace some portion of income; (c) a mandatory "second pillar" that is essentially an individual savings account but can be constructed in a variety of ways; (d) voluntary "third-pillar" arrangements that can take many forms (individual, employer sponsored, defined benefit, defined contribution) but are essentially flexible and discretionary in nature; and (e) informal intrafamily or intergenerational sources of both financial and nonfinancial support for the elderly, including access to health care and housing. For a variety of reasons, a system that incorporates as many of these elements as possible, depending on the preferences of individual countries as well as the level and incidence of transaction costs, can, through diversification, deliver support to aging populations relatively more effectively and efficiently.

The main changes to the World Bank's perspective are related to an enhanced focus on basic income provision for all vulnerable elderly as well as an enhanced role for market-based, consumption-smoothing instruments for individuals both within and outside mandated pension schemes. The World Bank increasingly recognizes the importance of initial conditions and the extent to which conditions in a particular country necessitate a tailored or tactically sequenced implementation of the multipillar model.

This chapter has two parts. The first part outlines the framework for the World Bank's thinking on pension reform, including its origins and scope. The second highlights key issues pertaining to design and implementation and focuses on three issues related to financial markets: financial market readiness, regulation, and supervision; costs and fees; and retirement-income products.

A Framework for Pension Reform

A framework for analyzing pension systems and their reform should be based on some core principles and the capacity to achieve a flexible and context-specific set of social and economic outcomes. It should not narrowly prescribe the structure, implementing institutions, or operations of a system. On a practical level, the application of such a standard requires the articulation of goals and criteria against which a proposed reform can be evaluated.

Goals of a Pension System and Reform

The primary goals of a pension system should be to provide adequate, affordable, sustainable, and robust retirement income, while seeking to implement welfare-improving schemes in a manner appropriate to the individual country:

—An adequate system is one that provides benefits to the full breadth of the population that are sufficient to prevent old-age poverty on a country-specific absolute level in addition to providing a reliable means to smooth lifetime consumption for the vast majority of the population.

—An affordable system is one that is within the financing capacity of individuals and the society and does not unduly displace other social or economic imperatives or have untenable fiscal consequences.

—A sustainable system is one that is financially sound and can be maintained over a foreseeable horizon under a broad set of reasonable assumptions.

—A robust system is one that has the capacity to withstand major shocks, including those coming from economic, demographic, and political volatility.

The design of a pension system or its reform must explicitly recognize that pension benefits are claims against future economic output. To fulfill their primary goals, pension systems must contribute to future economic output. Reforms should, therefore, be designed and implemented in a manner that supports growth and development and diminishes possible distortions in capital and labor markets. This requires paying attention to the secondary aspects of pension formulation, creating positive outcomes for development by minimizing the potentially negative impacts on labor markets and macroeconomic stability, and leveraging the positive impacts through increased national saving and financial market development.

Review and Extension of the Original Concept of Pension Reform

The evolution of the international and the World Bank's perspective on pension reform over the past decade reflects the extensive experience with reform in countries and an ongoing worldwide dialogue between academics and international organizations as well as within the World Bank. This process has contributed to the depth in understanding of the nuances and challenges of pension reform and reinforced the need to move away from a single-pillar design in nearly every circumstance. Experience has demonstrated that a multipillar design is better able to deal with the multiple objectives of pension systems—the most important being poverty reduction and income smoothing—and to address more effectively the kinds of economic, political, and demographic risks facing any pension system. Advance funding is still considered important, but the limits of such funding in some circumstances are also seen much more sharply. The main motivation for the World Bank to support pension reform has not changed. Instead it has been strengthened by the past decade of experience: most simple pension systems do not deliver on their social objectives; they create significant distortions in the operation of market economies and are not financially sustainable when faced with an aging population. At the same time, the original concept of a specific three-pillar structure—(a) a mandated, unfunded, and publicly managed defined-benefit system, (b) a mandated, funded, and privately managed defined-contribution scheme, and (c) voluntary retirement savings—has been extended to include two additional pillars: (d) a basic (zero) pillar to deal more explicitly with the poverty objective and (e) a nonfinancial (fourth) pillar to include the broader context of social policy, such as family support, access to health care, and housing. This proposed multipillar design is more flexible and, where feasible, better addresses the main target groups in the population.

The extensive experience in implementing pension reforms in a range of settings since the early 1990s has motivated a review and refinement of the framework in terms of the appropriate objectives and path of a reform effort. From the World Bank's perspective, the evolution of thinking and policy on pensions is characterized by five main additions:

—*A better understanding of reform needs and measures.* This includes (a) assessing the need for reform beyond fiscal pressure and demographic challenges to address issues such as socioeconomic changes and the risks as well as opportunities from globalization; (b) understanding the limits and other consequences of mandating participation in pension systems, particularly for low-income groups, for which risks other than old age may be more immediate and much stronger; and (c) reassessing the continued importance, but also the limitations, of prefunding for dealing with population aging in recognition of the importance of associated behavioral changes, including enhanced labor supply and later retirement.

—The extension of the reform model beyond the three-pillar structure to encompass explicitly as many as five pillars and to move beyond the conventional concentration on the first and second pillars. Experience with low-income countries has brought into focus the need for a basic or zero (noncontributory) pillar that is distinguished from the first pillar in its primary focus on poverty alleviation in order to extend old-age security to all of the elderly. Experience in low- to middle-income countries has heightened awareness of the importance of the design and implementation of the third, voluntary pillar, which can effectively supplement the basic elements of a pension system to provide reasonable replacement rates for higher-income groups, while constraining the fiscal costs of the basic components. Last, but not least, is recognition of the importance of a fourth pillar for retirement consumption that consists of a mixture of access to informal support (such as family support), other formal social programs (such as health care), and other individual financial and nonfinancial assets (such as homeownership) and the need to incorporate their existence or absence explicitly into the design of the pension system and old-age security.

—An appreciation of the diversity of effective approaches, including the number of pillars, the appropriate balance among the various pillars, and the way in which each pillar is formulated in response to particular circumstances or needs. Some pension systems function effectively with only a zero pillar (in the form of a universal social pension) and a third pillar of voluntary savings. In some countries, the introduction of a mandatory second pillar is required to gain popular acceptance for a reform of the first pillar, while the political economy of other countries makes a reformed (first-pillar) public system in conjunction with voluntary schemes the only realistic alternative.

—A better understanding of the importance of initial conditions in establishing the potential for reform and the limitations within which reforms are feasible. There is now greater awareness of the extent to which the inherited pension system as well as the economic, institutional, financial, and political environment of a country dictate the options available for reform. This is particularly important in establishing the pace and scope of a viable reform.

—A strong interest in, and support of, country-led features in pension design and implementation that are often innovative. These include (a) a nonfinancial or notional defined-contribution system as an approach to reforming or implementing an unfunded first pillar; (b) use of a single clearinghouse and other approaches to reduce costs for funded and privately managed pillars; (c) the transformation of severance payments into combined unemployment

and retirement-benefit savings accounts; and (d) public prefunding under an improved governance structure as introduced in a number of high-income countries. While all of these features are promising, they depend on close attention to country circumstances and require close monitoring and evaluation, as transferability to other countries cannot be assumed.

Three Key Concepts in Considering Pension Reform

Although the essential policy formulation explicitly recognizes country-specific conditions and leads to implementation of the multipillar model in a variety of ways, from the World Bank's perspective, three key concepts should be considered.

First, all pension systems should, in principle, have elements that provide basic income security and poverty alleviation across the full breadth of the income distribution. Fiscal conditions permitting, this suggests that each country should have provisions for a basic pillar, which ensures that people with low lifetime incomes or who only participate marginally in the formal economy are provided with basic protections in old age. This may take the form of a social assistance program, a small means-tested social pension, or a universal demogrant available at higher ages (for example, age seventy and up). Whether this is viable—and the specific form, level, eligibility, and disbursement of benefits—will depend on the prevalence of other vulnerable groups, availability of budgetary resources, and design of the complementary elements of the pension system.

Second, if the conditions are right, prefunding for future pension commitments is advantageous for both economic and political reasons and may, in principle, be undertaken for any pillar. Economically, prefunding requires the commitment of resources in the current period to improve the future budget constraints of government and to support retirees; it usually contributes to economic growth and development. Politically, prefunding may better guarantee the capacity of society to fulfill pension commitments because it ensures that pension liabilities are backed by assets protected by legal property rights, regardless of whether the funding is through government debt or other types of assets. The decision to prefund, however, requires careful consideration of benefits and costs, as net benefits are not automatically assured and political manipulation can make prefunding illusory. This decision also requires a close look at the implementation capacity of a country.

Third, in countries where prefunding promises to be beneficial, a mandated and fully funded second pillar provides a useful benchmark (but not a blueprint) against which the design of any reform should be evaluated. As a benchmark, it serves as a reference point for the policy discussion and as a means to evaluate crucial questions about welfare improvement and the capacity to finance the transition from pay-as-you-go to funded regimes. The efficiency and equity of alternative approaches to retirement savings, such as a significant reliance on voluntary individual or occupational systems, should be evaluated in relation to this benchmark.

Criteria for Evaluation of Reform

The application of a goal-oriented and context-specific flexible policy framework also necessitates the formulation of various criteria against which a reform proposal is evaluated in comparison with the existing arrangements. These include criteria directed to both the content and the process of reform.

The World Bank uses four groups of criteria to judge the soundness of a reform proposal:

—Does the reform make sufficient progress toward the goals of a pension system? Will the reform provide reasonable protections against the risks of poverty in old age by efficiently allocating resources to the elderly? Does it provide the capacity to sustain consumption levels and provide social stability across the full range of socioeconomic conditions that are prevalent in the country? Does the reform meet distributive concerns? Does it offer access to retirement savings and poverty protection on an equivalent basis to all people with significant economic participation, including informal sector workers and those performing mainly noneconomic work? Is the burden of transition financing equitably distributed between and within generations?

—Is the macro and fiscal environment capable of supporting the reform? Have financial projections been thoroughly evaluated over the long-term periods appropriate to pension systems and rigorously tested across the range of likely variations in economic conditions over these time periods? Is the proposed financing of the reform within the limits reasonably imposed on both public and private sources? Is the reform consistent with the macroeconomic objectives and available instruments of government?

—Can the public and private structure operate the new (multipillar) pension scheme efficiently? Does the government have the institutional infrastructure and capacity to implement and operate publicly managed elements of the reform? Is the private sector sufficiently developed to operate the financial institutions required for any privately managed elements?

—Are regulatory and supervisory arrangements and institutions established and prepared to operate the funded pillar(s) with acceptable risks? Is the government able to put in place sustainable and effective regulatory and supervisory systems to oversee and control the governance, accountability, and investment practices of publicly and privately managed components?

Experience also dictates that the process of pension reform is very important. Three groups of process criteria are, therefore, also relevant:

—Is there a long-term, credible commitment by the government? Is the reform effectively aligned with the political economy of the country? Are the political conditions under which the reform will be implemented sufficiently stable to provide a reasonable likelihood for a full implementation and maturation of the reform?

—Is there local buy-in and leadership? Even the best technically prepared pension reform is bound to fail if it does not reflect the preferences of a country and is not credible to the population at large. To achieve this goal, the pension reform has to be prepared primarily by the country itself, by its politicians and technicians, and be communicated effectively to, and accepted by, the population. Outsiders, such as the World Bank, can assist with advice and technical support, but ownership and public support must come from the client country.

—Does it include sufficient capacity building and implementation? Pension reform is not simply a change of laws, but a change in how retirement income is provided. Accomplishing this typically requires major reforms in governance, the collection of contributions, record keeping, client information, asset management, regulation and supervision, and benefit disbursement. With the passage of legislation providing for reform, only a small part of the task has been achieved. A major emphasis on and investment in continued capacity building and implementation, as well as continued work with international and bilateral institutions beyond reform projects or adjustment loans, are required.

Design and Implementation Issues

Through its pension reform activities in client countries and the work of other institutions and analysts, the World Bank has developed a better understanding of good and best practices—of what works and what does not—in an increasing number of design and implementation areas. In a variety of other areas, however, open issues remain, and the search for good solutions continues. The areas include issues related to the design of the various pillars and their relative weight, financial sustainability, administration, implementation, and political economy and lessons from multipillar pension reforms in the world's regions. This section discusses best practices and open issues in three areas of major interest related to fully funded pensions: When is the financial sector ready for fully funded pensions, and how should they be regulated and supervised? How should fees and costs of funded individual accounts be contained? Can the private market deliver the required annuities once contributors to fully funded systems retire—an often overlooked issue, but one of increasing relevance as both the population and fully funded pension systems age.

Readiness of the Financial Market and Regulatory and Supervisory Issues

The introduction of mandated funded pension pillars has given rise to considerable debate inside and outside the World Bank, and it will take many more years before a clear consensus is reached. This section addresses three major issues that have arisen: (a) Can funded pensions be introduced in a rudimentary financial market environment, and if so, what are the minimum conditions? (b) What are the good or best regulatory practices that countries should follow? (c) What are the good or best supervisory practices that countries should follow?

READINESS, MINIMUM CONDITIONS, AND SYNERGIES. Not all countries are ready to introduce a funded pillar, and those that are not should not do so. Nevertheless, the introduction of a funded pillar does not need perfect conditions, with all financial products available from the very beginning, since the pillar is introduced gradually and creates synergies for moving toward improved financial markets. Hence minimum conditions need to be satisfied, and these can be highlighted when discussing three types of countries and their financial market readiness.[1]

There are three main types of financial markets: (a) those that are incomplete but the segments that operate are sound, are associated with high per capita income, have a credible macroeconomic policy framework, and have open capital accounts (but domestic and international financial instruments are not perfect substitutes); (b) those that are incomplete and the segments that operate are predominantly unsound, are associated with low per capita

1. Impavido, Musalem, and Vittas (2002).

income, have a long history of macroeconomic policy imbalances, and have closed capital accounts; and (c) those that have an intermediate position between the two.

Countries with incomplete but sound financial systems that have relatively high per capita income, credible macroeconomic policies, and free capital movements offer the best case for funded pension and annuity systems. This is true for several reasons. First, (voluntary) funded pension and annuity products are luxury financial services. They are demanded at high rather than low per capita income (that is, at high per capita income, the time preference or discount rate is lower, which increases the valuation of purchasing coverage for future contingencies, and family ties are weaker, which reduces self-insurance within the family). Second, credible macroeconomic policy provides an enabling environment for the development of long-term financial instruments (for example, pension savings and annuities). Third, even if financial markets are incomplete (for example, embryonic capital markets), if banks are sound, they provide a vehicle for channeling long-term savings into long-term loans to borrowers (government, enterprises, and individuals). Finally, open capital accounts do not constrain pension funds from investing in the local market.

The second type of countries—those with chronic macroeconomic imbalances and other limitations—provide little room for the development of funded pensions and annuities. Long-term savings instruments cannot prosper in a macroeconomic environment with high and volatile inflation, and pensions and annuities are not affordable at low per capita income. Furthermore, the financial systems of these countries are essentially limited to the banking sector, which usually is weak. Although it would be possible to invest abroad, these countries, by having weak domestic financial institutions, should have closed capital accounts. Hence, before trying to develop these instruments, the authorities should focus on establishing a credible long-term macroeconomic framework and strengthening prudential regulation and supervision of banks. These two conditions are necessary for the successful development of funded pensions and annuities.

In the third, intermediate category of financial systems, there are a variety of cases. There are countries with credible macroeconomic policy, a relatively sound banking system, and an open capital account. However, they may have very incomplete financial markets (underdeveloped securities markets, insurance, pensions, and mortgages) and relatively low per capita income. Nonetheless, these countries have the preconditions for developing funded pensions and annuities, although their relatively low per capita income represents a scale barrier for many domestic financial markets. Initially, the portfolios of these funds would be composed primarily of government bonds and banks' long-term certificates of deposit. In addition, they could have small fractions in shares, foreign securities, and possibly leasing companies. As financial markets develop, investment regulations should allow more diversified portfolios by allowing large investments in shares, foreign securities, corporate bonds, and asset-backed securities and small investments in venture capital companies.

These countries will obtain secondary benefits from the development of funded pensions and annuities. Gains from financial sector development will initially be concentrated in development of the government bond market and long-term lending through banks. In a second stage, secondary benefits will also come from development of the corporate bond market and asset-backed securities, and in a still later stage the stock market may benefit. The development of funded pensions and annuities will encourage financial market innovation through development of the fund management industry and improved financial regulations, including stronger minority shareholder rights, transparency, and corporate governance. They also will provide competition to the banking system and foster efficiency and innovation in financial markets.

In summary, instead of a full-fledged financial system with a full array of efficient institutions and financial instruments, the following minimum conditions are needed for the successful introduction of a funded pillar:[2] (a) the presence of a solid core of sound banks and insurance companies, (b) a long-term commitment by government to pursue sound macroeconomic policies, and (c) a long-term commitment to financial sector reform through the establishment of a sound regulatory and supervisory framework for pensions and insurance products and providers.

WHAT REGULATORY PRACTICE TO FOLLOW? Seasoned practitioners of development respond to the call for application of best-practice regulations in developing countries by posing a question: If the countries could apply these practices, would they still be developing countries and World Bank clients? Applied to contractual savings, the question implies that the best practices may be beyond low- and middle-income countries for some time.[3] Nevertheless, the many pension reform programs in middle-income countries

---

2. Vittas (2000).
3. OECD (2004).

in Latin America and Central and Eastern Europe have created a rich body of experience. This subsection presents the main lessons from this experience.[4]

For a country following the open-end fund concept (as Chile), the World Bank strongly suggests initially applying strict regulations and relaxing them gradually as sound financial markets develop. The strict initial rules include limited choices for participants, the licensing of specialized providers under the rule of one fund–one account, uniform pricing and limited forms of fees, detailed investment limits, extensive disclosure, minimum return rules and state guarantees, and proactive supervision. The reason for the initial "Draconian rule" is essentially twofold. On the one hand, the new compulsory system starts with a weak capital market, limited traditions, and a lack of familiarity. On the other hand, strict regulations offer safeguards, control moral hazard, overcome opposition to the funded scheme, and are better able to prevent early failures. However, it is imperative to relax the rules as the market develops and the system matures.

The less controversial regulations should be applied to mandated funded schemes from the very beginning. These include (a) appropriate licensing and capital requirements for providers; (b) full segregation of assets, sponsors, management firms, and custodians and the use of external custodian banks; (c) asset diversification and the rules of asset management (the qualifications and licensing of internal or external managers); (d) asset valuation rules (mark-to-market) and rate-of-return calculations (the mutual fund instead of the savings account model); (e) periodic actuarial reviews and financial audits; (f) transparency and information disclosure; and (g) effective supervision and consistent application of sanctions.

The more controversial regulations, for which there remains uncertainty regarding whether and when they should be applied, include (a) controls on market structure and choice (should only special institutions and products be permitted, and is there a trade-off between choice and costs?); (b) funding, investment, and portability rules; (c) legal investment limits versus the prudent-man principle (can the latter be applied in an unsophisticated market?); (d) limits on commissions and switching; and (e) profitability rules and guarantees.

---

4. Carmichael and Pomerleano (2002); Hinz and Rao (2003); Rocha, Hinz, and Gutiérrez (2001); Vittas (1998a, 1998b).

What Supervisory Practice to Apply?

Again, many practices are not controversial and should be applied early on. A few others are still uncertain, and the verdict is still out about what works best and under what conditions.

The less controversial practices and tasks for the supervisory body include (a) the need for a politically independent, proactive, well-financed, and professional staff; (b) the vetting of the applications for licensing; (c) the undertaking of off-site surveillance and on-site inspection; (d) the elaboration and issuance of regulations; (e) the consistent and timely application of sanctions to rectify problems and establish a credible deterrent to abusive practices; (f) the publication of reports and statistics; and (g) collaboration with other regulators.

The more controversial rules and questions for supervision include (a) creation of a single-purpose or dedicated supervisory agency; (b) establishment of effective collaboration with other regulators and supervisors for the many institutions offering retirement-income products; (c) the best way to guarantee the independence of the supervisory body in a weak political environment; and (d) oversight and accountability of the supervisor.

Often a major decision related to the supervision of funded pensions is whether to establish this as an independent authority (as in Chile and most Latin American countries) or to integrate these functions with the supervision of similar financial entities, such as banks and insurance companies (as in Australia, Hungary, and the United Kingdom, among others). Both models have proven to be effective in achieving the objective of sound and reliable supervision, so there is no simple answer to the organizational question. The appropriate approach is likely to be a function of the design of the system and effectiveness of the existing supervisory bodies. Pension funds that operate in a highly specialized manner as very distinctive financial institutions can be effectively supervised by independent authorities, while those that function as adjuncts to existing financial institutions are best addressed by an agency with integrated authority. The form of the institution is secondary to the independence, adequacy of resources, quality of staff, and clarity of mandate. The most compelling impetus for an integrated supervisor is the need for consistency and coordination of oversight across similar financial institutions, which may be better facilitated in a single authority. A central counterargument is that an integrated supervisor with a weak governance structure will face conflicts of interest in controlling the activities of institutions within its authority that compete or play multiple roles in a pension system (for example, asset managers, banks, and insurance companies) or will be weakened in its ability to protect the system in the face of competing priorities.

How to Contain Fees and Costs

The amount of fees or charges levied on financial retirement products is an area of considerable debate and research. For critics of a funded pillar, these fees are much too high, in particular compared with the (best) unfunded benchmarks. This reduces the net rate of return on contributions, sometimes to unacceptably low levels, and thus reduces or even eliminates the potential return advantage of a funded pillar. Moreover, the structure of fees is often nontransparent and anti-poor, which prevents a broader pension coverage of lower-income groups. Supporters of a funded pillar (including the World Bank) recognize the need to bring fee levels down and to rework fee structures. But they see the problem as much more manageable, with fee levels in client countries much more in line with those of popular financial services in developed countries and falling after start-up costs have been covered. Still, various areas require closer investigation in and across countries and regions.[5] This subsection concentrates on three issues dealing with the measurement of fee levels and the approaches for their reduction or limitation.

MEASURING AND COMPARING FEE LEVELS. Across countries, charges or fees (administrative charges and management fees) on long-term financial products, such as pensions, are levied in many different ways. Some are one-off fees, usually a fixed sum payable either up-front or at maturity. Others are ongoing and can take the form of a fixed fee per period, a percentage of contributions or premiums, or a percentage of assets. One main problem with international comparisons is that products offer different services and pension systems have different structures. For example, some plans have guaranteed minimum returns or guaranteed minimum pensions, while others do not. Obviously, everything else being equal, guaranteed products should have higher fees. Also, some plans provide better services, such as higher rates of return and immediate benefits to plan members, and could justify being more expensive. Finally, funded pillars that rely on the public pillar to collect contributions (for example, Argentina) should have lower administrative costs than those that are independent of government.

---

5. First stock-taking exercises include those by James, Smalhout, and Vittas (2001); OECD (2001); Whitehouse (2000); World Bank (2003); and Yermo (2002).

A national and international comparison of fee levels requires a comprehensive and life-cycle-type approach in which all types of charges for, say, a full working life are considered and, for example, the gross amount and the net accumulated amount are compared at retirement.[6] Time-specific comparisons of fees on flows (contributions) and stocks (assets) alone are of little value.

LIMITING FEES VIA REGULATION OF STRUCTURE. Countries have taken different approaches to regulating the fee structure of pension funds. For example, Australia, Hong Kong (China), the United Kingdom, and the United States have few, if any, explicit restrictions on charges and instead regulate charges under the broader "prudence" or "reasonableness" standards. This is partly explained by the fact that private pensions in the United States are largely voluntary, while in other countries they are built on preexisting voluntary systems. Most World Bank client countries limit the structure of charges, and quite a few have restrictive regimes in that companies are limited to two charges (an asset-based and a contribution-based charge), one of which is subject to a ceiling (asset-based charge), while the other can take any value.

It is still unclear to what extent these limitations on the structure lead to effective lower fee levels or what they imply for the longer supply structure (number of funds) or demand structure (scope of coverage). It appears that these limitations may be of lesser relevance than other elements of the second-pillar design and implementation.[7] A simple and transparent fee structure with well-thought-through price caps is probably a useful approach when such a new pillar is introduced. But these limitations need to be reviewed regularly and adjusted with other pillar characteristics if deemed necessary; it is quite likely that they will be relaxed as time progresses and individuals become more familiar with the system.

LIMITING FEES VIA SPECIAL ORGANIZATION OF PROVIDERS. Several models of pension fund management are aimed at reducing fees by reducing costs. The basic idea is that, in competitive markets, costs are the major determinant of fees. Moreover, reformers should be concerned with the real cost of producing the services. International experience indicates that close-end funds (those limiting membership to employees of a firm, industry, or profession) have lower fees than open-end funds, perhaps because they incur lower marketing costs. Some countries use a centralized competitive-bidding

---

6. Whitehouse (2000).
7. For a first assessment of four European and Central Asian countries, see World Bank (2003).

process to outsource fund management (Bolivia, Kosovo, and Latvia, but not Sweden). These systems have resulted in lower fees, although it is not clear whether the related reduction in worker choice is sustainable. In this regard, the experience of the Federal Thrift Savings Plan in the United States (covering only federal government workers) is encouraging. Its gross expense ratio has declined steadily as fund assets have grown, from an average of 0.67 percent of funds in 1988 to 0.07 percent in 1999.[8] It is by far the lowest fee structure in the industry. Another important case for reducing fees while providing almost unlimited investment choices to plan members is the Swedish scheme. The majority of Latin American and some Eastern European countries adopted a model of open-end and specialized fund managers, with countries differing in terms of centralization or decentralization of collection and record-keeping systems. These models have produced relatively high management fees, especially in their early years. Although their fees are not higher, and in some cases are lower, than those of personal and stakeholder plans in the United Kingdom, there is still room for reducing them by addressing the issue of industry concentration.

Deregulation of fees and market contestability (for example, providing options to plan members) promote competition but require strong disclosure of information. Fund managers have to provide affiliates with statements of their accounts. In addition, at least once a year they need to provide affiliates with basic information about the pension fund management company (ownership, managers, directors, and audited financial statements, including the auditor's report) as well as information on the fee structure and rate of return relative to the respective system's average, taking into account the long-term view. The greater the choice and contestability, the greater the incentive of fund managers to spend money on public relations and marketing—costs that eventually are passed on to worker-affiliates.

Again, it is too early to make strong recommendations, but the experience so far suggests three promising approaches. First, limit costs by saving on the administrative costs of contribution collection, account administration, and so forth (that is, adopt the clearinghouse approach). Second, limit the incentives for marketing expenditures by pension funds through blind accounts or constraints on the ability of individuals to change funds as a result of laws or exit fees. Last, but not least, limit asset management fees by such means as the use of passive investment options, employers' choice of financial provider, or competitive bidding for a restricted number of service suppliers.

8. Hustead and Hustead (2001); James, Smalhout, and Vittas (2001).

Can the Private Annuity Market Deliver?

A privately managed, funded pillar (mandated or voluntary) requires the provision of annuities that transform at retirement an accumulated amount into a lifelong income stream (that is, until death). This requirement has often been neglected when fully funded pillars are set up, but it raises a number of issues for which good answers are not always available. For example, how much annuitization is required, in what form, and at what age (or ages if plan members are given the option of purchasing annuities through time) in order to improve risk management? What type of providers should offer what products? To what extent can and should unisex life tables be applied? What prudential and business regulations should be applied? What risk-sharing arrangements can or need to be put in place between providers and annuitants? What is the appropriate allocation of the risk of future changes in mortality among public and private sources? What role is there for governments in ensuring that appropriate financial products are available to back indexed annuity contracts? This subsection concentrates on five issues: What type of providers should be allowed to offer annuities? What kinds of products should be allowed? When must a private annuity market be ready? Should there be price indexation of annuities? How should we deal with the main challenge: risk bearing?

WHAT TYPE OF PROVIDERS SHOULD BE ALLOWED TO OFFER ANNU-ITIES? Because of the insurance nature of annuity products, the insurance sector is bound to represent the largest set of annuity providers in any country. Pension funds (occupational and individual) may also provide annuities, especially if they provide defined benefits. Among insurance companies, there is an issue whether general life insurance companies should be allowed to sell annuities or whether specialized annuity companies should be licensed under the regulation (as in Mexico, for instance). On the one hand, life insurance companies may "hedge" the longevity and mortality risks when selling annuities and (say) term life products. On the other hand, information disclosure in the insurance industry is poor in practically all jurisdictions. Accounting standards are mostly opaque, and, from the point of view of consumer protection and transparency, an argument can be made for specialized annuity companies, especially to provide annuities from mandatory schemes.

WHAT KINDS OF PRODUCTS SHOULD BE ALLOWED? Annuity markets are characterized by large asymmetric information between suppliers and demanders. This results in adverse selection and a difference between an actuarially fair price for an average individual and the typically insured of some 10 to 15 percent even in well-developed markets. This also results in complex products that compete on price as well as many other characteristics. It also results in differences in prices between deferred annuities (for example, where individuals pay premiums periodically through their active life) and annuities bought at retirement. Last, but not least, it results in price differences between individual and group insurance. To address the issue from a public policy perspective, a few needs stand out: (a) the need for comprehensive consumer information and protection for all products, (b) the need for standardized products as benchmarks for consumers, (c) the need for employers to be included in the selection of products, and (d) the need for policymakers to pilot innovative solutions (such as the auctioning of whole pension cohorts in a mandated pillar).

WHEN MUST A PRIVATE ANNUITY MARKET BE READY? At the inception of pension reform in client countries, a functioning life insurance sector typically is not available and need not be so. These reforms concentrate initially on the accumulation phase, with the payout phase some ten or more years away. But can a reform be launched without a view to the insurance sector? For example, the choice of individuals to join the second pillar may depend on available products and their characteristics (such as indexation and joint annuities). It is probably the case that if a financial sector fulfills the minimum requirements for launching such a reform, the insurance sector can (and must) be built over a period of five or so years. Major contributions to its development would be the adoption of a modern law establishing an operationally independent regulatory and supervisory authority, encouraging actuarial training, promoting reinsurance arrangements with highly reputable reinsurers, and opening up to well-established foreign life insurance companies from reputable jurisdictions, in the form of either joint ventures or privatized public institutions. For very small jurisdictions, considerations need to be made about unification or integration of several supervisory authorities, especially securities, insurance, and pensions.[9]

SHOULD THERE BE PRICE INDEXATION OF ANNUITIES? For annuities to provide real consumption smoothing to individuals, they need to be price indexed; otherwise, even moderate inflation over a lengthy period of retirement will lead to a major fall in the real value of the annuity. For insurance companies to provide indexed annuities at reasonable prices (if at all) requires access to price-indexed assets, preferably in the form of price-

9. Impavido, Musalem, and Vittas (2002).

indexed government bonds. Various countries have started to provide such bonds (Chile, Sweden, the United Kingdom, and the United States), but they are far from universal and often not long term. Even if indexed government bonds are available, insurance companies offering indexed annuities must forgo other more profitable investments and must therefore charge a higher price to annuitants than they would for nominal annuities. Therefore, indexation involves a difficult trade-off between the higher financial security of older pensioners and the lower payouts they will receive when young. This trade-off needs to be taken into account by governments when projecting the replacement rates that the new system will generate.[10] Moreover, if governments want to ensure (or mandate) the availability of price-indexed annuities, they will need to issue the appropriate inflation-indexed or other specialized instruments to enable this market to develop. This, however, potentially imposes significant distributional trade-offs because in nearly all developing (and many developed) countries the beneficiaries of indexed annuities are higher-income groups, while all will bear the costs of providing the financial instruments that enable indexed annuities to develop.

HOW SHOULD WE DEAL WITH RISK ISSUES IN ANNUITIES? Two issues are addressed around the question of who should bear the risk. The first concerns rating or differential underwriting of survival probabilities (such as genetic testing, for instance). One of the disadvantages of pooling risks is that good types (in the case of annuities, those who die early) subsidize bad types, giving rise to the pooling premium. For some groups of pensioners—for example, those with health impairments or those with poorer socioeconomic backgrounds—the terms on which pooling takes place may mean a high probability of subsidizing other parties to the pool because of the lack of homogeneity of lives.

Disallowing access by insurance companies to this information increases asymmetric information, adverse selection, and the danger of a breakdown of the market. Providing this information for both sides of the market leads to segmented risk pooling and the exclusion of some groups (those with identified high survival rates), for which public provisions may have to be established. The introduction of rating would eliminate the nonstochastic component (that is, those elements that would induce strong adverse selection) from the pooling equilibrium. In other words, types systematically better than the average from the standpoint of suppliers of annuities (that

10. Impavido, Thorburn, and Wadsworth (2004).

is, those who die early) would be better off, while types systematically longer-lived than the average would be worse off compared to a no-information situation.

The other main issue concerns the question of who should bear the risk of rising life expectancy and uncertain future investment income. Some demographers have been predicting large increases in life expectancy due to scientific breakthroughs. Some economists have been predicting prolonged drops in stock prices or bond interest rates due to aging populations who cash in their stocks and use them to buy more stable bonds. Evidence from many countries indicates that these companies now return the government bond rate to annuitants over their expected lifetime; that is, the "money's worth ratio," discounted at the government term structure, is close to 100 percent.[11] A large increase in longevity or a decrease in investment income may bring losses to these companies, including the possibility of insolvency and failure to keep their promises to annuitants.

How should we deal with these risks? Who is best equipped to deal with them? At least three approaches are relevant here. In the first approach, insurance companies continue to bear the risks, but with careful government regulation to ensure that their reserves are large enough to cover unexpected shocks. Such reserves and regulations have significant costs, so we would expect them to be factored into the prices (or money's worth ratios) offered annuitants.

The second method explicitly shares these risks with annuitants by allowing and possibly encouraging variable annuities whose value varies annually depending on actual longevity and investment outcomes. Annuitants get a higher expected return than they would under fixed-rate annuities, but they also bear some of the risk, which may be difficult for low-income pensioners. Also, they may not understand the complex terms of the variable annuity, and companies may take advantage of their lack of information. Obviously, if this approach is taken, government has a large responsibility for providing consumer information and for standardizing the terms of payout variation to facilitate comprehension and comparability.

The third method of assigning risk places a heavier burden on government, which might offer a minimum pension guarantee, sell longevity-indexed bonds, or provide the annuities directly. This enables the broadest possible intergenerational risk sharing, but it also creates the danger that government will be faced with a large contingent liability many years in the

---

11. See, for example, James, Vittas, and Song (2001).

future. The "best" solution for the annuity dilemma remains an unresolved and controversial issue.

Conclusion

Substantial progress has been made in pension reform, in the context of a changing environment. The history of reform and the interactions of policymakers, pension experts, and representatives of developing and industrial countries have made clear the continued relevance of the main objectives of pension systems—to protect low-income elderly and to smooth consumption.

Pension designs have been reformed and modified—the inappropriateness of a single pillar has become increasingly clear, as have the advantages of a multipillar approach, as affordable. Pension reforms are increasingly being tailored to country circumstances. At the same time, a number of new questions have arisen—in some cases modifications of old issues—that pension systems must answer to be effective. This short chapter has concentrated on issues arising in the fully funded pillar of pension systems. A fuller discussion of these issues and others is contained in the longer volume on which this paper is based.[12]

References

Carmichael, Jeffrey, and Michael Pomerleano. 2002. *The Development and Regulation of Non-Bank Financial Institutions.* Washington: World Bank.

Hinz, Richard, and G. V. Nageswara Rao. 2003. "Approach to the Regulation of Private Pension Funds in India: Application of International Best Practice." In *Rethinking Pension Provision in India,* edited by Gautam Bhardwaj and Anand Bordia. Invest India/Tata McGraw-Hill Series. New Delhi: Tata McGraw-Hill.

Holzmann, Robert, Richard Hinz, and Bank Team. 2005. *Old-Age Income Support in the 21st Century: An International Perspective on Pension Systems and Reform.* Washington: World Bank.

Hustead, Edwin C., and Toni Hustead. 2001. "Federal Civilian and Military Retirement Systems." In *Pensions in the Public Sector,* edited by Olivia S. Mitchell and Edwin C. Hustead, pp. 66–104. University of Pennsylvania Press.

Impavido, Gregorio, Alberto R. Musalem, and Dimitri Vittas. 2002. "Contractual Savings in Countries with a Small Financial System." In *Globalization and Financial Systems in*

12. Holzmann, Hinz, and Bank Team (2005).

Small Developing Countries, edited by James Hanson, Patrick Honohan, and Giovanni Majnoni. Washington: World Bank.

Impavido, Gregorio, Craig Thorburn, and Mike Wadsworth. 2004. "A Conceptual Framework for Retirement Product: Risk Sharing Arrangements between Providers and Annuitants." Policy Research Working Paper 3208. Washington: World Bank.

James, Estelle, James Smalhout, and Dimitri Vittas. 2001. "Administrative Costs and Organization of Individual Accounts: A Comparative Perspective." In *New Ideas about Old-Age Security,* edited by Robert Holzmann and Joseph Stiglitz. Washington: World Bank.

James, Estelle, Dimitri Vittas, and Xue Song. 2001. "Annuities Markets around the World: Money's Worth and Risk Intermediation." CeRP Working Paper 16/01. Moncalieri, Italy: Center for Research on Pensions and Welfare Policies.

OECD (Organization for Economic Cooperation and Development). 2001. *Private Pension Systems: Administrative Costs and Reforms.* Private Pension Series 2. Paris.

———. 2004. *Supervising Private Pensions: Institutions and Methods.* Private Pension Series 6. Paris.

Rocha, Roberto, Richard Hinz, and Joaquín Gutiérrez. 2001. "Improving Regulation and Supervision of Pension Funds: Are There Lessons from the Banking Sector?" In *New Ideas about Old-Age Security,* edited by Robert Holzmann and Joseph Stiglitz. Washington: World Bank.

Vittas, Dimitri. 1998a. "Institutional Investors and Securities Markets: Which Comes First?" Policy Research Working Paper 2032. Washington: World Bank, Development Research Group, Finance.

———. 1998b. "The Role of Non-Bank Financial Intermediaries." Policy Research Working Paper 1892. Washington: World Bank, Development Research Group, Finance.

———. 2000. "Pension Reform and Capital Market Development: 'Feasibility' and 'Impact' Preconditions." Policy Research Working Paper 2414. Washington: World Bank, Development Research Group, Finance.

Whitehouse, Edward. 2000. *Administrative Charges for Funded Pensions: An International Comparison and Assessment.* Social Protection Discussion Paper 0016. Washington: World Bank.

World Bank. 2003. "Administrative Charges in Second Pillar Pensions in ECA: A Case Study Approach." Washington: World Bank, Europe and Central Asia, Human Sector Development Unit.

Yermo, Juan. 2002. "The Performance of Funded Pension Systems in Latin America." Paper prepared for the Office of the Chief Economist, LAC Regional Study on Social Security Reform. Washington: World Bank.

Contributors

Gerard Caprio
World Bank

Indermit Gill
World Bank

Morris Goldstein
Institute for International Economics

James A. Hanson
World Bank

Robert Holzmann
World Bank

Patrick Honohan
World Bank

Robert E. Litan
*Ewing Marion Kauffman
    Foundation and Brookings
    Institution*

Fernando Montes-Negret
World Bank

Thomas Muller
World Bank

Brian Pinto
World Bank

Anna Wong
Institute for International Economics

Index